Cake Decorating
For Dummies

Cheat Sheet

A Cake Decorating Kit Checklist

These items represent the cool hardware you'll need for your decorating endeavors and adventures. Your kit could be a fancy carrying case, a few shelves in a kitchen cabinet, or both.

- Icing tips, such as #1–#10 for dots, lines, and scripting; #16, #18, #21, and #32 for forming stars; #48 for basketweaving; #67 for forming leaves; #104 for creating flowers; and a flower nail such as a #7
- Disposable pastry bags
- Couplers for the pastry bags
- Icing offset spatulas, 4-inch and 9-inch
- Ruler
- Various sizes of baking pans, such as 9-inch rounds, 10-inch square, 9-x-13-inch rectangle, 12-x-18-inch rectangle, and Bundt
- Cardboard rounds to support the cake
- Cooling racks
- Cookie, fondant, and gum paste cutters
- Cake tester
- Bench scraper
- Pastry brush
- Decorating comb
- Turntable
- Layer leveler
- Candy and oven thermometers
- Parchment paper
- Toothpicks and bamboo skewers for sketching
- Modeling tools
- A color wheel

Ingredients to Have on Hand for Cake Decorating

To bake and decorate cakes, always strive to have the freshest, highest-quality products and varieties on hand. Some of your most common ingredients include

- Cake flour
- Unsalted butter for baking and mixing frostings
- White granulated sugar
- Confectioners' sugar for frostings and icings
- Eggs, at room temperature
- Whole milk
- Pasteurized egg whites for royal icing
- Coloring gels, in a variety of colors, to shade frostings
- Baking powder
- Baking soda
- Flavorings and extracts
- Edible embellishments such as hard candies, chocolates, nuts, fruits, sprinkles, sanding sugars, and nonpareils, as well as marzipan for modeling
- Nonedible embellishments such as candles and fresh flowers

For Dummies: Bestselling Book Series for Beginners

Cake Decorating For Dummies®

Cheat Sheet

Frosting Your Cake Perfectly

To frost your cake, follow these easy steps. They're for a double-layer, 9-inch cake but are easily adaptable for other sizes:

1. Gather your tools, including wax paper, offset spatulas, and a silicone brush.

2. Have your bottom cake layer on a cardboard round (or the board it will sit on), and place strips of wax paper underneath it around its borders.

3. Use the silicone brush to gently sweep off excess crumbs, and then use a wide-angled spatula to spread an even layer of frosting on top of the bottom layer. Put the second layer on top and again sweep off excess crumbs.

4. Spread another layer of frosting on top of the cake and all around the sides. You've now formed your crumb coat. Refrigerate the cake for the frosting to crust over.

5. Remove the cake from the refrigerator and use an offset spatula to spread frosting cleanly and evenly, beginning first on top and then frosting the sides. Use the spatula to achieve a flat, smooth look, adding and removing frosting for a finished, polished presentation.

Last-Minute Cake Decorating Ideas

Even when you're in a time crunch, you can still turn out a cake that will draw oohs and ahs. Consider these swift toppings and methods:

- Top your cake with chocolate shavings or curls.

- Group nonpoisonous fresh flowers, such as roses or daisies wrapped with a grosgrain or organza ribbon, atop your confection.

- Use a stencil and sift confectioners' sugar or cocoa over your creation.

- Decorate cake plates with sauces — such as hot fudge or raspberry purée — that complement a cake slice.

- Place evenly spaced milk chocolate, butterscotch, cinnamon, white chocolate, or mint chips all over your cake for a Swiss dot effect.

- Use hard candies, sours, or jelly beans to create festive swirls, spell out a name, create a flower, or form a geometric pattern.

- Create a tableau with small fruits, or if it complements the cake's flavor, thinly slice and place citrus fruits in a decorative pattern.

A Pre-Showtime Quiz for Your Cake

Before the cake's to be presented, make sure it looks the best that it can:

1. Examine the cake's silhouette: Is it even? Does frosting completely cover the cake? Are the borders clean?

2. Are there too many decorations? If so, can a piece easily be edited out?

3. Did you double-check the spelling and appearance of any writing?

4. Is the cake board clean?

5. Is the cake board sturdy enough to transport the cake safely?

For Dummies: Bestselling Book Series for Beginners

Cake Decorating FOR DUMMIES®

by Joe LoCicero

BICENTENNIAL
1807
WILEY
2007
BICENTENNIAL

Wiley Publishing, Inc.

Cake Decorating For Dummies®

Published by
Wiley Publishing, Inc.
111 River St.
Hoboken, NJ 07030-5774
www.wiley.com

About the Author

Family lifestyle expert **Joe LoCicero**'s obsession with cakes and instruction began with the Flintstones-themed cake his mom served for his fifth birthday. Before the cake was doled out, Joe explained to everyone the importance of embellishing a cake with frosting and figures. He developed an immediate interest in deconstructing and designing desserts, and by the time he was in seventh grade, his carrot cakes had become such a hit that local organizations auctioned them off at fundraisers.

More recently, the Southern-bred LoCicero has spent the last 15 years in Los Angeles working in the entertainment industry as a party planner, writer, columnist, and marketing consultant. He also works wonders as a cake decorator, accomplished home chef, creative instructor, and entertaining guru.

Having organized big-budget parties for network, studios, agents, and stars, Joe founded Chartreuse Cake in 1999, which specializes in themed, fantastically crafted cakes for large gatherings such as birthday parties, bridal and baby showers, signature events, and private screenings. His Red Velvet Cake and its wide variety of decorations is his most requested. Chartreuse Cake has also catered meals for independent films, and dessert buffets for celebrities. LoCicero also continues to offer one-on-one home cooking instruction.

In 2004, Joe and his wife founded Practical Whimsy (www.practicalwhimsy.com), a company that celebrates family style with products, recipes, party tips, and of course ideas for cakes. Joe and his wife champion the importance of family supper and celebrations and have given presentations on those topics to corporations, organizations, and educational institutions including MTV, Paramount, Viacom, Turner Broadcasting, Loyola Marymount University, and Southern California's Discover Conference.

Joe's column on entertaining, "Practical Whimsy: Southern Hospitality, Hollywood Style," is a regular feature in *Y'ALL: The Magazine of Southern People,* and he's the author of a number of books, including *The Complete Idiot's Guide to Clear Thinking* and *Streetwise Meeting and Event Planning.* Additionally, Joe is the Food Contributor for momready.com.

LoCicero has been featured in *Cosmopolitan, Woman's World,* several daily newspapers in the U.S. and Canada; radio outlets including Sirius' *Martha Stewart Living Radio;* and network affiliate news programs.

LoCicero lives in Los Angeles, where he cooks dinner every night for his wife, Lori, and their two young children. They have cake as often as possible.

Dedication

To Dalton, whose love for cakes, zest for life, and ever-burgeoning outpouring of new ideas provide a happy, constant source of inspiration.

Author's Acknowledgments

I truly regard cake decorating as a way to celebrate the infinite number of happy occasions that can bring friends, colleagues, relatives, and immediate family together. In that spirit, I'm so thankful to my nieces and nephews — Eli, Mary Elle, Samuel, Tucker, Savannah, Ethan, Paulina Jane, and Alex — who take cake and celebrating very seriously and have fueled my passion for cakes, served as excellent taste testers, and proved to be unending idea factories. And to my delightful daughter Garcy, who has already shown me that I was, in fact, prepared to have a girl, particularly one who has such fabulous, discriminating taste.

I've realized that people can be just as passionate about enjoying cake as I can be about making and decorating them. Jill and Mark Illsley, Maureen FitzPatrick and Doug Armstrong: Your unending support and encouragement, your graciousness, and your ever-present humor humble me.

I'd also like to thank Kristy Wylie and Shari Kaufman, two champions of my cakes who never missed the chance to express their sheer delight, spread the word, and show me the importance of never making light of a talent you've been given And I appreciate all my friends and colleagues at Paramount, Disney, Turner Broadcasting, and Sony who heaped praise on myriad confections, instilling more pride, happiness, and publicity than they'll ever know.

To those who willingly enter the Practical Whimsy test kitchen and help us so immeasurably — namely the incredibly talented Sarah Kent and Julie Jones. Your assistance in so many areas was absolutely invaluable. You make us smile and never let us down.

At Wiley, I so appreciate my Acquisitions Editor Stacy Kennedy's passion for this project and understanding of my vision; Project Editor Tim Gallan's steadfast commitment and easygoing style; Copy Editor Elizabeth Rea's cheer and verve; and Pam Mitchell's expert recipe testing.

In Jacky Sach, I am always happily amazed at what a dedicated advocate I have. I'm so lucky to be in league with such a smart, savvy agent who never wavers from helping me accomplish the ideals I strive for. And that sense of humor: Don't get me started!

I also want to point out my parents, Joe and Gloria, whose zeal for good food and love of us all propelled us to believe that we can do anything. And finally, to my favorite cake lover, my amazing Practical Whimsy coconspirator/wife Lori, who let me have an actual chartreuse-colored cake for our wedding . . . and had no idea what she was getting us into when she ordered me that Martha by Mail cake decorating kit oh-so-long ago.

Publisher's Acknowledgments

We're proud of this book; please send us your comments through our Dummies online registration form located at www.dummies.com/register/.

Some of the people who helped bring this book to market include the following:

Acquisitions, Editorial, and Media Development

Senior Project Editor: Tim Gallan

Acquisitions Editor: Stacy Kennedy

Senior Copy Editor: Elizabeth Rea

Technical Editor and Recipe Tester: Pamela Mitchell

Editorial Manager: Christine Meloy Beck

Editorial Assistants: Erin Calligan, Joe Niesen, David Lutton, Leeann Harney

Illustrator: Liz Kurtzman

Photographer: T. J. Hine Photography, Inc.

Food Stylist: Lisa Bishop

Cartoons: Rich Tennant (www.the5thwave.com)

Composition Services

Project Coordinator: Lynsey Osborn

Layout and Graphics: Brooke Graczyk, Joyce Haughey, LeAndra Hosier, Stephanie D. Jumper, Heather Ryan

Anniversary Logo Design: Richard Pacifico

Proofreaders: Melanie Hoffman, Betty Kish

Indexer: Steve Rath

Publishing and Editorial for Consumer Dummies

Diane Graves Steele, Vice President and Publisher, Consumer Dummies

Joyce Pepple, Acquisitions Director, Consumer Dummies

Kristin A. Cocks, Product Development Director, Consumer Dummies

Michael Spring, Vice President and Publisher, Travel

Kelly Regan, Editorial Director, Travel

Publishing for Technology Dummies

Andy Cummings, Vice President and Publisher, Dummies Technology/General User

Composition Services

Gerry Fahey, Vice President of Production Services

Debbie Stailey, Director of Composition Services

Contents at a Glance

Table of Contents

Recipes at a Glance

Embellishments

Kids' Cakes

Cakes for Grown-Ups

Bridal and Baby Shower Cakes

Wedding and Anniversary Cakes

Year-Round Cakes

Quick and Easy Cake Ideas

Introduction

I often hear moms and dads, girlfriends and boyfriends, wives and husbands say, "I really wanted to decorate a special cake for this birthday (or party, or dinner, or . . . insert occasion here), but it just seemed too hard," or "I meant to come up with a cake, but I ran out of time," or "I'd like to do that, but I'm not that creative." If you're guilty of using these excuses or others like them, banish them from your mind because an admirable desire to bake and decorate a beautiful cake for someone (or some event) means that you already have the perfect running start. Add some cake flour, confectioners' sugar, a few techniques, and a couple of easily attainable supplies and you'll be pleasantly amazed at how easy and fun it can be to produce a delicious, lovely cake that becomes the smashing centerpiece of a celebration.

From a very early age, I was enthralled with cakes as the four kids in my family got to select whatever birthday cakes we wanted. I often requested a sunshine orange cake with orange frosting; my sister's favorite was strawberry through and through; one brother favored milk chocolate cake, frosting, and filling; and my other brother routinely asked for a choo-choo chocolate chip ice cream cake with chocolate frosting. Eventually, we graduated to more innovative tastes and accoutrements, like the coconut cake that hosted a big top and circus on parade and the banana peanut butter cake that featured a wild configuration of Flintstone toys. I also started to understand how cake delighted grown-ups as much as (if not more than) it did kids, and as an adult planning events and parties for networks, studios, and Fortune 500 companies, I realized that celebrations and opportunities to enjoy cake are everywhere. Particularly delicious, eye-catching cakes can put anyone in a festive mood and make any event that much more memorable.

No doubt you have much to celebrate with friends, family members, and colleagues. And a cake is that winning component that makes everyone realize that where they are, who they're with, and what they're doing is special. Although you certainly may order the cake from a local bakery or supermarket (and occasionally, you may have to), the taste, look, charm, and feelings conveyed by a homemade decorated cake are simply unparalleled. Be it at a birthday party, bridal shower, wedding reception, anniversary celebration, graduation, holiday gathering, date night, awards banquet, retirement party, bon voyage soirée, or dessert buffet, your own specially created cake is always welcome.

For your cake decorating endeavors, you can draw inspiration from a variety of sources: some common, some unique, some understandable, some unfathomable. Inspiration may come in the form of haute couture fashion design, a vintage piece of china, a college football game, a cereal box, a state map, an advertising relic from a certain decade . . . and of course the person or event being honored.

About This Book

This book shares the basics and beyond necessary to bake, frost, fill, and decorate a variety of cakes. Because I cover varying degrees of difficulty, this book truly is accessible to all. Each cake commands different skills for all the activities that complete the cake's look: mixing up batters, whipping up frostings and fillings, modeling frosting roses or marzipan miniatures, getting desired results from assorted icing tips, handling frosting-filled pastry bags, and selecting the perfect embellishments to be eaten or just simply marveled at. But ultimately, the beauty of cake decorating is that it can be very simple and elegant or extraordinary and detailed.

You can use the tips, tools, guidelines, and instructions herein to create your own designs, or you can rely on the proven recipes and directions I provide to bake and decorate tested (and happily tasted) cakes for a variety of occasions and celebrations. Regardless of your choice, you can use the information I provide on an assortment of techniques and a wide range of embellishments to complete, accomplish, and perfect stunning creations.

I promise that, in no time at all, you'll be creating, baking, and decorating your very own cakes that will amaze, impress, and delight . . . and bring incalculable rewards for your time and effort.

Conventions Used in This Book

Baking is one culinary art in which using precise ingredients and following a recipe to a T are absolute musts. If you're not the type to read a recipe before diving in, here's my gentle plea to change your ways for the better.

For optimal results, keep the following recipe conventions in mind as you embark on each new cake project:

- Most of the cake recipes call for cake flour, which is a lighter, finer version of all-purpose flour that makes cakes more tender.
- Confectioners' sugar (also known as *powdered sugar*) is 10X.
- White granulated and brown sugars are cane sugars.
- Butter is unsalted. Do not substitute margarine or vegetable spread.

✔ Extracts (vanilla, almond, and so on) are pure (not imitation), unless otherwise indicated.

✔ Salt is finely granulated table salt, not kosher or sea salt.

✔ Oil is all-vegetable. Avoid other kinds of oil (such as peanut), and definitely steer clear of any type of olive oil.

✔ If water is called for, use filtered water.

✔ Unless otherwise directed, mixing should be done with a stand mixer rather than a hand mixer.

Occasional patches of text highlighted in gray are known as *sidebars,* and they contain information that I think may come in handy or interest you. Although I'm fond of the details doled out in sidebars, reading them isn't required for your understanding of the text or your ability to execute any of the projects. (But if you do read the sidebars, you'll have some great conversation starters to use at parties and an even deeper understanding of cake trivia, origins, and such.)

Foolish Assumptions

Call me crazy, but in writing this book, I assumed a few things about you, the reader:

✔ You love cake or are eager to impress with cake.

✔ You know your way around a baking aisle or have a friend to guide you.

Beyond that, anything goes: You may be ready to try cake decorating for the first time; you may have done some cake decorating in the past but want to expand your repertoire, ratchet up your skill level, add a few techniques; or both. In any case, you don't need to have any experience whipping up prize-winning confections in order to get something from this book. You just need an appetite for sweet success.

How This Book Is Organized

This book is divided into six parts that cover cake decorating from all angles, from an overall look at its primary components to preparing layers and frostings to be embellished in various ways, with a variety of techniques, for a myriad of occasions and celebrations. The parts also cover serving in style, taking shortcuts, and getting kids involved.

Part I: Getting Ready to Decorate with Ease and Expertise

This part offers up everything you need to know about gathering all the tools you need for cake decorating, setting up your very own cake station, and filling your pantry with the finest ingredients for the most delicious and most impressive cakes.

Part II: Preparing the Canvas of Cake

The chapters in this part delve into the details for determining how your cake should look and embracing some easy artistic concepts with which to design it. With design in hand, you prepare to make the cake from scratch and set it up for the decorating process.

Part III: Topping, Filling, and Embellishing Your Creations

With a luscious cake baked and waiting, this part tackles demystifying and deconstructing the cake decorating process with foolproof recipes and instructions for topping the cake with frostings and icings, spreading the layers with complementary fillings, and embellishing the creation with the perfect accoutrements, designs, and accompaniments.

Part IV: Sweetening Life's Special Occasions

Nothing says "celebrate" like a cake at a gathering, party, or event. Part IV looks at some of the most popular times for cakes, and showcases raves-winning, delicious creations with easy-to-follow directions. And, since most parties build up to that moment when the cake will be served, these ideas won't let partygoers down. In addition to a comprehensive selection of cakes you'll love to make and decorate, you'll also glean — in different chapters — tips on baking with kids, commanding popular shower power moves, and dream up even more occasions for cakes.

Part V: Thinking Outside the Cake Box

This part addresses a few things sure to get your heart racing: transporting your finished cake, creating a cake in a flash when an occasion surprisingly pops up, and turning your cakes into an exciting new moneymaking venture. If you're so inclined to start a cake decorating business, you find out what you need to consider and how to get your venture up and running and successful.

Part VI: The Part of Tens

The indispensable reference information in this part includes the ten best places to find cake supplies and inspiration, ten ways to cut and serve a cake, ten easy alternatives to conventional baking and frosting practices, and ten techniques to try when your cake just doesn't come out according to plan.

Icons Used in This Book

You'll notice a few symbols repeatedly scattered throughout this book. These icons are intended to point out useful information and advice.

This icon alerts you to information that's time-saving, creatively instructive, or otherwise helpful in your cake decorating adventures.

This icon points to something that you should pay close attention to and keep in mind as you consider and put what you read here into practice.

When you see this icon, take heed: It's attached to safety essentials and ways to prevent mistakes and mishaps in your preparation, baking, and decoration.

This icon highlights some pointers and details that deal more with the science of baking than the art of it. Skipping this text won't harm your efforts, but I promise that your head won't swim and you'll be more enlightened if you decide to read it.

Where to Go from Here

Obviously, I love cake decorating and just can't get enough of it. The endless design possibilities, flavor combinations, vibrant colors, amazing tastes, and happy cake eaters coalesce for a remarkably fulfilling experience.

If you're just starting out, you may want to flip to Part I to find out about getting the cake decorating tools and ingredients you need for the job as well as map out space in which to work. Then you may want to segue into mastering a few basic recipes and trying some simple designs.

If you already have some experience decorating cakes, you may want to head to the chapters containing recipes for cakes and frostings and add those to your repertoire. Or you may turn to Chapters 11 and 12 to pick up a new embellishment technique or two, like working with different icing tips, modeling with marzipan, or crafting buttercream roses.

Part IV, the home of recipes and instructions to create specific cake designs, is a great place to start if you have experience in decorating or if you have a child's birthday party, a cousin's wedding, or another special occasion on the horizon. The cakes in these chapters will cheerily light up a celebration and cake eaters' faces.

If someone you want to impress is coming over tonight and you don't have time to go through the whole process of cake decorating, skip directly to the fast fixes in Chapter 19.

Cake decorating is a marvelous union of art, baking, your point of view, and your knack for celebrating in style. I encourage you to relish every moment of the process, from concept to creation, because few pursuits can boast such satisfying, vibrant, heady — and delicious — results.

Part I

Getting Ready to Decorate with Ease and Expertise

The 5th Wave   By Rich Tennant

Because angel food cake is easy to make, that's why. If you want something else for a change, make your own dessert.

In this part . . .

Everyone loves to see cake at a gathering, party, or event. This part puts you squarely — and delightedly — on the path to tapping into your well of creativity and swiftly building skills for designing, baking, and decorating amazing cakes. You delve into setting up your very own cake station, collecting the tools you need, and considering how to style a cake your way.

Chapter 1

Acquiring the Skills and Creativity

In This Chapter

▶ Linking baking skills with your creativity and tastes

▶ Working through the cake process

▶ Becoming a cake designer

▶ Embracing all cake opportunities

Cake decorating requires both skill and creativity . . . but you can do it for every occasion that calls for a celebration! With an understanding of some basic mechanics (and maybe a few secrets), you can create amazing, memorable cakes that impress and delight partygoers, event attendees, and families alike.

Truth be told, who needs an occasion to bake and decorate a cake? When you get wrapped up in the sheer enjoyment of dreaming up a cake's design, mixing batters and making frostings, selecting the perfect accompaniments and colors, and the tasty results that undoubtedly bring smiles aplenty, you don't need an occasion to create a delicious masterpiece.

If you peruse magazine pages or fancy bakery cases with cakes that you think your work can't possibly match up to, fear not! All you need is the instruction in this book, the inspiration provided by your family, friends, and events . . . and a love of cake!

Bridging Baking and Creativity

From a very young age, practically everyone loves to eat cake. (Do you have pictures of yourself on your first birthday with cake smeared all over your hands and face? I do.) For most people, the word "cake" conjures up images of sweet times, fun gatherings, and memorable celebrations.

On its own, a cake certainly can be beautiful and delicious. But a decorated cake, particularly one with well-executed flavors and designs that's stunning in its own right and appropriate for the occasion, takes the event to another level, delights all those in attendance, and — perhaps most important — makes the celebrant or honoree feel even more special.

Chefs and bakers sometimes are referred to as *culinary artists* because, in many ways, food influences expression and creativity like more conventional art forms. There may be sweet ingredients you can't wait to try, an imported candy in the perfect color that inspires you to create a whole design around it, or a restaurant dessert that you're eager to recreate.

Cake decorating, as an art and activity, allows you to express yourself in so many ways. You build upon an array of talents such as baking, cooking, pairing flavors, thinking up and drawing designs, creating and assigning colors, mastering tip techniques, and modeling embellishments. In addition to executing the final cake design, you also infuse your personality and artistic expression into how the cake is showcased and served.

And cake decorating can be as simple or complex as you like. You can transform cake layers and sizes into a towering masterpiece, like a multitiered chocolate cake castle with edible stone walls and gum paste flowers climbing multiple stories, or a simple confection, like a double-layer round white cake with raspberry filling and swirls of buttercream frosting on the outside. You can elaborately script a message in chartreuse frosting or feature rows of different colored shredded coconut. You can top it with pink roses or festoon it with silver dragees. Experimenting with and practicing different techniques helps you swiftly take on more delicate or demanding decorations.

Gathering the Tools and Ingredients

Cake decorating requires that you acquire — and know how to use — a variety of tools and equipment. Some items are common enough that you're likely to have them on hand already, but others may require some Internet shopping or visits to stores that specialize in cake decorating. If you don't plan ahead and keep yourself organized, all the things you need and use in cake baking and decorating could take over your kitchen! Like many activities and hobbies, cake decorating needs a home base. One organization item I recommend you put together is a cake decorating kit that includes tips, flower nails, pastry bags, and other items. Although some apparatuses and goods, such as odd-sized baking pans and decorating turntables, may not fit in a kit, they do fit in with your endeavors, so you need to have them on hand as well. Further, cake baking and decorating relies on an assortment of typical ingredients, some of which all aspiring and practicing bakers are familiar with. Other ingredients, like food coloring gels and embellishments, are quite unique to cake decorating.

Cake decorating utilizes a space that doesn't have to be massive but does have to be efficiently appropriated and used. Trust me: You absolutely don't need a five-star kitchen to work on your masterpieces. Keen organization skills help you make the most out of your existing counter space for sufficient elbowroom.

Picking Up the Skills

The art of cake decorating breaks down into several skill sets, which you eventually combine (effortlessly, of course) to create your cakes. From the first hint of a desire to decorate cakes, it's important to remember that cake decorating is a process; you get to mix things up and get your hands dirty with decorations, but you also need to spend time thinking about your cake and planning your design and execution.

Baking the foundations

The foundation for your work — that is, moist and delicious cakes — means that you have to tackle baking with verve. And baking — believe it or not — has rules you should follow for ultimate success. For instance, to get the most out of your baking efforts, use key ingredients, line your pans, and take care to mix the perfect batters.

When your cakes come out of the oven, you must prepare them . . . much like an artist readies a canvas. From leveling to torting to crumb-coating, you depend on a host of strategies to create the optimal surface for decorating.

In Part II of this book, I provide some master cake recipes, such as Delicious Yellow Cake, A Most Excellent White Cake, and Cocoa Chocolate Cake. When you get these cakes under your belt, you can experiment with them in a variety of ways to create new and different flavors.

Spreading on the layers

Before segueing to decorate the outside of the cake with designs and embellishments, you may want to consider adding a filling other than frosting between the cake's layers. Fruit curd, whipped cream, and nut spreads can all complement the cake and frosting flavors while adding another flavor dimension.

After baking and filling your cake, you head into the favorite cake-covering domain of many: frosting . . . gobs and gobs of frosting. Buttercream, chocolate ganache, and cream cheese (all of which I give you recipes for in Part III), are delicious standards. Of course, even though frostings are fun to mix and master, other cake coverings, including icing, fondant, and glaze, have their own distinct advantages, too.

Decorating with tips and embellishments

Oftentimes, when people dream of a tasty and perfectly decorated cake, they can't help but imagine frosting lined up in rosettes or stars, in ridges around a cake's circumference, spelling out names and greetings, or even forming complete pictures. These decorations are all made possible thanks to icing tips, of which there are many different kinds to use for cake decorating. You can almost certainly replicate in frosting any frill, design, or picture you have in mind thanks to the tips that you guide to outline and fill in designs. Because there are so many different tips available to you, and because the designs you create using them can range from simple to highly complex, Part III covers tips from all angles: the staggering array of available tips, the amazing effects they can produce, and how you can pick up tip skills with some guidance, instruction, and a little practice.

Icing tips unleash a veritable juggernaut of choices and effects, while embellishments also enhance cake designs. Embellishments are edible and inedible, common and uncommon, accoutrements, trimmings, frills, and figures. They range from fresh flowers you pick up or order from a nursery to candies you find on a grocery store aisle. An inedible embellishment may be a wedding cake topper made out of fine bone china or a car made out of pressed tin. Or you may choose to apply a few more techniques to craft embellishments out of frosting, as in roses or hyacinths; out of marzipan, as in miniature, realistic versions of fruits and vegetables; or out of gum paste, as in flowers.

Setting up, striking down

Your cake no doubt will be a stunning creation in its own right, but you should keep in mind how it will be presented just before it's served. You never want your amazing work of art just to be plopped down on a table next to a garbage can or in a dark corner surrounded by the wires of a nearby coffee pot! Set up your cake for success by placing it properly on a sturdy, decorated cake board and taking care with transportation, and showcase and serve your cake in a venue that does it — and cake eaters — justice.

After the lights dim on the big event, you (hopefully) won't have any leftovers because your cake will have been such a hit. But if you do find yourself with remaining cake, don't let it go to waste! Carefully storing, refrigerating, and freezing both just-baked cake layers and frosted finished cakes guarantees that your cake always tastes as good as its first outing.

Infusing Your Own Taste

After you master some basic recipes and techniques, a good deal of the fun of cake decorating lies in bringing your own tastes, talents, preferences, and personality to the proceedings. For your creation, you're part architect and part fashion designer . . . and the best part is that you actually get to eat your work of art.

When you're wearing the architect hat, you figure out your cake's structure and size and how the layers and embellishments will hold up. And much like a fashion designer working on apparel, you get to decide your own look, texture, and overall appearance using frostings, icings, and embellishments instead of fabrics. Draw upon your own preferences and palette while taking into account the celebration and the honoree being feted with cake.

For the most impressively decorated cake, you have to start with a plan, so hunker down and map out what your cake will look like. With only a vague image in mind, you're on the road to disaster if you take a stab at decorating willy-nilly with an icing bag filled with an arbitrarily colored frosting. Some people want to race right on to picking up that icing spatula and getting that frosting on the cake, but they're really missing out. Part of cake decorating's charm and allure definitely plays into laying out how your particular confection will look and how you plan to achieve it and then doing your best to follow that path or — if need be — improvising to get your desired result.

In putting your own creative spin on a cake, you need to consider several points regarding the event, party, or occasion, and the honoree (or honorees). To make sure that you devise the right cake plan for the occasion, your cake research entails finding out about the celebrant's likes and dislikes, the theme of the party, the colors involved, the feel of the location, and so on.

Your plan may involve deftly following a pattern, adapting a design from a template, or coming up with your own design from scratch. Whatever design route you decide to take, you'll be choosing colors, considering shapes and sizes, plotting out the design in the space available, and factoring in curves, lines, and outlines.

Calling All Occasions

With cake decorating, you quickly realize that opportunities for a wonderfully decorated cake are limitless. Consider making cakes for these special events:

- Kids' birthday parties
- Grown-up dinner parties
- Baby showers

- ✔ Bridal showers
- ✔ Weddings
- ✔ Anniversaries
- ✔ Graduations
- ✔ Housewarmings

And these holidays:

- ✔ Valentine's Day
- ✔ Easter
- ✔ The Fourth of July
- ✔ Halloween
- ✔ Thanksgiving
- ✔ Christmas
- ✔ New Year's Eve

Part IV of this book arms you with recipes and instructions for creating cakes for a variety of special occasions and a variety of honorees. From whimsical birthday cakes for boys, girls, or both, to themed creations that prove that cakes aren't just kids' stuff, baby and bridal shower cakes, to wedding and anniversary confections, and cakes for many holidays in between, your memorable creations add to the events and stand the test of time. Some of the designs I provide feature elements particular to the occasion, such as fondant, frosting flowers, or kid-friendly decorations. And each chapter in this part reviews considerations you should bear in mind when making cakes for kids (both boys and girls), men, and women.

Recognizing Possibilities

Your cake decorating ventures (and adventures) may be so entertaining, thrilling, and fulfilling that you decide to switch careers or make cake decorating a part-time job. Taking cake decorating to the next level isn't as simple as making cakes and selling them to friends and family. When starting a cake decorating business, you have goals to consider, a workspace to locate, equipment to get your hands on, and marketing strategies to implement.

So whether you decide to take it up as a career or simply enjoy it as a hobby, cake decorating will provide you — and countless others — constant opportunities to celebrate life's occasions . . . and eat cake!

Chapter 2

Assembling Your Cake Decorating Kit

In This Chapter

▶ Gathering the tools for cake decorating

▶ Storing your supplies

I n a sense, the magic of cake decorating begins with your very own cake decorating kit that's tailored to your needs, wants, skills, and aspirations.

Depending on the level of decorating you're taking on, this kit could be a durable box, a plastic case, or an entire cupboard; it includes all the goods, gadgets, and tools you need to turn out decorated cakes. You may already have some of the items for your kit, but others may be new and mysterious. So this chapter helps with the intimidation factor by explaining the uses and various functions of your kit items along with where you can get them in the first place.

The items included in this chapter cover quite an extensive range of equipment that assists in baking, leveling, frosting, filling, and decorating. Don't feel like you have to run out and buy everything listed here all at once or like you can't give cake decorating a go without having every single item on hand. Throughout the chapter, I point out the items that are absolutely essential, and you can choose to add other items to your cake decorating kit as you become increasingly proficient in some areas or veer off in new decorating directions.

Targeting Tips and Flower Nails

Closely associated with cake decorating and integral to your endeavors, tips, couplers, and flower nails are the tools that will need a special place in your kit because they will help you create and craft a host of fabulous designs. While just the terms may initially seem intimidating, fear not: They won't be only a trusty addition to your kit, you'll enjoy them as some of your most valuable resources.

Starting with essential icing tips

When it comes to stocking your cake decorating kit, you have dozens of icing tips to choose from, but you're likely to rely on only a handful of tips over and over again in your cake decorating escapades. Because of that, you can start off with a simple collection of some standard sizes.

Before I get into specific tip sizes, I recommend that you work with nickel-plated tips, which should be washed by hand. Plastic tips are widely available — and usually you can run them through a dishwasher for easy cleanup — but they aren't as reliable as metal tips in design or execution.

Based on my experience, a collection of round tips in a variety of sizes will serve you well; when you're just getting started, you'll repeatedly call on round tips #1 through #10. These tips are appropriate for a range of techniques that are both simple and stunning and include piping dots and strings, scripting, forming block letters, and writing messages. You should also gather the following more-specialized tips:

- Star tips, such as #16, #18, #21, and #32
- Basket weave tip, such as #48
- Leaf tips, such as #67 and #352
- Petal tips, such as #102, #103, #104, and #125

A variety of tips are shown in Figure 2-1.

Rather than purchase individual tips, many people opt for tip sets, which include many of these essential tips; sets range from student sets that have less than 10 tips to professional ones that boast more than 50 tips. (I was pretty ambitious from the get-go, and my first kit had more than 30 tips, which I continue to supplement.) Standard tips run less than $1 each, so if you start out with a small tip set, you certainly can keep adding on at a relatively slim cost.

When you purchase your tips, make sure to buy a tip cleaning brush, too. A very worthy and very inexpensive investment, the tip cleaning brush helps you get deep into pointed tips to remove any frosting residue that running water (or a wadded-up, damp paper towel) just can't get!

Regardless of whether you buy individual icing tips or a set, take the opportunity as soon as possible to test every tip, practicing with each one to see its particular design and to start thinking about how you can integrate each one into your cake decorating. As you play around, remember that some tips can give more than one effect: As you pipe, turn the tips over on different sides to maximize the frosting effects.

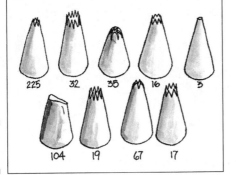

Figure 2-1:
Icing tips.

For a more-detailed discussion of all kinds of tips and their forms and functions, check out Chapter 11.

Adding couplers

To fit a tip onto a pastry bag, you need a *coupler,* which consists of two parts:

- ✓ A round plastic cone that you fit inside the pastry bag
- ✓ A coupler ring that you screw over the tip on the outside of the bag

I like having lots of couplers handy (see Figure 2-2) because they allow me to ready several different colored frostings all at once. Also, couplers are useful when your cake design involves different piping designs in the same color frosting: Instead of preparing a pastry bag for each tip you need to use, you just outfit one bag of frosting with a coupler and then change the tips.

For some reason, cake decorating kits sold as a complete lot rarely include more than one or two couplers. Invest in at least a few more; they're inexpensive, and having them on hand is guaranteed to save you time.

Fixating on flower nails

A *flower nail* is a spindly tool with a large, circular flat head; as you can see in Figure 2-3, it looks very much like its name suggests. However, the head of a flower nail is much larger than that of any nail you'd find in a hardware store. Flower nails come in different sizes, but a #7 is a good standard size for your decorating kit.

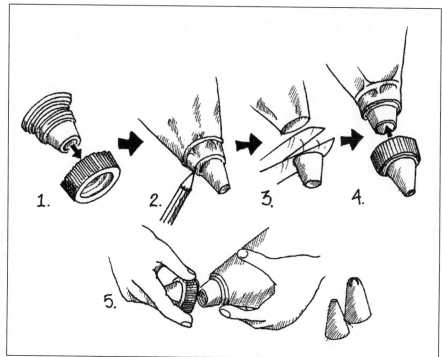

Figure 2-2:
Putting a
coupler on a
pastry bag.

The head of a flower nail is big enough to craft a single frosting rose bloom on, but even if rose-making doesn't interest you, you also can use it for creating other types of flowers.

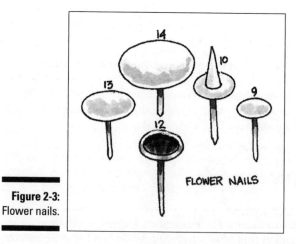

Figure 2-3:
Flower nails.

Picking Out Paper Goods and Pastry Bags

A few disposable goods are completely indispensable in your cake decorating efforts. The following items don't necessarily fit into a cake decorating caddy, but they should be on hand in your pantry:

- ✔ **Parchment paper:** You use parchment paper to line your baking pans, particularly big ones and pans that you're filling with tender batters. In addition, parchment paper also provides a good practice surface to test out designs beforehand with your frosting-filled pastry bag. Purchase parchment paper either by the roll or in packs of 12-x-16-inch sheets.

- ✔ **Wax paper:** If you decide to frost and decorate a cake on the platter or tray that you plan to serve it from, placing wax paper strips under the edge of the cake before you decorate and then removing them after you're done keeps your serving platter, plate, or board free of any smudges or frosting drips that could detract from a neat presentation.

    Wax paper also provides a handy assist when creating multiple frosting flowers and storing flowers until you're ready to apply them to your cake. Attach a square to a flower nail with a dab of frosting, and pipe a flower directly onto the wax paper. Then remove the wax paper square from the nail, attach a clean square, and pipe the next flower.

- ✔ **Plastic tumblers:** Clear, plastic tumblers are great for holding frosting-filled pastry bags upright or for holding empty bags upright while you fill them with frosting.

- ✔ **Paper bowls:** Mixing frosting and colors in paper bowls means easy cleanup.

- ✔ **Plastic spoons:** Mixing frosting and colors with plastic spoons is a great way to cut down on your cleanup time.

- ✔ **Cupcake liners:** Keep cupcake liners in stock, and be on the lookout for liners that are pretty but out of the ordinary. For instance, a pattern sold around the holidays actually may be suitable for year-round use.

- ✔ **Disposable pastry bags:** You have more than one option for pastry bags, but I almost always veer toward disposable ones. I find that it's just plain easier to toss a frosting bag away after you're done using it rather than try to clean out the excess frosting and then dry it. If you prefer, you can use reusable decorating bags — just be sure to keep them clean and dry so that they're always ready for your next cake decorating adventure.

- ✔ **Cardboard rounds and squares:** Typically, you set each layer of a cake on a cardboard round or square (depending on the shape of the layer) to provide stability to the cake, to keep it from cracking or breaking as you move it around, and to make it easier to move during the decoration and boarding process.

Sizing Up Pan Shapes

Baking pans are a necessity. Invest in chef-quality ones, which, although expensive, more than make up for the cost with durability and results. Good pans produce cake layers that are higher and more level. Chef-quality pans have perpendicular sides, which give your cake straight and clean lines (rather than slanted ones) for a much more professional look.

As far as pan shapes are concerned, you can get a lot of decorating mileage out of just a few basics.

Rectangular and square

Rectangular cake pans produce some of the most common cake shapes, like *quarter-sheet, half-sheet,* and *sheet cakes.* Typically, these sizes are for cakes for crowds, big and small. While this terminology is consistent among bakers, I've found that the sizes for these cakes actually varies. As a general guideline though, a quarter-sheet cake is 9″ x 13″, a half-sheet is 12″ x 18″, and a full-sheet is 18″ x 24″. Therefore, a full-sheet could be "put together" by having the more regular 12″ x 18″ size on hand. The rectangular cake pans you should have are the 9-x-13-inch and the 12-x-18-inch. In addition, for variety, I recommend picking up a 10-inch square pan as well.

When you have only one pan of a certain dimension, you double your baking time when you need two layers. Consider getting two pans in the 9-x-13-inch and 10-inch sizes. The 12-x-18-inch pan is big enough and deep enough that it's unlikely that you'll stack two such generous layers.

Round and oval

Round cakes are perhaps the most ubiquitous cake shape. Because smaller rounds are perfect for cakes for small dinner parties and family gatherings, invest in two 8-inch or 9-inch rounds. If you occasionally take on bigger parties and like a little variety, consider having 10-inch, 12-inch, and 14-inch rounds on hand, too. I'm also a fan of the 6-inch round pan; a decorated cake that size makes a simple thank-you to someone, and it also provides a nice accent to a bigger cake.

Oval cakes have been in vogue lately, so if you're into the modern look, you may want to have this type of pan as well.

Cupcake tins

If you opt to go the cupcake route on a cake recipe, you're likely to need two cupcake tins, each one with 12 wells. A nonstick surface is only necessary if you don't plan to use cupcake liners.

Bundt

Some bakers like Bundt pans because they can just pour in the batter and not worry about leveling and layering. I developed a fondness for these pans when I was mastering the Tunnel of Fudge recipe from scratch.

Traditional Bundt pans allow you to create interesting shapes with cake (such as the doll dress cake in Chapter 13 and the jack-o'-lantern cake in Chapter 17) with a minimal amount of work. I recommend that you have at least one Bundt pan in your equipment cupboard. Nonstick varieties are available but not necessary. And while you can certainly invest in a cavalcade of different shapes and sizes of Bundt pans, I suggest you at least have one traditional-shaped one.

Specialty shapes

In recent years, you may have noticed that cooking stores and even chain stores are flooded with an assortment of cake pans in all sorts of shapes. These specialty pans aren't necessary for general cake decorating, but if a particular shape catches your attention and triggers your creativity, go for it!

Unfortunately, cakes don't always turn out like the pictures on pan packaging, so if you plan to use a specialty shape pan for a special occasion, do a trial run and bake a cake in it ahead of time to avoid any mishaps with your final product. Also, many specialty pans turn out cakes with raised or indented features, and baking a test cake gives you the opportunity to figure out the best way to spotlight the intricate design. For example, you may want to sprinkle the cake with powdered sugar or coat it with a thin icing that settles into the design's fine lines.

Boarding Cakes

Every cake needs a home. Cake plates and cake pedestals are standard for round cakes. However, for larger cakes — such as quarter-sheet, half-sheet, and full-sheet cakes, my favorite vehicle is a 16-x-22-inch hardwood pastry board that's ¾-inch thick. Other options for cake boards include foam core, cardboard, plywood, and Masonite.

If you work with only one cake at a time, you need only one pastry board, which you can easily dress up to go with the cake or the occasion. For example, you can cover the board with wrapping paper and then heavy cellophane wrap to keep it clean. Or you can dress the board with an assortment of decorative foils that are available online or at national craft stores. (I cover cake board decorating in Chapter 7.)

Don't cover your cake board in aluminum foil. Sure, it does the job, but it isn't the most attractive covering. You have so many options for coverings, and the shiny, wrinkly presence of plain aluminum foil will definitely detract from your delicious, beautiful cake.

Gathering General Utensils

You may already have some of the items in this category of goods in your kitchen. In the cake decorating process, they're the workhorses that both fortify and enhance your endeavors.

Ruler

A ruler is a must when measuring out designs and transferring the width, height, and length of a sketch to the actual cake. You may also need it to figure out the lengths of frosting strings, garlands, swags, and borders.

Cookie, fondant, and gum paste cutters

Cookie cutters provide you with ready-made outlines and stencils for filling in with sanding sugars and nonpareils. (Plus, you can incorporate different-shaped cookies into your cake design.) Gum paste cutters are specifically sized for shaping flowers, and fondant cutters come in a nice range of graduated sizes for layering or creating other designs with rolled fondant. Most of these different kinds of cutters come in either metal or plastic; I find that metal cuts more easily, but plastic's easier to clean . . . so in the end, it's your pick!

Cooling racks

After that cake comes out of the oven, it has to cool somewhere, and the crisscross wirework of cooling racks provides optimal ventilation. To accommodate a variety of cake shapes and sizes, have two sizes of racks on hand — a 10-x-16-inch and a 14½-x-20-inch. Also, because you have to invert cake layers when they come out of the oven, it's a good idea to have two cooling racks of each size for flipping the cake over.

Buy stainless steel or nickel-plated cooling racks so that you don't have to contend with rust.

Pastry brush

A pastry brush, preferably one with silicone bristles, is a great tool for sweeping the crumbs from your just-baked cake. Getting the crumbs off your cake surface and sides makes your crumb coat more effective (because there are fewer crumbs to cover up), which keeps your frosting as crumb-free as possible.

Use a dedicated pastry brush for your cake decorating work. Although pastry brushes clean up well in a dishwasher, it's better not to worry about what scents or residue may remain on the brush from that barbecue chicken you basted or the roasted vegetables you brushed with olive oil.

Rubber spatulas

No kitchen utensil works quite as effectively for scraping every last drop of cake batter or frosting out of a mixing bowl as a flexible rubber spatula. Rubber spatulas also are perfect for gently folding whipped egg whites or whipped cream into a recipe. Stock up on different shapes and sizes.

Large spatula

I recommend also getting a stainless-steel spatula (or turner) that will make moving a cake layer — from cooling rack to cake board, for example — easier. The wood-handled spatulas I use for this are 14-inches long, with the stainless steel "blade" or "lifter" portion measuring 10-inches long by 3-inches wide.

Thermometers

To make cake baking and decorating easier and more accurate, you need a candy thermometer and an oven thermometer. A candy thermometer is about

12 inches long and has a clip on the back side so that it can hang down into your pot for an accurate temperature reading. Look for a stainless steel variety that's dishwasher-safe. A candy thermometer is necessary when preparing cooked frostings and fillings, such as caramel and lemon curd, in which the mixture has to reach a certain temperature for the desired flavor and consistency. Some recipes call for a mixture to be heated to the *thread* or *soft-ball stages,* both of which are clearly marked on a candy thermometer.

An oven thermometer helps you keep your oven's temperature in check. You may have set the oven to 350 degrees F, but it may not actually be that hot — or it could be hotter. An independent gauge, the oven thermometer clips to an oven rack so that you can easily read the oven's actual temperature. If the reading doesn't match up with your oven setting, then you can make the necessary adjustments to get the temperature you need.

Cake tester

You can certainly rely on toothpicks or bamboo skewers to test a cake for doneness, but I suggest having something more permanent. This skinny, stainless steel rod usually measures between 5 and 7 inches.

Rolling pins

A rolling pin — which can be wooden, marble, or metal — is a must for working with rolled fondant. Depending on how often you work with marzipan, gum paste, and fondant, you may also consider purchasing smaller, nonstick rolling pins designed specifically for working with those confections.

Toothpicks, bamboo skewers, and dowels

This trio of wooden tools works wonders for your cake decorating in a variety of capacities. Their most obvious duties include:

- ✔ **Toothpicks:** Handy for mixing colors into marzipan or fondant and for testing for doneness (if you don't have a metal cake tester)
- ✔ **Bamboo skewers:** The perfect tools for sketching out a cake's design on a frosted cake
- ✔ **Dowels:** Provide internal support to tiered cakes

Tooling Around with Decorating Specifics

The tools covered in this section help you refine your cake design and allow for a more polished and professional look.

Decorating comb

This type of comb has no place on a vanity! Drawing it over a layer of frosting creates evenly spaced rows, lines, and V-shaped patterns across the top of a cake or along its sides. Cake decorating combs come in varying lengths. Some have a straight side that produces no texture, and others may have teeth on both sides. Different widths distinguish the teeth on each side of a dual-sided comb (see Figure 2-4).

Turntable

The turntable can be absolutely invaluable in decorating. Invest in one and you'll wonder how you ever decorated without it! With this device, your cake sits on a platform that rests on a rotating wheel of sorts. You can stay in one position while you spin your cake around to frost and decorate it on all sides. With a turntable, you also get an even visual perspective of all sides of the cake.

Plastic turntables with pedestals are fairly inexpensive. You can also find turntables that have pedestals that angle up, which make decorating even easier (especially when you're working on a time-consuming and involved design like a basket weave). If you want to step up from plastic, sturdier turntables are available with cast-iron stands and aluminum tops.

Figure 2-4:
A decorating comb is a great tool for adding texture to frosting.

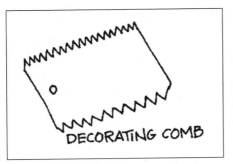

DECORATING COMB

Leveling assists

A level cake that provides a flat surface for designs is a cake decorator's dream. And achieving a level cake is easier than you think with this trio of tools.

Levelers

Cake levelers allow you to slice off a cake's dome or crown so that you're left with a completely level, flat surface. Typically, this apparatus consists of a sharp blade or wire stretched between two short steel poles with a handle on the top. You adjust the blade to the height of your cake top, set the poles on your work surface, and slide the blade across the cake, taking off just enough to make the entire layer level. Levelers come in both large and small varieties to accommodate various sizes of cakes.

Particularly sturdy and sharp levelers can also *torte* layers, allowing you to split a cake into two or three layers that you then fill.

Bake even strips

These insulated strips fit snugly around a cake pan to insure moist, even cake layers and prevent cracked or domed tops. You soak the strips and then place them around the circumference of the pan before baking. Essentially, the strips retard baking on the outer edges for more evenness throughout.

Heating core

Recommended for cakes that are 10 inches or larger in diameter, a heating core distributes heat so that larger cakes bake more evenly. This hollow stainless steel element is about 3½ inches in height and 4 inches in diameter. You place it in the center of the cake pan and then fill the pan and core with batter. When the cake is done baking, you remove the core, pop out the piece of cake that's inside it, and use that piece to plug the hole in the cake layer. After you frost the cake, the repaired hole is unnoticeable.

Icing spatulas

Icing spatulas are essential for coating your cakes. These spatulas are quite different from the ones you may use to flip burgers or fried eggs: They look more like knives with rounded blades and usually feature wood or molded plastic handles.

In the icing spatula arena, I prefer offset or angle-blade spatulas. I find that they're more flexible and give my cakes a smoother finish. I recommend that you get two sizes of the offset kind: a 4-inch one and a 9-inch one. In addition, you'll also get a lot of use out of a straight 8-inch spatula, which is particularly good for crumb coating. A variety of spatulas is shown in Figure 2-5.

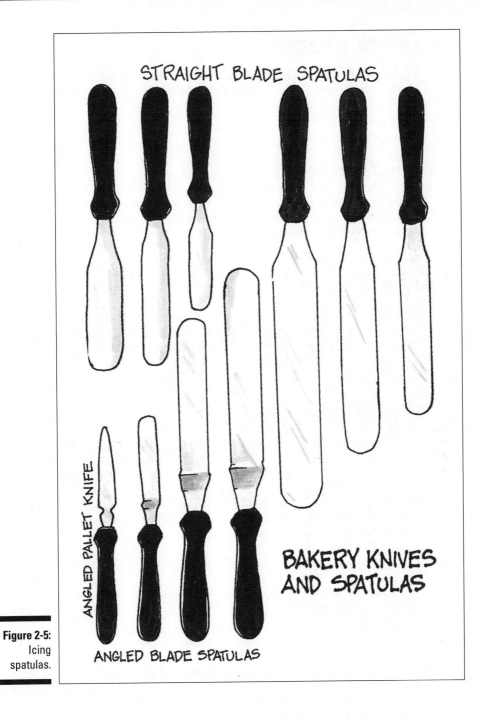

Figure 2-5:
Icing
spatulas.

Bench scraper

Usually about 6 inches long, a bench scraper is an ideal tool for smoothing out the frosting on a cake's sides or circumference. The scraper typically has a molded plastic handle on one side that allows for easy guiding of the other straight-edged side.

Fondant smoother

This tool, which is somewhat shorter than a bench scraper, helps smooth out the draping of rolled fondant for an even finish. You gently glide the fondant smoother across the surface of the cake to take out any wrinkles or bumps.

Modeling tools

Usually made from plastic, a modeling tool set is ideal for shaping creations out of gum paste and fondant. The typical set includes a ball tool to cup and smooth petals, a veining tool for lining up realistic-looking veins in leaves, and a shell tool to emboss patterns.

A color wheel

Color plays an important part in cake decorating for your frosting base, the colors you use to tint frosting, and how you pair colors for different designs. A color wheel, which you can find at art and craft stores, helps you see how certain colors contrast with each other for a dynamic effect or blend together for a complementary tone. You may not even realize some of the colors available to you until you take a few spins on the color wheel and see the limitless possibilities that await you and your cake!

A color wheel has rotating pieces of cardboard stacked on top of each other that let you see gradations of color and how a color mixes with another one to create a third hue (see Figure 2-6). Most color wheels also give you a brief primer on color definitions such as primary, secondary, and tertiary as well as tints, tones, and shades.

Chapter 5 offers tips for introducing and using color in your design, and Chapter 7 covers the process of mixing colors for your cake decorating work.

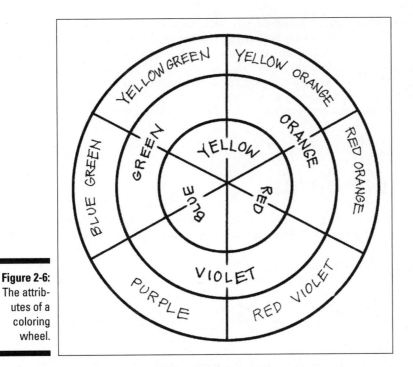

Figure 2-6:
The attributes of a coloring wheel.

Keeping All Your Tools Together

After you collect all your cake decorating kit items, where do you put them? I recommend a portable caddy that will easily store and, if necessary, transport your most vital items. Craft and cake decorating supply stores carry storage boxes that are made specifically for cake decorating, but you can also be inventive. You may find just what you need at a sporting goods store, hardware store, or craft store. I've seen people repurpose or christen anew a tool kit, art caddy, sewing kit, and even a fishing tackle box for their cake decorating headquarters.

A caddy can't hold your baking pans or cooling racks, but it should have a place for your tips, spatulas, pastry bags, decorating comb, and so on. Whatever box or caddy you go with needs to be augmented with tip holders, which are molded plastic cones that keep your icing tips clean, upright, and easy to identify when decorating. If you buy a tip set, you can just hang on to the box it comes in. Or you can purchase a tip storage case, which usually is pretty inexpensive.

You may also want room inside the box or caddy to store your coloring gels (which I cover along with other related cake foodstuffs in Chapter 4). If you put your gels in the same caddy as your other tools, make sure that you sequester them appropriately, like in a sealed plastic bag, so that if one accidentally breaks open, it doesn't ooze all over everything else. No matter how into color you are, you probably aren't too keen on having your tips, icing bags, ruler, and sundry other supplies stained a bright shade of leaf green or neon pink.

Finding the Goods

With the vast array of retail outlets available on the Internet, it's easier than ever to get your cake decorating kit up and running . . . and staying the course.

Before you pull out your wallet, I recommend wandering through a cake decorating store or the cake decorating aisles at a national craft chain store to familiarize yourself with what's out there. Look at the inventory, touch (but don't open!) the supplies, read the packaging, and ask questions of a knowledgeable salesperson. Just don't buy everything you see all at once!

Decorate a few cakes with just the core supplies. Then take another look at the additional offerings to see if any have potential to earn a place in your cake decorating kit.

In addition to the cake decorating supply stores and national craft store chains, cooking stores often devote at least some space to cake decorating. Big box stores also may have a few supplies in their kitchen and housewares sections. For a complete listing of my recommendations for where to buy cake supplies, check out Chapter 21.

Chapter 3

Planning Your Workspace

· ·

In This Chapter

▶ Organizing your kitchen to facilitate baking and decorating

▶ Checking out necessary appliances and equipment

▶ Getting your oven in shape

▶ Dealing with refrigeration and freezing

· ·

*T*his chapter focuses on laying out the most productive area for designing, baking, frosting, filling, and decorating your creation. I show you how best to use the space you have, and I describe the equipment you need to maximize your cake decorating potential. With the proper set-up and equipment, your cake decorating will flourish (rather than be derailed) . . . no matter what your current kitchen looks like.

My initial cake decorating endeavors growing up were in the crushed confines of a kitchen that, decked in the harvest gold hues of the 1970s, was the constantly humming hub of a very busy household. When I first started turning out cakes professionally, I worked in a tiny bungalow kitchen with uncooperative tile counters and a slanted floor that tested both my patience and the oven's ability to bake even cake layers. So I can say from experience that, however small, old, or peculiar your kitchen may be, you can make a cake decorating space that works for you!

Organizing Your Kitchen: What Goes Where

You may have visions of lengthy, polished, stainless steel counters, several deep sinks, and a bounty of double ovens, but you really don't need a million dollar dream kitchen to accomplish all your cake baking and decorating.

What you do need is to keenly analyze your particular workspace and adapt it for your adventure. Besides delineating the area where the actual cake decorating will occur (see the next section for that information), you'll need to figure out the best place for appliances — large and small — for access and efficiency. You also need to determine the kind of counter space that will work for you and adopt some tidy habits for a smooth-running endeavor.

The must-haves in a cake-friendly kitchen are the kitchen components that do figure into your entire cake venture. They include the following:

- ✔ Refrigerator for chilling layers, frostings until they're ready to tint and in between uses, and your finished cake
- ✔ Oven for baking
- ✔ Stovetop for cooking frostings and fillings
- ✔ Mixer for preparing batters, frostings, and fillings
- ✔ Freezer for freezing layers (optional)
- ✔ Microwave for melting and softening
- ✔ Food processor for chopping nuts, chocolate, embellishments
- ✔ Spice or coffee grinder for preparing ingredients that should be finely powdered

Creating a decorating zone

Survey your kitchen to determine where you may set up shop to decorate. Fortunately, because decorating largely takes place after baking, you can get all your baking ingredients and equipment such as cooling racks out of the way before bringing in frosting, coloring gels, piping bags, and embellishments. Because you can't just work anywhere you set down a cake, keep in mind the room you'll need to decorate and the access you'll need to your tools and supplies, including your tinted frostings and embellishments, appliances such as a mixer or spice grinder, and equipment such as a sink.

If you have a cake board, a turntable, or cake cardboard rounds, lay them out in the workspace to get a real sense of the room each item takes up. If you don't have those accessories, lay out your baking pans to get a rough idea of space allotment. If you don't have enough room in one part of your kitchen to work with your decorating equipment, keep moving around until you find the right-sized space.

Also get a sense of the accessibility of the tools you call on in decorating your cakes. You don't always use all these utensils and decorating assists on every project, but it's helpful to get an idea of the space they take up and the space you need to use them. These include (but aren't limited to)

- ✔ Cups, glasses, or clear tumblers to hold frosting bags upright
- ✔ Bowls in which to mix coloring gels into frosting
- ✔ A tray of tips

 ✔ Icing spatulas

 ✔ Decorating combs

The space you decide on for decorating doesn't have to be exclusively for decorating; it just has to serve you during the actual course of decorating. So if you have to shuffle around or remove counter staples (such as a toaster or coffee maker), you can put them back after you're done.

If possible, don't set up your decorating space where you may repeatedly bang your head into an upper cabinet as you work, and the burners of a stove don't qualify as a working counter space.

Promoting accessibility and efficiency

Much is written about the *kitchen triangle,* the workspace pathway between the refrigerator, sink, and oven, but I don't worry so much about that for cake baking and decorating. More important is making sure that all the ingredients for the task are lined up, that all the appliances and apparatuses are in working order, and that all the accoutrements are collected, stacked, and close at hand.

Nothing can stifle (and possibly stop) the cake baking and decorating process like a missing ingredient, a burned-out mixer, or an oven that doesn't reach the desired temperature. If you spot potential problems and troubleshoot from the outset, you're in for a much smoother operation.

Purchase a couple of clear plastic containers (with lids) in which you can collect only the tools, accessories, and nonperishable embellishments that you plan to use for a particular cake. If you don't have the space to lay out everything you need, the containers provide a handy resource to pull from so that you aren't interrupting the cake process to sift through lots of utensils and foodstuffs to find what you need.

Checking out the counter space

In terms of the counter space itself, you really need a smooth, level surface on which to work.

Countertops made of Corian, stainless steel, granite, or Caesarstone are ideal for rolling out fondant or marzipan on because they're seamless. However, if you have tile countertops, for example, you don't need to remodel your kitchen to decorate a cake. You can roll out materials on a large cutting board or durable piece of heavy plastic, or you can purchase even bigger cutting boards — made of stainless steel, for example — on which to do your decorating. Several cake equipment retailers, such as www.kitchensource.com and www.frigodesign.com, sell these types of cutting boards online. If you get one and things are still rocky, lay damp kitchen towels underneath the large cutting board when you're working to anchor the board and offer you a stable surface for decorating.

Giving yourself a little elbow room

Regardless of whether you're in a commercial space, an expansive kitchen, or one that could pass for a cooking closet, get rid of the clutter. Baking and decorating a large cake is made more difficult than it actually is when you're squeezed for room.

Interestingly enough, more space doesn't necessarily mean more organization; even when working out of a commercial or commercial-grade kitchen with long gleaming countertops, you still have to stay on top of keeping the area clean and constantly putting things away. So as you finish each task, put away all the tools involved. Don't sabotage yourself!

To aid your progress and process further, begin your decorating with an empty dishwasher or sink, and clean as you go along. Also have a full roll of paper towels and a clean stack of kitchen towels at the ready to tackle inevitable spills and messes quickly.

Hauling Out the Heavier Equipment

In beating batters, making frostings, incorporating ingredients, and fashioning embellishments, you must rely on an assortment of small appliances to efficiently and effectively get the job done.

Kitchen mixers

I'm very passionate about my particular mixer. I started with a guaranteed refurbished one from a kitchen outlet store that I still have (and that works perfectly) even though the volume of cakes I produce necessitated getting a professional-grade one.

When it comes to choosing a kitchen mixer, you have many options and manufacturers available to you. To narrow the field, I recommend that you first visit manufacturer Web sites to gets specs and terminology for the models you're interested in so that you can ask educated questions, understand the answers, and conduct effective follow-up. Then check the Web for feedback on certain models and visit a store that lets you operate mixers to see how they are in action.

Don't choose a model because you're into the color, it matches your kitchen, or it's on sale. I've had to use mixers that were beautiful to look at but didn't get the job done well at all. Make sure that you fully investigate a mixer's functionality and comparison shop before you make a decision, particularly if you're thinking about making a substantial investment. I've found that, in the case of stand mixers, you get what you pay for! It's not worth buying a cheap mixer over and over again if one $250 model can last for decades (and many more expensive models certainly do).

I vastly prefer a stand mixer to a hand-held one. Although a handheld mixer is good for small, quick jobs or to have around as a backup, the recipes you mix for cake decorating projects really require a powerful stand mixer, preferably one that has at least a five-quart capacity with a 325-watt motor.

For best results when making frostings, batters, and fillings, your mixer should come with both a balloon whisk and paddle attachments.

Food processors and grinders

Both full-size and mini food processors are exceptionally handy in chopping ingredients, such as nuts or dried fruits, or pulsing small quantities of fresh fruits, needed for some batters, frostings, and fillings. Here again, take the time to fully investigate the models out there, and find the one that best suits your needs.

Grinders — either spice or coffee — also are useful for pulverizing substances — such as coffee crystals — into a fine powder that's easy to incorporate into a batter or frosting. You should designate an inexpensive coffee grinder just for nuts and spices so that your nuts don't taste like coffee and your coffee doesn't taste like nuts.

Pasta makers

This equipment recommendation may come as a surprise, but depending on how much work you do with fondant or gum paste, you may want to invest in a pasta maker.

Although not an absolute necessity for your kitchen, a pasta maker is very useful for rolling out fondant to make bows, ribbons, and strips. It's also a timesaver for flattening pieces of gum paste for parts of flowers.

Ideally, you can borrow a pasta maker or work with someone who already has one to determine if it's a piece you think is a must-have. Some kitchen mixers come with pasta maker attachments, too; if yours does, try it out before you decide whether or not to buy a freestanding pasta maker.

Firing Up an Accurate Oven

Whether you have a double oven or tiny range, your cake depends on a good heating environment. You may be surprised to know that there are actually two kinds of ovens available for baking. Knowing about each kind will assist you in turning out the best cakes. Further, cake decorators also revel in the speed and convenience a microwave oven can provide for a host of related duties.

Conventional vs. convection ovens

Conventional ovens heat from below. At the bottom of the oven chamber is an electric heat source that uses air (heated by gas or electricity) to cook the food (or bake the cake). Conventional is the most common type of oven used in today's kitchens. As a result, baking instructions in recipes generally assume that this is the type of oven the reader has.

Some ovens simply don't have the capacity for large pans, so if you're working with a size or shape of pan for the first time, put the empty pan into your empty, cool oven to make sure it fits.

Most ovens are 27-inches or 30-inches. But, if you have the money to spend and the space to put it, I'd go with a 36-inch oven. While certainly not absolutely necessary for the home baker, the accommodation for multiple cookie sheets and large cakes — and the time you save in baking multiple layers all at once — is worth the investment.

And if you're currently in the market for an oven, do yourself a favor: Take your baking sheet and cake pans down to the appliance store and get a first-hand look and feel for how everything fits.

Advanced bakers tend to prefer *convection ovens* for their dependability. In convection ovens, an embedded fan circulates hot air around the baking pan for faster and more even baking. What's more, convection ovens don't have the hot spots or cool spots that may plague conventional ovens. Generally, convection ovens should be set at a lower temperature than a conventional oven. Commonly used in commercial operations, convection ovens have definitely gained in popularity in home use despite their higher cost.

In either case, be familiar with your oven's idiosyncrasies: if it runs hot or cold pertaining to temperature, or if you need to check before suggested "done" times because your oven's generally a few minutes off.

Perfecting temperatures

A good cake depends on a heating environment that you can measure accurately. With some ovens, the temperature you set doesn't match the actual temperature inside the oven; if you aren't aware of the discrepancy, you're in for some frustration. When the temperature is off, baking times are woefully unpredictable, and you're left with an underbaked cake soup or an overcooked cake brick — neither of which is the moist and delicious creation you had in mind.

Invest in an oven thermometer to monitor the temperature inside your oven. Too often, cake problems can be traced to the fact that the oven just isn't the temperature you think it is. If you're aware of the fact that your oven is too hot or too cold, you can lower or raise the temperature to make up the difference. However, to make sure that your temperature problems aren't a symptom of a bigger problem or continue to worsen, I suggest calling a professional to inspect your oven.

Before you turn on the oven, make sure that the racks are in the position you need them to be to bake your cake. Further, after you place your cake in the oven to bake, don't open and close the door excessively. Checking for doneness near the end of the baking time is fine, but up until then, pop the oven light on and use the window to check on your cake. Each time you open the oven door, the temperature drops — as much as 100 degrees in some models!

The microwave has its place, too

Although not normally the oven you use for actual baking, a microwave is a supreme help when it comes to melting chocolate, heating cream and milk, and softening butter. As you probably know, microwave ovens vary widely (and wildly) in terms of cubic feet, wattage, and settings. If you're new to using it in cake decorating assistance, give yourself time (and at least a few tries) to get the results you want.

Refrigerating and Freezing

Before you even begin to pull out ingredients to mix your batter, assess your refrigerator space. Ask yourself:

- Do I have enough room for the cake's layers?
- Do I need room to accommodate fillings or frostings before they're applied to the cake?
- Do I have enough room for the finished cake?

If necessary, clear out some space and rearrange moveable shelves to accommodate what you expect to refrigerate. Remember that you don't have to fit the layers, fillings, and finished cake in there all at once. However, making the necessary arrangements beforehand saves you frustration and reduces the chance that you'll have to watch a whipped cream filling melt while tossing out a dozen leftovers.

Personally, I recommend a "French door bottom freezer" refrigerator. This type has dual, same-sized refrigerator doors, and a pull-out freezer drawer below the doors. In this style — unlike a typical side-by-side — you're able to have shelving that's the width of the refrigerator, and you don't sacrifice depth because the freezer compartment (which also is the width of the refrigerator) is directly below the refrigerator unit. A 20 cubic feet model is fine, but if you have the space and many cakes in your future, by all means check out the 25 cubic feet possibilities.

The freezer may not be an appliance that you expect to use much in cake baking and decorating, but I recommend that you put it to good use by mixing up an extra batch of cake batter when you're making a cake, bake up both cakes, and freeze the extra layers. In so doing, you'll want to make sure that the layers can be positioned flatly; you don't want to be standing them up on end. While they can be stored in a freezer that's part of a side-by-side refrigerator (depending on how much else is in your freezer), I recommend a freezer compartment that affords your cake layers the entire width of the refrigerator.

Cake layers wrapped in plastic wrap and then in aluminum foil keep for 30 days. You may hear that you can keep cake frozen longer, but I don't recommend it. In addition, I also advise against freezing frostings or fillings. To defrost cake, pull the layers out of the freezer and keep them wrapped until they're completely thawed.

Chapter 4

Stocking Your Pantry

. . . .

. . . .

*T*o make, bake, and decorate stunning cakes, you must start with the finest, freshest ingredients. The best-looking cakes should taste delicious, too. To ensure that you don't let your dessert-loving audience down, use the utmost care in understanding and selecting all the ingredients you need.

In this chapter, I help you evaluate all those baking essentials that work together to create your sweet culinary masterpiece. You find out which ones you should plan on keeping on hand so that baking and decorating a cake is a more immediate proposition. Armed with the information in this chapter, you'll see that assembling a cake's components doesn't have to be overwhelming or intimidating at all.

The Lowdown on Baking Staples

Whatever cake you decide to tackle, you're almost guaranteed to need the following elementary yet essential ingredients: flour, sugar, eggs, and a fat, such as butter or oil. In addition, you'll call on a host of other foodstuffs to make sure your cake rises, is moist, tastes flavorful, and has a delicate crumb. Because you require these ingredients in your cake making (and some go into frostings and fillings, as well), it's a good idea to keep them stocked in your pantry.

 Some baking ingredients have longer shelf lives than others; this section includes guidelines for storage and freshness. Familiarize yourself with your ingredients by smelling them, tasting them (if appropriate), and knowing their normal compositions, aromas, and appearances. You'll be more primed to spot any offending ingredient that's not worthy of your confection.

Cake flour and all-purpose flour

All-purpose flour is generally used for a range of baked goods and foods. However, as far as cakes are concerned, I prefer to use cake flour. Most of the recipes in this book (and often, for cakes in general) call for cake flour. It's more finely textured than all-purpose and has less gluten in it, which means that it produces a more delicate, tender cake.

If a recipe lists cake flour as an ingredient, do your best to follow it; you'll definitely notice a positive difference in your cakes. However, if your recipe calls for cake flour and you have only all-purpose flour, simply omit 2 tablespoons from each cup of cake flour called for in the recipe. Conversely, if you're substituting cake flour for all-purpose flour, add 2 tablespoons for each cup of all-purpose flour called for in the recipe.

In the baking aisle of your grocery store you may come across self-rising flour, which has baking powder already mixed in. Steer away from this type of flour for the sake of simplicity and the ability to control your ingredients. By using all-purpose or cake flour instead of self-rising, you can add baking powder according to your recipe's specifications and follow the recipe more accurately.

When you get your flour home, empty the box or wrapper it comes in into a clear plastic or glass container with an airtight lid. If you have both all-purpose flour and cake flour, keep them straight by labeling the outside of the containers.

Even though flour keeps for months in airtight containers, take note of the expiration dates on the original packaging and mark them on your flour containers. Stale flour is no friend to a cake!

Sugars

Cake recipes often call for granulated white sugar, which is the most popular staple for sweetening baked goods. During baking, white sugar also lends that nice golden color to white and yellow cakes. Occasionally, recipes call for brown sugar; they usually specify whether you should use light (or golden) brown or dark brown sugar. Light brown sugar imparts a smoky molasses flavor, whereas dark brown sugar carries a stronger caramel taste.

Frostings often rely on confectioners' sugar. Being a fine powder, confectioners' sugar dissolves well so that your frostings and fillings don't have a grainy taste. This sugar is also an essential ingredient in fondant and gum paste.

Store all types of sugar in airtight containers. Even though they're fairly easy to tell apart, you should label the containers to avoid any missteps.

Butters, oils, and shortening

Fats bring richness to your cakes. Most of the cake and frosting recipes in this book call for butter, and by that I mean unsalted sweet butter. The butter you buy should be in a carton stamped with a "Use by" date, that you should definitely honor.

In baking cakes and making frostings, don't use margarine or spreads of any kind. The fat content of these products is lower than that of butter, so they don't yield the same texture. And worse, the taste just isn't the same.

In terms of oil, you should stock up on all-vegetable oil for baking. You're probably aware of several other kinds of oil that are available — such as safflower, olive, and even grapeseed — but you should stick with vegetable oil for cake baking. In addition to oil, you use shortening, available in both tubs and sticks, for both frostings and greasing your baking pans.

Some brands of shortening come in a butter flavor variety, but stick with the regular, unflavored version. The butter flavor interferes with the intended flavor of your cake.

Oil and shortening don't have indefinite shelf lives. Pay attention to expiration dates; even if the product hasn't officially expired, if a tub or bar of shortening or a bottle of oil smells rancid, don't use it! I'm often asked, "How do you know if oil or shortening has gone bad?" Believe me, it's a no-brainer; the smell of a rancid fat is one you'd never associate with something edible.

Eggs and egg whites

Fresh eggs are key to your cake turning out perfectly. Be sure to check the sell-by date stamped on the egg carton before you buy them, and store them in the carton (rather than in a tray that may be part of your refrigerator) to keep them as fresh as possible.

When a recipe calls for egg whites (think royal icing) and doesn't include a step for cooking them, buy a carton of pasteurized egg whites rather than separating whites from raw eggs. When you use pasteurized egg whites, you don't have to heed warnings about food-borne illnesses to pregnant women, the elderly, or young children, all of whom shouldn't eat raw eggs. Pasteurized egg whites generally need to be used within a few days of opening the carton.

Baking powder, baking soda, and cornstarch

Both baking powder and baking soda are leavening agents that work with other ingredients in your cake to make it rise. You can keep them in the containers they came in, but make sure to keep them only until their expiration dates. After a time, baking powder and baking soda lose their potency, making them worthless to your cake batter.

Recipes for glazes and fruit fillings often call for cornstarch, a thickening agent. Keep it in the original container, and use it by the expiration date for best results.

Chocolate

Here's a topic that gets almost everyone excited, and depending on your household's cravings, it may be hard to keep stocked in your pantry . . . but do try! In addition to cocoa (see the next section), chocolate is a key ingredient in many cakes — including chocolate, marble, fudge brownie, and white chocolate — and frostings, including ganache.

For baking, you can use chocolate chips (milk chocolate, semisweet, and white) and baking squares (semisweet and bittersweet). The chips are typically sold in 12-ounce packages; the squares are divided into 1-ounce portions, typically eight to a box. Store chocolate in a cool, dry place but not in the refrigerator.

Grocery stores in larger cities and upscale chains usually carry a variety of better or higher-end chocolates, but it comes down to taste preference: Some prefer chocolate with a high percentage of cacao, whereas others are happy with the taste of a common candy bar. Regardless, when purchasing chocolate for cake baking and decorating, check the ingredients: For best results, cocoa butter should be the fat listed, and you don't want to use a product full of such nonchocolate ingredients as palm kernel or cottonseed oil.

If a recipe calls for you to chunk or grate chocolate, don't use a food processor, which will just produce a mess. For chocolate chunks, place the chocolate squares or bar on a cutting board and use a serrated knife to chop it. Or if the chocolate is wrapped up, skip any mess by hitting it several times against the cutting board to break up the bar. For grated chocolate, chill it and then use the fine side of a box grater or a handheld microplane grater to finely shred it.

Spices and seasonings

You should have an array of spices and seasonings at the ready to either heighten an existing flavor or incorporate a new or complementary one. Keep the following ingredients in your pantry:

- ✔ Cinnamon, ground
- ✔ Cocoa
- ✔ Espresso powder
- ✔ Ground cloves
- ✔ Ground ginger
- ✔ Ground nutmeg
- ✔ Salt

Spices can be expensive, so you may be tempted to buy them in bulk at a warehouse store. But unless you plan to bake many cakes regularly with the same spices, stick with smaller quantities. Dry spices lose their potency after time, and some can even go rancid, so you don't want them sitting in your cupboard for years on end. Keep track of the purchase dates of your spices by labeling the bottles, jars, cans, or tubs with permanent marker.

Opening the Dairy Case

Recipes for both cakes and frostings call for dairy products galore. In each case, be mindful of expiration or sell-by dates. Pull fresh, perishable dairy goods out of a cold case in your grocery store, and, of course, if you notice a foul odor, curdling, or mold, get rid of the product even if the stamped date says it should be fresh!

Fresh milk

You may need whole milk for your cake batter or heavy cream for a chocolate ganache. Some cake batters rely on the smooth tang of buttermilk, and some fillings need a splash of half-and-half.

I generally recommend steering clear of reduced-fat, lowfat, or fat-free milk when baking or making frosting. Particularly if you substitute a fat-free product for a full-fat one, the taste and overall result is disappointing. However, reduced-fat buttermilk is fine if that's all you can get your hands on.

Canned milk

Evaporated milk and sweetened condensed milk are thicker and richer than regular milk due to their manufacturing processes that remove water. Also, sugar is added to produce sweetened condensed milk. Both kinds of canned milk are delightful additions to frostings and fillings.

You can determine the shelf life of canned milk by checking out the expiration date printed on the top, bottom, or wrapper of the can.

Other dairy products

Depending on the recipe, you may use such other dairy products as cream cheese, sour cream, or yogurt. In all cases, stick with full-fat versions (unless a low-fat recipe calls for otherwise). Particularly in the case of cream cheese, don't substitute reduced-fat Neufchatel; it tastes fine but doesn't hold up volume-wise to cream cheese's fluffiness.

Coloring Agents

Color undeniably plays a vibrant, fun, and impressive role in cake decorating. Although other ways to color — including sprays, markers, and even airbrushing — exist, you're most likely to use gels and pastes to tint your frostings.

They generally don't carry expiration dates, but you can't hold on to food coloring gels and pastes forever. Over time, they can separate or change color, either lightening or darkening your intended shade. I recommend not keeping gels and pastes for more than a year after purchase. Use a permanent marker to write the date you bought the product on its label. And keep the gels and pastes in a cool, dry area of your pantry or an area that's not exposed to heat, moisture, or harsh light.

Gels

Food coloring gels often come in ¾-ounce plastic squeeze bottles. Typically, the color of the gel is marked by a round dot in that color on the bottle's flip-top.

Some gels in popular colors come in larger quantities. Cake decorating kits usually include a combination of 8 to 12 of the most popular colors, such as black, blue, sky blue, red, pink, fuchsia, green, violet, brown, orange, teal, and yellow. Food coloring gels are readily available on the Internet as well as in cake decorating supply stores. You may not find the colors you want in larger chain craft stores, which tend to have limited stock of gels but plenty of pastes to choose from.

These bottles of coloring gel are different from write-on gels available in the baking aisle of your grocery store. You use that type of gel, which is more translucent than frosting, to write messages on a cake. Write-on gels have little effect in adding a hue to a white frosting.

I'm partial to using food coloring gels rather than pastes to color frostings. Squeezing the coloring gel into the frosting a drop at a time makes for less mess and easier maneuvering than adding pastes to a mixture.

Pastes

Food coloring pastes, which usually come in ½-ounce pots, are more concentrated in color than their gel counterparts. Pastes are widely available in larger chain craft stores as well as cake decorating supply stores in individual pots or in sets of 8 to 12 popular colors (see the preceding section for the most common colors).

Pastes sometimes yield a truer color than gels for the hue you're trying to achieve. However, you need some utensil — such as a toothpick — to add the paste to the frosting. And, needless to say, you shouldn't use the same toothpick twice or you may get mixed colors or bits of buttercream or royal icing in your paste pot (an unsanitary proposition at best).

Gathering Flavorings and Other Liquids

You need several liquid accoutrements for your cake making adventures to add flavor, make gum paste and fondant, and accent batters.

Extracts and flavorings

On the flavor front, pure vanilla extract and almond extract are must-haves. Depending on the favorite tastes in your household, you also may want to include lemon extract, orange extract, anise (which has a licorice flavor), and peppermint extract.

When it comes to extracts, use pure extract rather than the imitation counterpart. The flavor of pure extract truly tastes more pure and intense than that of imitation extract, and it doesn't include any artificial ingredients. However, if you're eager to use a flavor that you can't find in the pure form, the imitation is okay.

If you're preparing white frosting with vanilla extract as one of its ingredients, know that the frosting will turn slightly ivory in color. If you want the frosting to remain true white, you have to use a clear vanilla extract, which is only available in the imitation form.

In addition to extracts, you have a wealth of other flavorings — also known as *candy oils* — to pick from to satisfy a recipe's needs or to fulfill someone's special request. The possibilities really are endless and exciting. For instance, these are widely available on the Internet and through specialty kitchen stores:

- ✔ Black walnut
- ✔ Blueberry
- ✔ Butterscotch
- ✔ Caramel
- ✔ Cherry
- ✔ Coconut
- ✔ Cream soda
- ✔ Eggnog
- ✔ Hazelnut
- ✔ Macadamia nut
- ✔ Passion fruit
- ✔ Peach
- ✔ Peanut butter
- ✔ Piña colada
- ✔ Root beer
- ✔ Violet

But be mindful in using flavorings because they're more concentrated than extracts, so a little goes a long way. If you're adding flavoring to a batter or frosting, begin with as little as ⅛ teaspoon, take a taste, and gradually add more to your liking. (You can always add more flavoring, but you can't take it out after the fact!)

Additional flavorings are in the form of soaking syrups, such as those you see in a coffee house, and liqueurs. Both liquids may be used to moisten layers of cake while adding flavor. Occasionally, you also may need a liqueur to flavor a cake batter.

Other common liquids

In your cake-filled escapades, these last few staples are good to have on hand:

- ✔ **Corn syrup:** A common sweetener that comes in both light and dark varieties and lends a subtle caramel flavor (light) or a more dramatic one (dark); called for in fondant and gum paste recipes

- ✔ **Honey and maple syrup:** Ingredients that add depth and also shade flavors with a different, rich sweetening effect

- ✔ **Fruit juice:** Contributes both liquid and flavoring to a recipe; use freshly squeezed for best results

- ✔ **Vinegar:** Interacts with other ingredients for both taste and leavening purposes

Embellishing with Pizzazz

Reserve room in your pantry for a bounty of goodies that lend charm, sophistication, or just plain good humor to your cake creation. These are the fun foodstuffs!

This section covers a few categories of goods to consider using for decorations and, in some cases, adding to batters, frostings, and fillings. Be on the lookout for any other treats that thrill you in color or appearance. (I address actually enhancing your cakes with embellishments in Chapter 12.)

Candies

Practically anything goes when you're decorating with candy. It's a good idea to keep bags of your favorites handy in case inspiration strikes and you need them for a cake. Plus, if you don't use the candy, you can always just eat it! Candies commonly used in cake decorating include:

- ✔ Bubblegum
- ✔ Candy canes
- ✔ Candy corn
- ✔ Conversation hearts
- ✔ Jells and gummis
- ✔ Jelly beans

✔ Licorice

✔ Lollipops

✔ Marshmallows

✔ Peppermints

✔ Sours

✔ Stick gum

✔ Taffy

Chocolates

Chocolates come in many shapes, from round candy-coated chocolates to chocolate kisses, from chocolate chips to chocolate squares or bars. You can use the variety of shapes to create elaborate designs or illustrations, or simply make curls and shavings off a block of chocolate.

I recommend using chocolate as soon as you can. But for having some on hand, semisweet chocolate can keep up to a year in your pantry. However, you should keep packages sealed in resealable bags for optimum freshness. As for milk chocolate and white chocolate, freeze those varieties if you're not using them immediately, wrapping them in a plastic, resealable bag when you do.

Colorful additions

You have access to a kaleidoscope of amazing colors in the variety of sprinkles, sanding sugars, and nonpareils on the market. Use them as simple, festive decorations or as part of a more intricate design. Like spices and coloring gels, these additions also don't keep forever. Most likely, they won't be stamped with a "use by" date, but don't keep them past a year from when you bought the container. And remind yourself by writing the date on the container with a permanent marker.

Part II
Preparing the Canvas of Cake

The 5th Wave   By Rich Tennant

"What a wonderful swirled icing effect! How ever did you do it?"

In this part . . .

Ready to put on your design hat and grab an apron?
This part tells you how to create — and bake — your
cake from scratch and prepare an exceptional canvas to
host the design you have in mind.

Chapter 5

Prepping for the Cake Decorating Process

In This Chapter

▶ Gathering details on the occasion

▶ Applying cake terminology to the process

▶ Selecting appropriate and tasty flavors

▶ Coming up with an inspired design

The occasion's coming and you've committed to having a cake there. Or maybe you'd like to commit to have a cake there but don't feel experienced enough in the cake decorating department. Rest assured: Rather than stop by a bakery or order one at the discount warehouse, you can craft your own great-tasting, awe-inspiring cake.

Cake decorating isn't just about the decoration, though; many aspects factor into the equation of producing the best cake for an occasion. That's why I refer to cake decorating as a process. This chapter examines the first part of the process, when you spend some time thinking about the occasion and figuring out what kind of cake — from the shape and size to the flavors and the design — is the most appropriate.

Considering the Occasion and the Atmosphere

Here's where your cake design starts. If you didn't take time to assess the upcoming event, you'd just put out a plain white or chocolate cake and call it a day. But with all the opportunities for delicious and beautiful cakes, who wants to just do that?

To make your cake memorable and truly special, analyze the event it will be featured at. When I use the word "analyze," I don't mean that you have to embark on some laborious, intense process. Gathering all the information you need to influence and inform your cake's taste and design should be both fun and educational.

Surveying the celebrant and celebration

Before tackling the cake for an occasion, I like to spend some time with the person in charge of the event and ask him or her some important questions. Each question addresses distinct, distinguishing characteristics of the event, the person being feted, and ultimately, the cake that will be a culinary centerpiece.

Some questions relate directly to the cake, but some just give you a better idea of the event. You want your cake to be ideally suited to both the celebrant and the celebration, so it's best to become familiar with what will be going on at the event.

The following questions pertain to a wide spectrum of events: birthday parties, baby showers, team league award ceremonies, anniversary banquets, and evening weddings. Use this list as a guide for the upcoming event for which you're supplying a cake.

- What is the celebration? Does it have an official name?
- Is someone in particular being celebrated (such as a birthday honoree, a wedding couple, or a baseball team)?
- How would you describe the celebrant?
- What are his or her interests, hobbies, and favorites?
- Does the celebrant have a favorite cake flavor? Frosting flavor? Filling?
- When is the event being held (both day and time)?
- How long will the event last?
- Is this an annual event, or a one-time-only affair?
- Where is the event taking place?
- What is the tenor or atmosphere of the event?
- How is the event space being decorated?
- Are there predominant colors to take into account?
- Is there a particular theme to consider?
- Is there a touchstone, heirloom, memento, or mascot that should somehow factor into the cake decoration?
- Will there be flowers at the event? If so, what kinds and what colors?

Taking theme and audience into account

In all the information you gather, you obviously want to focus on the celebrant and event. But you have two other major considerations as well: theme and audience.

If the event doesn't have a theme, you're free to create one for your cake that works with what you know about the celebrant. But if the event does have a theme, you have to make sure that your cake fits in. In other words, a Santa Claus cake isn't right for a birthday party unless the birthday falls on December 25th or the celebrant looks like St. Nick. And a soccer field cake doesn't play well at a wedding (although featuring it as the groom's cake isn't unheard of).

These may be extreme examples (and I know of worse ones!), but they illustrate my point that if you don't factor in the event's theme, your cake will be hopelessly incongruent with the affair. You want your cake to be in the spotlight because it's an appropriate celebration of the event, not because it's completely out of place.

In addition, realize that your theme should be carried out on a cake that fits in with the people attending the event and ultimately eating the cake. Sure, you may think a passion fruit puree with chopped lychee is a tasty filling for a white chocolate cake, but is a gang of 6-year-olds really going to enjoy it? Regarding the audience, the rule of thumb is to avoid going too complex for an audience that loves simple and to shun the too unusual for a group that revels in the norm. Basically, in considering your taste and design, strive to be age and theme-appropriate, and you're off to a winning start.

Calculating how much cake to make

In many instances, your design starts with the shape of a cake: hexagon, square, circle, petal, heart, oval, or rectangle. When you know the shape, you can narrow down the size of that shape based on the selection of cake pans available. Most shapes come in many sizes; for example, round pans usually start at 6 inches in diameter, and a rectangular or sheet cake can be anywhere up to 18-x-24-inches in size.

I often get asked this question: How can I be sure that I'll have enough cake? I always err on the side of having too much cake. Leftovers are easy to dole out, and people are compelled to return for seconds when the cake tastes good. Ultimately, you never want someone to be left with an empty plate because there was a run on the cake. Too much cake is better than not enough, but let's be real, too: A sheet cake for 40 looks ridiculous at an intimate gathering of 6, so some thoughtful planning is necessary.

If you're planning to be at the event to cut the cake, decide beforehand how the cake can be cut (and even make it a step in your design process). Even go as far as sketching up a sample cutting template or diagram. If it's an oddly shaped cake or features several layers, it's helpful to know ahead of time how to efficiently parcel it out into appetizing pieces of cake. If you don't plan to be at the event, create cutting guidelines for whoever does the honors. For more information about the different shapes of cakes, and how many servings they can yield, check out Chapter 22.

Be prepared to adjust your cutting plan to slice smaller but still substantial pieces of cake if more guests than were expected show up.

Table 5-1 has some general guidelines for common cake sizes and their yields.

Table 5-1	Cake Sizes and Yields	
Size and Shape of Cake	*Number of Layers*	*Number of Servings*
8-inch heart	2	10
9-inch round	2	12
9-inch hexagon	2	12
7⅞-x-10¾-inch oval	2	14
10-inch square	2	16
9-x-13-inch rectangle	1	18
12-x-18-inch rectangle (half-sheet)	1	36

Picking Up Cake Decorating Lingo

Like any specialty, cake decorating has its own words and phrases that are uniquely special to the art and craft of the process. As you embark on creating an amazing design perfect for the occasion at hand, familiarizing yourself with this jargon sets you on course to dive in and master the recipes and designs for delicious, memorable cakes.

Understanding the tools

As far as tools and utensils are concerned, you depend on *icing spatulas* to spread your frosting, smooth it out, and make it conducive to decoration. In addition, you may decorate your cake with different applications of frosting. To do so, you place the frosting in *pastry bags* and use *couplers* to attach *tips* in various sizes and designs. Those tips, along with the pressure you apply to the pastry bag, produce different effects. A tool that fits in the tip category (but isn't actually a tip, per se) is the *flower nail,* which you use as a platform on which to pipe the petals, ruffles, edges, and stamens of flowers, from roses to lilacs and chrysanthemums to carnations.

For the cake itself, you put each layer on a cardboard base for easier movement and transporting during the decorating process, and you may need to place it on an elevated *turntable* to make it easier to decorate. You need to prepare a *cake board* to host the finished cake; the board may be made of wood, foam core, or a similar sturdy substance and be covered with your choice of decorative materials. Whatever you use may need to be wrapped again with a protective layer — such as thick cellophane — that's easy to wipe off so that your final presentation is neat and tidy and not smudged with frosting.

Gathering components and coverings

You may want to flavor the cake using *extracts* or *flavorings.* White, yellow, and chocolate are the most common types of cake, but your imagination can run wild with red velvet, lemon, spice, and Tahitian vanilla flavors. You pair the cake with any number of *frostings* for spreading on the top and sides of the cake. The popular buttercream frosting may take on any of a number of flavors. A *stiff decorator frosting,* which is more rigid than buttercream, is best for piping decorations. Other leading choices for frosting feature cream cheese and chocolate *ganache,* which is made with whipping cream and semi-sweet chocolate.

The frosting you plan to use on the outside of your cake also can serve as the *filling* in between the cake layers. Or you may opt for a completely different but complementary taste for the cake's filling. A filling can be a mousse or jam or can contain fruit or nuts.

Instead of traditional frosting, you may cover the surface of your cake with any of the following:

- ✔ **Icings,** which are traditionally thinner than frostings, can sport a shiny or matte finish. *Royal icing,* made with confectioners' sugar and pasteurized egg whites, hardens upon drying for a lasting effect.

- ✔ **Glazes,** which are made from heating sugar and water to produce syrup, are a shiny coating for nuts and fruits atop a cake.

- ✔ **Rolled fondant,** a smooth covering made from confectioners' sugar and corn syrup (among other ingredients), gets carefully rolled out and laid over a cake.

For decorating, you may choose to *tint* frostings, royal icing, and fondant with *food coloring gels* or *pastes,* available in a lively, rainbow assortment of colors.

You add them to achieve the desired shade for your effect, embellishment, lettering, or design.

Prepping the surface

After you bake your cake, you need to *level* the top to create a perfectly flat canvas on which to create your masterpiece.

Preparing your cake for decoration may be a bit of a construction project: You may be working with several layers and need to construct *tiers*. Tiers usually require you to insert *dowels* into the layers to add support so that each layer doesn't cave in when another layer's placed on top of it. Other than tiers, you may be cutting cakes to fit together to form a bigger shape or working with a *cake mold* of a particular shape.

When you initially frost your cake, you cover it with a *crumb coat,* which is a thin layer of frosting that seals in crumbs. You refrigerate it and then, when that coat hardens, you'll frost over it for a finished, seamless, smooth final frosting coat.

Adding embellishment

Embellishing is often thought of as the most fun part of cake decorating because, in this stage, you explore piping techniques, and place and position edible and inedible embellishments on your cake.

In determining your embellishments, you work from a plan — either a *blueprint* of your very own design, a *stencil* you're filling in, a *pattern* you're following, or a *template* you're using as a guideline.

Piping refers to using a tip to apply frosting in any number of applications and effects, including *rosettes, shells, string work, lace work,* and *garlands,* among others, as well as *borders* around the top and bottom edges of your cake.

You use icing tips and piping techniques to form *letters* or *scripting* for a message. Specialized piping techniques include the *basket weave,* which involves arranging rows of finely-grooved piping to produce a woven effect that looks very much like a basket. In addition, you can pipe out large amounts of frosting to form figures, such as clowns, dolls, or animals. And by using your icing tips and a flower nail, you can create flowers to enhance your cake's design.

Other edible embellishments include chocolate, nuts, fruits, and nonpoisonous flowers as well as coconut, nonpareils, sprinkles, a variety of candies, and sanding sugars. Inedible embellishments include just about anything, from a wedding cake topper to tiny vintage toys or a ballerina ornament.

In addition to being a cake covering, you can use *fondant* as an embellishment; fondant cutters allow you to create shapes or letters. Further, you can mold gum paste and marzipan into figures and shapes: *Gum paste,* which is edible but not very tasty, is great for shaping into flowers, and *marzipan,* which is edible and tasty (it's made from ground almond paste), is often molded into fun, colorful vegetable shapes.

Picking Flavors for the Cake and Frosting

You have an infinite number of possibilities where the flavors and kinds of cakes, frostings, and fillings are concerned. Simply perusing the variety of boxed cake mixes and tubs of frostings available at your local grocery store will give you an idea of the choices that await you when you prepare cakes and frostings from scratch.

You want your cake to be as impressive on the inside as it is on the outside. With the endless flavor combinations available, take the event and celebrant into considerable account by asking yourself the following questions:

- ✔ Has there been a special request for a specific kind of cake and frosting? If so, does it need to be tweaked (either because a recipe doesn't exist or because it's so nontraditional that people at the party may not like it)?

- ✔ If a special request runs the risk of turning many event attendees off, can you incorporate that flavor into cupcakes served on the side or a tier to be removed from the main cake?

- ✔ If you're not dealing with a special request, what cake and frosting combination will be the most delectable and enjoyed by everyone in attendance?

- ✔ Are any flavors or ingredients off-limits? (For example, a birthday cake for a 1-year-old shouldn't contain nuts because of concerns regarding allergies or choking; the honoree at a retirement party may be allergic to strawberries.)

- ✔ Is there a theme that the cake and frosting flavors should follow? Harvest, tropical, and springtime themes immediately conjure up scents associated with delicious, definitive flavors such as cinnamon, coconut, and lemon, respectively.

- ✔ Is there a color scheme for the event that a certain flavor naturally ties in with? (For example, a red, white, and blue color scheme is perfect for a cake with three layers: one strawberry, one blueberry, and one marshmallow.)

Having answered these questions, one flavor combination may immediately spring to mind. If not, chart out a few options and test out some flavor pairings or peruse store shelves to get a sense of what you can create from scratch for this occasion.

Devising a Design

The final step in the planning process for a decorated cake is finalizing a design and committing to the actual cake.

The design process breaks down into four stages:

1. **Brainstorming an array of choices to find the perfect idea**
2. **Deciding on the best design and draw up the blueprint**
3. **Assigning the right colors to the design**
4. **Assessing whether or not the cake you're planning fits the bill in terms of the event, theme, celebrant, and other relevant factors**

Finding inspiration

Spend some time brainstorming ideas and gathering inspiration for how you want the cake to look. In starting out, you may have an exact idea, a general idea, or no idea at all; regardless, the right inspiration helps you fine-tune your creation or coax it to fruition.

Your inspiration can come from anywhere: the Empire State building, a fashion movement of the 1960s, your son's comic books, or a 1920s etiquette book. Don't assume that you have to settle for a teddy bear-shaped cake or a square that says "Happy Birthday" unless you think a more-traditional design is perfect for the celebration. But if you're convinced that you can't come up with a better idea, think again.

When you have an upcoming occasion to plan a cake for, you may be surprised at what jumps out at you as a possibility for a cake design. Take a look around you, and peruse photos that fit in with the theme of the party or event for the featured cake. In some cases, an honoree or celebrant knows exactly what he or she wants the cake to look like, such as the shape of a football helmet, a parachute, or a re-creation of a high school prom. You may not have a detailed vision of such images, but remember that the Internet is loaded with photos to help you out. Simply enter the theme or look into your favorite search engine and browse the results.

Taking stock of your options

Mull over the various ways you can design your cake based on your inspiration. Depending on the time you have and your eagerness to explore, you may want to pull out a pad of paper and sketch out a few of the ideas you have in mind.

You may want to ease into your design. For instance, if your original plan of building a pirate ship cake from scratch seems overwhelming, don't be afraid to step back and take a simpler approach.

Consider your skill set before committing to a cake design. Cake decorating should be an enjoyable, continuing activity . . . not one that you immediately abandon after a frustrating first go. To that end, realize that every design — or the thought of a design — carries a multitude of choices; be open to all possibilities. For example, rather than build a pirate ship out of cake, you could draw one on the cake's surface and fill in the ship's spaces with crushed candies. If drawing the pirate ship on the cake seems too daunting, find a toy pirate ship or a cake topper set of pirate paraphernalia and pipe waves of blue frosting around it.

After you come up with the perfect design, make a rough sketch of it. Don't worry if you weren't an art major or think you can't draw; you can sketch just fine for cake planning purposes. The sketch is a visual, handheld guideline that you can easily muck around with and make adjustments to for the exact look you're trying to achieve with your cake. Believe me: You don't want to be standing over your cake with only a mental snapshot of what the cake should look like. To sketch out your design, you need the following:

- ✔ Sketchpad of plain white paper
- ✔ Drawing pencil
- ✔ Pencil sharpener
- ✔ Set of colored pencils
- ✔ Gum eraser

Discerning colors

Part of the design process is assigning colors to your sketch, the blueprint for your final cake. Use your colored pencils to color in your sketch and see how the color combinations you're expecting to use look on your design.

Each season, the fashion industry adopts a hot color palette of the hues that are "in." If possible and appropriate — and particularly for cakes and celebrations for grown-ups — you may want to use some of those colors for your cake. You can either check out fashion magazines for the latest shades, or type "color trends" or "hot colors" followed by the current year into your Internet search engine and investigate the sites that pop up. You can also visit one of my favorite sites for color at www.pantone.com. Pantone's business is color. It's a company that facilitates both communication and technology about color for a variety of industries, and it offers a plethora of the current season's eye-catching hues and other related valuable information on their site.

Don't choose a color for the cake just because it's your favorite (unless it's for your own birthday!) or because you think a few colors pair well in your mind. Use your coloring pencils to experiment and actually see what goes with what. You may be surprised to find that, when you see hues side by side, they aren't anything like what you expected . . . or they look better than you thought, giving you more confidence in your design.

Chapter 7 offers further advice and instructions regarding finding and mixing colors and coming up with the best shades for your work.

Greenlighting your plan

Having come up with the design for your cake and given it the colors that work best, you must determine if your planned cake will be the event's definitive culinary centerpiece. You want the celebrant to revel in the cake's taste and creation and all the cake eaters to remember it as a vibrant, delicious cake.

For a final review, consider this last set of questions to ensure that you're embarking on a successful cake decorating adventure. If you're comfortable with your answers, you're well on your way to an amazing amount of fun in the kitchen.

- ✔ Have I tested this flavor combination of cake, frosting, and, if appropriate, filling? Am I sure the flavors complement one another?
- ✔ Will the majority of the cake eaters like the cake's flavor?
- ✔ Is the design congruent with the celebrant's style?
- ✔ Is the design appropriate for the event?
- ✔ Do the colors pair well with each other and with the event?
- ✔ Is the design too complicated for my skill set?
- ✔ Before I begin baking, do I have the design clearly mapped out?
- ✔ Before I begin decorating, have I reviewed and tweaked the design sufficiently?

Chapter 6

Baking the Perfect Cakes

Cakes can attract attention for eye-catching designs, but unfortunately, they sometimes fall flat when it comes to taste. Don't sacrifice taste for decoration, or vice versa. With a little care, attention, and an indispensable collection of recipes, you can take your creation to the next tier — shining an even bigger spotlight on your decorating because the cake itself tastes so good!

The foundation for your soon-to-be masterpiece begins with a cake that's moist and delicious. In this chapter, you're treated to the techniques that are keys to a visually exciting cake's basic — but important — beginnings: measuring ingredients, pouring batter, lining pans, and taking cakes out of the oven. Plus, you get recipes that will become the staples of your baking endeavors, providing the perfect inside tastes to accompany your cake decorating. After all, the goal is to make a cake that people want to admire *and* eat!

Comprehending the Language of Cake Baking

Before you fire up the oven and get your stand mixer whirring, you need to be familiar with a few terms that you're bound to see in almost every recipe you tackle.

  ✔ **Greasing:** *Greasing your pan* refers to spreading butter or shortening all over the insides of your cake pans before pouring batter into them. Recipes often tell you also to *flour the pan* after greasing it by shaking a few teaspoons of flour around the pan to completely cover the surface. These steps ensure that, after baking, a cake comes out of the pan without sticking to the bottom; when you flip the cake onto a cooling rack, it should come out perfectly intact.

✔ **Preheating:** *Preheating* the oven so that your cake goes in at the desired temperature is of paramount importance. Otherwise, your cake is subjected to a longer baking time while it sits in the oven waiting for it to reach the desired temperature. Another downside to not preheating your oven is that it takes longer to heat because a big cake's in there waiting to bake.

✔ **Sifting:** *Sifting* is a technique that involves measuring dry ingredients (most often flour) into a sieve or sifter and then passing it through the mesh of that apparatus. Sifting allows you to break down (or eliminate) compacted clumps that may have settled in your dry ingredients. If you don't catch 'em, these clumps become balls in your batter and also prevent proper leavening, which allows your cake to rise to its best occasion.

✔ **Creaming:** *Creaming* usually refers to mixing softened butter (or whatever type of fat you're using, such as shortening or a butter/shortening mixture) and sugar together until you have a completely smooth mixture. It's usually the first step in mixing your cake ingredients. The quickest and easiest way to cream butter and sugar is to use the paddle attachment on your stand mixer.

✔ **Folding:** To *fold* ingredients, you use a rubber spatula to gently draw the addition into the batter. Recipes usually call for folding when you need to incorporate stiffly beaten egg whites or freshly whipped cream into a batter. The technique requires a delicate touch because you don't want to destroy the air and lift of the beaten or whipped ingredient.

Measuring Up

In measuring your ingredients, precision is key. You may be surprised to find out that baking cakes actually is very scientific. (It's no surprise to me when I find out that a medical doctor, like my brother, or a chemist is an excellent baker!) Whereas some cooking almost pleads for you to add a dash more of this or that, complement the ingredients with others, or give your own twist to the listed instructions, cake baking commands (and even demands) that you stick to the prescribed regimen.

For some liquid ingredients — such as milk, cream, buttermilk, or oil — you should rely on a glass measuring cup. Using a glass measuring cup is easier in the long run because you get an exact visual on your measurement. It also makes for easier pouring of liquid ingredients. For precise measuring, set the glass measure on your work surface and fill it while checking the measure at eye level. Don't pick up the measuring cup to check the measure. To get an even, accurate measure, leave the cup on your work surface and bend or kneel down to check it.

Following are a few general recommendations for measuring:

- ✔ **Consider having on hand two sets of measuring cups and spoons: one for liquid ingredients and the other for dry ingredients.** This convenience cuts down on your preparation time and allows you to easily segue between measuring out different ingredients.

- ✔ **Take your time and measure your ingredients out before you start mixing things together.** Your cake batter will come together much more quickly if everything's measured and ready to go.

- ✔ **For ease in clean-up, consider lining your work surface.** Wax paper and aluminum foil both work well to catch spills and drips, especially from milk and eggs, and they make clean-up a breeze.

- ✔ **Don't measure over the batter you're mixing.** If you need only a small amount of an ingredient — such as salt, vinegar, or vanilla — you may be tempted to simply spoon out a bit as the mixer is running. But one slip and it's time to start over. After all, a little vinegar goes a long way (and a lot of vinegar really ruins a cake batter!). Once an ingredient's mixed in, there's no getting it out, so err on the side of caution and measure over another bowl.

If your recipe calls for dry ingredients measured by weight (or if you're extra excited about measuring), invest in a kitchen scale, which determines quantity more precisely than a volume measurement. Scales come in both manual and electronic versions; in either case, make sure that weigh-ins account for both ounces and grams. If you opt for a manual scale, get one with a removable weighing bowl or tray, and make sure the numbers are easy to read. I prefer a digital kitchen scale just because it tends to be more compact (which makes it easier to store), and I like that a digital display expresses the weight clearly and quickly. Plus, I like that I can put my own bowl on it for quick and easy measuring.

Flour

Before you measure out flour for a cake recipe, stir and aerate it first with a balloon whisk to break up any lumps. Stirring the flour first also leads to more accurate measuring.

Gently spoon the flour into a stainless steel or plastic measuring cup (don't scoop it straight out of the container). Then level the flour by scraping a knife across the top of the cup. You don't want to pack the flour into the cup, so take care not to press the knife down too hard as you level.

If a recipe calls for flour that's not sifted, you simply measure it out as I describe and add it to the recipe. However, recipes mentioning "sifted flour" need particular attention:

- ✔ If a recipe calls for "flour, sifted," you measure out the flour, sift it, and then add it to your recipe.

- ✔ If a recipe calls for "sifted flour," you measure out a little more flour than what's called for, sift it, and then precisely measure the amount you need from the sifted flour.

You can buy presifted flour, but it may still need to be sifted. When flour sits on a grocery store shelf, it settles, meaning that lumps inevitably form. Therefore, I recommend that you always sift flour, even if the package says it's presifted.

Sugar

Measure sugar in much the same way as you measure flour (see the preceding section). Even though sugar is less likely to clump than flour, make sure that yours is lump-free. Stir it up first, scoop the sugar into your measuring cup, and then level it with the flat side of a knife.

If a recipe calls for light or dark brown sugar, you need to pack it firmly into your measuring cup (and still make sure that it is level). When you add brown sugar to the mixing bowl, the sugar should hold the shape of the cup it came from.

Butter and shortening

Measuring butter is fairly easy: On sticks or bars, follow the tablespoon and cup indications on the wrappers. In your local grocery store, you can find 1-pound packages of butter, each containing four bars. Each 4-ounce bar is 8 tablespoons, or ½ cup.

Some cake recipes may call for shortening, or in some cases, you may be able to substitute shortening for butter. If you're using shortening, opt for packaged shortening that comes in bars. Like sticks of butter, you can measure off tablespoons and cups quickly and neatly without having to scoop shortening out of a container to fill measuring cups or spoons.

Eggs

When preparing eggs for a recipe, crack them into a separate measuring cup or bowl. Preparing the eggs separately has two advantages:

- ✔ On the rare occasion that you get a bad egg (literally), you don't ruin your entire batter by mixing the bad egg in.
- ✔ If a bit of shell comes away as you crack the egg, it's far easier to fish it out of your measuring cup (with a fork, of course!) than out of a mixing bowl full of other ingredients.

Spices, baking soda, and baking powder

Recipes usually call for dry ingredients like spices, baking soda, and baking powder in measuring spoon amounts. Dip the clean measuring spoon into the ingredient, and level it off with a knife's straight edge before adding it to your mixing bowl.

Sticky substances

For ingredients such as honey, molasses, or corn syrup, squeeze or pour the substance into a measuring spoon or cup rather than scoop it out.

Cover the measuring surface with nonstick spray so that the sticky goodness slides right out into your mixing bowl and you have a much easier time cleaning up everything.

Vanilla, vinegar, and other liquids

Simply pour liquid ingredients from the bottle into your measuring spoon or cup. Just be sure to pour them away from the mixing bowl in case you pour too much or a bit sloshes out as you're measuring!

Fruits, nuts, and the like

To measure chopped nuts, flaked coconut, or dried or grated fresh fruits (or vegetables, like carrots for a carrot cake), spoon the ingredient into a measuring cup and tap it down lightly to get an accurate measure. Then add it to your batter.

Prepping the Pans

To prepare the pans you're using for the particular cake you're baking, you need to grease, flour, and, with some cakes, line them with parchment paper (although not always in that particular order!).

For greasing pans, many cake bakers swear by shortening while others prefer butter. For a time, I would have suggested only shortening . . . but now I use only butter. In general, I avoid most nonstick sprays because I've found that they tend to leave a gummy residue on the bakeware after the cake's turned out. That said, I've had nice success with a cooking spray that includes flour, so if you're committed to cooking sprays, I suggest you look for that kind.

To line a pan, you put a piece of parchment paper into the pan after you grease it. This step is often necessary when baking large cakes — such as sheet cakes or wedding cakes — because it allows for more uniform baking and basically gives you a double-guarantee that the cake will turn out cleanly.

To line the pan:

1. **Grease and flour the entire pan.**

   Using a paper towel or piece of wax paper, spread butter or shortening all over the inside of your cake pan, and then shake a few teaspoons of flour around the pan to completely cover the surface. To get a light coating of flour, tap the pan against the heel of one hand as you move it around. When the pan's coated in flour, dump out any excess.

2. **Set the pan on the parchment paper right-side up, and trace around the bottom of the pan with a pencil. Then cut the shape out and place the paper in the bottom of your pan.**

3. **Grease and flour the parchment paper, following the procedure in Step 1.**

Lining a pan with parchment paper is completely unnecessary (not to mention difficult) for a Bundt or highly detailed pan. For these pans, grease all the

Experience of a cooking spray convert

I first tried cooking spray with flour when I was asked to make a rosebush cake that I designed to include 36 rose cakelets each baked in a very intricate blooming rose-shaped mold. I knew that getting butter into all the crevices of the molds would be an arduous, time-consuming, and ultimately unsuccessful task. A catering friend had mentioned having good results with a cooking spray with flour, so I decided to give it a try. The cakelets tumbled out of the molds perfectly, the molds weren't left sticky, and a new allegiance was born.

nooks and crannies using a nonstick spray with flour. For more advice on working with molds, see the sidebar "Baking with molds."

Mixing the Batter

Mixing up your cake batter is the fun part of cake baking because you see all the individual ingredients come together. Some recipes call for you to combine all the ingredients in a single bowl and just mix away. This kind of cake is referred to as a *dump cake*. However, mixing up the batter is a bit more complicated in many recipes, and it's another part of the cake baking process in which you really need to follow instructions.

Most of the basic cake recipes in this chapter begin with creaming butter and sugar. You should start with softened but not melted butter; cream the butter first, then add the sugar gradually. Beat the butter and sugar, basically drawing air into them, until the mixture is pale in color, light, and fluffy.

Many recipes tell you to add flour alternately with milk (or buttermilk or cream). When alternate adding is necessary, start and end with the flour. For most cakes, you should try to mix the flour in four even additions and the liquid, in between that, in three equal ones. Mixing these ingredients in alternate additions prevents the cake from becoming tough or full of tunnels.

During the mixing process, be sure to scrape the sides of the bowl at least two times with a rubber spatula. It's so disheartening to ready your batter for pouring and discover that a whole mess of ingredients settled at the bottom of the bowl and were never incorporated in the batter. The mess doesn't look pretty added as an afterthought to the top of your cake pans when you pour the batter!

If you get to the end of pouring the batter and realize that a disheartening amount of ingredients have settled into the bottom of the bowl, don't despair. Gently scrape the batter back into the mixing bowl. Use a wooden spoon to stir in the ingredients that went unmixed the first time. Then beat the batter just long enough to incorporate all the ingredients. For the whole process, work quickly, and don't overbeat. Pour the batter back into freshly cleaned, greased, and floured pans.

Because not everyone uses the same stand or hand mixer, times for mixing can vary: Two minutes of beating with one mixer could be more than two minutes on another and less than two minutes on a third mixer. So you should look for recipe watchwords, such as "creamy," "light and fluffy," or "just combined" to give you visual cues.

Wow! That's a lot of cake!

Las Vegas celebrated its 100th anniversary in 2005 with the world's biggest birthday cake. The cake weighed 130,000 pounds and was 102 feet long, 52 feet wide, and 20 inches tall. The cake's ingredients added up to 23,000 pounds of flour; 35,000 cups of sugar; and 130,000 eggs. The frosting, which weighed roughly 34,000 pounds, consisted of 42,000 cups of sugar; 10,200 cups of shortening; 5,200 cups of butter; and 5,200 cups of corn syrup. Five hundred volunteers spent 14 hours constructing and decorating the cake, which consisted of 30,240 half-sheet cakes. This undertaking makes all your baking endeavors much less daunting, doesn't it?!

Getting Down the Rules for the Perfect Cakes

Perhaps you're baking a cake for an anniversary celebration, your daughter's birthday, or a neighbor's homecoming. Whatever the event, stick to a recipe that you've already tried and now trust. The time will come when you can scan a recipe and attempt it without a preliminary outing because you're familiar with ingredients, proportions, and different flavorings. But for now, stick with and perfect a cake repertoire that you can turn to for most celebrations and cake-worthy opportunities.

If you really want to branch out but aren't totally comfortable with the cake you're attempting, give it a trial run. If it's too large, mathematically downsize the recipe, and do a taste test so that you can see and taste the cake's taste and texture, make minor adjustments (if necessary), and — most important — build your confidence for the main event.

You may get inspired and suddenly have an idea for a cake that you think will be perfect for the occasion, but unless you have time to test it beforehand, now's not the time to experiment. Do that on your own time!

Give yourself enough time! Your cake (and you, for that matter) will suffer if you rush through the baking and decorating process. This section covers the basic steps of cake baking, from beginning to end.

Reading up and getting ready

Before you start measuring and mixing, read through the entire recipe. You don't want to get midway through making a cake only to realize that you need to let the batter refrigerate for 90 minutes . . . and you were supposed to be at an event with the cake an hour ago.

As you review your recipe, assemble all your ingredients and measure everything out to make sure that you have what you need and you have enough of it.

Before you start mixing, preheat your oven, and select and prepare (grease, flour, and line) your pans. Use the shape of pan that the recipe suggests. Your cake may end up looking quite different than you want it to if you fill a different kind of cake pan with the batter without making any adjustments to the recipe.

Opt for shiny pans for best results. If you bake in a dark-colored or glass pan, lower the oven temperature 25 degrees.

Battering up and baking

If you're using only one pan, simply pour your batter into the pan after it's all mixed up, and smooth it with a rubber spatula to encourage a more level rise as it bakes.

If you need to divide your batter up into more than one pan, you have two choices for even distribution: Simply eyeball it, or if you're eager to be more exact, use a kitchen scale to ensure that your pans weigh the same when filled.

I don't recommend pouring batter into a measuring cup and doling out amounts into pans. Scraping batter in and out of cups tends to mess with its volume and delays getting fresh batter in the oven. The less you futz with it, the better!

Batter should come up to approximately two-thirds of the pan's height. Any less and you have a layer that looks too flat. Too much and your cake overflows into the oven. After you pour the appropriate amounts of batter into your pans, smooth the batter with a rubber spatula to encourage a more level rise as it bakes.

Set the pans in the oven on the middle rack, but make sure not to crowd them. If you need to, stagger the pans on different racks. There needs to be enough space between the pans for the heat to circulate and cook the cakes evenly. If you notice during the baking time that one layer seems to be cooking faster than the other, switch the pans' rack positions.

Opening your oven door too much during baking tampers with the oven's temperature and may cause your cake to deflate a bit. Instead of opening the door, use your oven light to check the cake's progress.

Leveling during baking

This step may seem a little silly but, during baking, you may notice that your batter swoops to one side or that there's more in the front of the pan than in the back. This unevenness could be the result of a maladjusted backing rack, a slightly tilted oven, or an uneven floor. If your cakes consistently come out lopsided, get out a toolbox level. On a cool oven, check the level of your racks and the oven itself, and also check the floor the oven sits on.

If the oven isn't level on your floor (or if your entire floor is actually uneven) you could prop up the oven with a shim (a thin piece of wood). However, I recommend having a handyman or kitchen contractor check out your situation because messing with the oven's positioning, particularly if it's a gas oven, can cause all kinds of problems if the remedy goes awry.

If you think that your oven rack is the culprit, pull it out of the oven and examine it. If it's warped, replace it. If the rack looks fine, it could be sticking to the inside of the oven at an angle or lodged into an off-kilter position because of baked-on food. Your best recourse with an uneven rack is to thoroughly check out the situation to determine the cause.

Knowing when a cake is done

Testing for a cake's doneness can be tricky. Many cake bakers espouse the virtues of a cake tester that, when inserted in the center of the cake, comes out completely clean, but I advocate the importance of a few moist crumbs attached to the tester. (If you don't have a tester, a toothpick works fine, too.) Too often, cakes are overdone. In addition to the cake tester test, look for other signs of doneness, including:

- The cake springs back when lightly touched.
- The cake has risen and is just pulling away from the sides of the pan.
- The cake doesn't jiggle when you pull the oven rack out to inspect it.
- The cake's color indicates that it's done, such as a golden brown top if it's a yellow cake.
- The cake has lost the sheen of a shiny batter.

Just as mixers vary for mixing, ovens vary for baking. So always take a baking time as a suggestion and make adjustments for your oven. Become familiar with how your make and model operates by paying close attention to baking times and results when you bake, well, anything. And use an oven thermometer to check the accuracy of your oven's temperature. If you set the oven for 400 degrees F, does it actually get that hot? If not, or if it hits 425 degrees, you need to adjust a cake's baking time accordingly.

Baking with molds

Cathedrals, Christmas trees, fire trucks, snowmen, roosters . . . you can get a cake mold in virtually any size, shape, or creation.

If you decide to use a cake mold, take note of its capacity. If you don't have the right amount of batter to fill the mold, the cake doesn't take on the desired shape. And too much batter results in a misshapen cake (and probably a drippy mess in your oven, too).

Before pouring batter into a mold, grease and flour it properly. Many cake molds have intricate designs and patterns that make greasing tricky. To ensure that you get all the crevices, use a nonstick spray with flour.

Cooling and extracting the cake

Before leveling (slicing off any slight peak to your cake layer) and frosting, your cake must cool completely. To cool your cake and get it out of the pan the right way, follow these steps:

1. **Let the cake sit in its pan for 10 minutes after you pull it out of the oven.**

2. **Insert the tip of a knife into the space between your cake and the side of the pan, and glide it carefully around the pan.**

3. **Place one cooling rack on the top of the cake, grab the rack and the cake pan, and quickly flip it all over, inverting your cake onto the cooling rack to cool completely.**

4. **Slowly and carefully pull the pan directly up and away from the cake. If you lined your pan with parchment paper, peel it off the facing side of the cake.**

5. **Lay a second cooling rack on the facing side of the cake (which is actually the bottom of the cake), and invert it again by holding both racks and flipping them.**

Avoiding cake-tastrophes

As you work to perfect your cakes, you may run into a few problems: Your cakes may seem dry, shrink too much, or contain tunnels, for instance. Don't dismay. Make sure that your oven is reaching the right temperature and that you're ready to check for doneness at the appropriate time. If the oven doesn't seem to be the problem, many times the culprit is undermixing or overmixing.

Being aware of potential cake problems at the outset can make you more mindful in your next endeavor. Check out these handy guidelines and try, try again. Don't let it intimidate you — it's only cake batter!

- **If your cake is dry, cracked on top, or appears to have shrunk,** you may have overmixed the batter. On the dryness front, you also may have skimped on the liquid ingredients.

- **If your cake has a coarse texture or has holes and tunnels running through it,** you may have undermixed the batter.

- **If your cake falls,** you may have tested too soon for doneness, or it may be underbaked.

- **If your cake doesn't rise properly,** the batter may have been overmixed or undermixed.

- **If your cake is stuck in the pan,** you may not have greased the pan or parchment paper enough, or you may have left the cake in the pan for too long after baking.

You may have to live with a few lumpy or dry cakes on your road to delicious perfection, but don't sweat it too much. That's why I advise you do a test run and give your cakes a preliminary sample.

Above all else, have fun when baking your cakes. When you relax, you enjoy the process more and — after just a bit of fine-tuning — your cake eaters can enjoy your efforts, too.

Perfecting the Basic Cake Repertoire

This section contains a handful of very important ingredient tips and some of the trustiest recipes to produce cakes that you can later lavish with stunning decorations and your own creativity. These recipes are all designed to fill two 9-inch round pans or one 9-x-13-inch rectangular pan. (Many of the recipes in this book start with these basic recipes but then are adjusted to produce larger cakes or to incorporate different flavorings.)

Lining up the ingredients

Keep the following tips in mind when gathering your ingredients to make the cakes in the next section:

- Don't substitute margarine for butter, and definitely steer clear of vegetable oil spreads, as the amount of fat in them varies. Furthermore, you should always use unsalted rather than salted butter so that you control the salt in the recipe (and don't have to contend with it if it's not an ingredient in the recipe). In addition, cut the butter into ½-inch chunks to make the creaming process easier.

✔ Most of the recipes in the next section call for cake flour, which I'm a huge fan of when it comes to cakes. Cake flour is milled from soft winter wheat, which produces delicate flour that really isn't interchangeable with all-purpose flour. Sifting cake flour is almost always a necessity in recipes, so I usually get that out of the way first, sifting the flour into a large bowl and then measuring out of that bowl.

✔ When a recipe calls for milk, I usually stick with whole milk. From time to time, I've substituted reduced-fat milk, but whole milk really is best. The lower fat content of one percent and fat-free milk detracts from the fat in the recipe and results in a less rich flavor.

✔ For eggs, size matters, and large eggs are the norm for the following recipes. However, if you must use an egg substitute, two large eggs generally equal ⅓ to ½ cup of substitute, and three eggs are roughly equal to ½ to ⅔ cup of substitute. With those guidelines (and the equivalents that are usually printed on egg substitute cartons), you can substitute accordingly.

✔ If a recipe calls for separate egg whites or egg yolks, you need to separate those parts of the eggs. The easiest method is to crack an egg over a bowl (not your mixing bowl!), let the yolk glide into one half of the shell, and let the white fall away into the bowl. You may need to transfer the yolk back and forth between the shells a few times before the white completely separates. Alternately, you can use an egg separating device that allows the white to strain through a slotted sieve, but I'm partial to the hands-only method (because it's fun and it leaves one less apparatus to clean up!).

Take care in handling raw eggs. Wash exposed surfaces (and your hands) with an antibacterial soap after handling eggs to prevent cross-contamination.

✔ In recipes that call for oil, use only all-vegetable oil, and definitely stay away from olive oil! That's one taste that you don't want in your cake!

Making the cakes (finally!)

Without further ado, here are some basic cake recipes. Remember to practice, have fun, and don't forget to enjoy the finished product.

A Most Excellent White Cake

This delicious white cake bakes up high-and-mighty and is a staple for all kinds of celebrations.

Tools: *Two 9-inch round cake pans*

Preparation time: *15 minutes*

Baking time: *45 minutes*

Yield: *12 servings*

4½ cups sifted cake flour

¾ teaspoon salt

1 tablespoon plus 1 teaspoon baking powder

7 egg whites

2 cups whole milk

9 tablespoons unsalted butter, slightly softened and cut into ½-inch pieces

2½ cups granulated white sugar

1½ teaspoons pure vanilla extract

1 Preheat the oven to 350 degrees F. Grease and flour two 9-inch round cake pans, and set aside.

2 In a large bowl, sift the salt and baking powder into the cake flour, and stir the mixture with a balloon whisk.

3 In a medium bowl, break up the egg whites with a fork, add the milk, and mix together lightly.

4 In a large bowl, cream the butter. Add the sugar, and continue beating until light and fluffy. Add the vanilla, and continue beating.

5 Alternately add the flour and egg white mixture to the butter mixture, beginning and ending with the flour. Scrape down the sides of the bowl twice during beating. Stop beating when the last portion of flour is just blended into the mixture.

6 Pour the batter into the prepared pans, and bake for 45 minutes, or until a cake tester inserted in the center of the cake comes out with moist crumbs attached.

7 Cool the cakes in the pans on wire racks for 10 minutes. Run a knife around the edges, and then invert the cakes onto racks to cool completely.

Cocoa Chocolate Cake

This take on chocolate cake bakes up nicely and makes a sturdy foundation for dreamy chocolate decorations and accompaniments, which I explore in Chapter 12.

Tools: *Two 9-inch round cake pans*

Preparation time: *15 minutes*

Baking time: *35 minutes*

Yield: *12 servings*

¾ cup unsweetened cocoa powder

2 teaspoons baking soda

¼ teaspoon salt

3¼ cups sifted cake flour

9 tablespoons unsalted butter, at room

2½ cups granulated white sugar

1½ teaspoons pure vanilla extract

4 eggs

2 cups whole milk

nd flour two 9-inch round cake pans, and set

wder, baking soda, and salt. Then whisk in the

sugar, and beat until light and fluffy. Add the

ure, one at a time, beating well after each

lour mixture and the milk to the egg mixture
flour. Each addition should be mixed until
he bowl twice during beating.

d bake for 35 minutes, or until a cake tester
ut with moist crumbs attached.

r 10 minutes. Run a knife around the edges,
ol completely.

Delicious Yellow Cake

Another staple for your repertoire, this yellow cake is popular for all occasions and pairs well with buttercream and milk chocolate frosting, which I cover in Chapter 8.

Tools: *Two 9-inch round cake pans*

Preparation time: *15 minutes*

Baking time: *40 minutes*

Yield: *12 servings*

1 tablespoon baking powder

½ teaspoon salt

3½ cups sifted cake flour

1¼ cups butter, at room temperature and cut into ½-inch pieces

2 cups granulated white sugar

1 teaspoon pure vanilla extract

5 eggs

1 cup whole milk

1 Preheat the oven to 350 degrees. Grease and flour two 9-inch round cake pans, and set aside.

2 In a large bowl, sift together the baking powder and salt. Then whisk in the cake flour.

3 In a large bowl, cream the butter. Add the sugar, and beat until light and fluffy. Add the vanilla, and continue beating.

4 Add the eggs to the butter mixture, one at a time, beating well after each addition.

5 With the mixer set on low speed, add the flour mixture and the milk to the egg mixture alternately, beginning and ending with the flour. Each addition should be mixed until just combined. Scrape down the sides of the bowl twice during beating.

6 Pour the batter into the prepared pans, and bake for 35 to 40 minutes, or until the cake springs back when lightly touched and a cake tester inserted in the center of the cake comes out with moist crumbs attached.

7 Cool the cakes in the pans on wire racks for 10 minutes. Run a knife around the edges, and then invert the cakes onto racks to cool completely.

Flavor-Friendly Sponge Cake

This easy-to-bake cake stores, transports, and freezes well. I developed this version as an ideal base for soaking up flavored syrups, which I cover in Chapter 10.

Tools: *9-x-13-inch cake pan*

Preparation time: *10 minutes*

Baking time: *30 minutes*

Yield: *12 servings*

2¾ cups sifted cake flour	*1½ cups granulated white sugar*
3 teaspoons baking powder	*5 eggs*
1¼ cups unsalted butter, slightly softened and cut into ½-inch pieces	*¼ cup whole milk*

1 Preheat the oven to 350 degrees. Grease and flour a 9-x-13-inch rectangular cake pan, and set aside.

2 In a medium bowl, sift the baking powder over the cake flour, and whisk together.

3 In a large bowl, cream the butter and the sugar until smooth, light, and fluffy. Add the eggs, one at a time, beating well after each addition.

4 With the mixer set on low speed, add the flour mixture and the milk to the butter mixture alternately, beginning and ending with the flour. Each addition should be mixed until just combined. Scrape down the sides of the bowl twice during beating.

5 Pour the batter into the prepared pan. Bake for 30 minutes, or until a cake tester inserted in the center comes out with just a few crumbs attached.

6 Cool the cake in the pan on a wire rack for 10 minutes. Run a knife around the edges, and then invert the cake onto a wire rack to cool completely.

The Best Carrot Cake Ever

This cake is a moist, delicious treat that pairs well with cream cheese frosting (see Chapter 8). I usually steer clear of self-rising flour, but I actually developed the recipe for this cake when I was in the seventh grade, and old habits die hard.

Tools: *Two 9-inch round cake pans*

Preparation time: *20 minutes*

Baking time: *40 minutes*

Yield: *12 servings*

2 cups sifted self-rising flour	*2 cups granulated white sugar*
1 teaspoon baking soda	*3 cups grated carrot (about 8 medium carrots)*
1 teaspoon salt	*1½ cups vegetable oil*
1 teaspoon cinnamon	*4 eggs*

1 Preheat the oven to 350 degrees. Grease and flour two 9-inch round cake pans, or spray a Bundt pan with a nonstick spray that contains flour.

2 In a large bowl, sift together the flour, baking soda, salt, cinnamon, and sugar.

3 Add the carrot, oil, and eggs to the dry ingredients. Mix until well blended, but don't overmix.

4 Pour the batter into the prepared pans. Bake for 40 minutes, or until a cake tester inserted in the center of the cake comes out with some crumbs attached.

5 Cool the cakes in the pans on wire racks for 10 minutes. Run a knife around the edges, and then invert the cakes onto wire racks to cool completely.

Vary It!: *For the Best "Light" Carrot Cake Ever, substitute 1½ cups lowfat yogurt for the oil.*

Rich Pound Cake

As far as decorations are concerned, this cake pairs well with basic confectioners' sugar icing (see Chapter 9).

Tools: *10-inch tube pan*

Preparation time: *15 minutes*

Baking time: *1½ hours*

Yield: *12 servings*

1½ cups unsalted butter, slightly softened and cut into ½-inch pieces

1 pound confectioners' sugar

6 eggs

1 teaspoon pure vanilla extract

2¾ cups sifted cake flour

1 Preheat the oven to 300 degrees F. Grease and flour a 10-inch tube pan, and set aside.

2 In a large bowl, cream the butter and gradually beat in the eggs and confectioners' sugar until light and fluffy. Then beat in the vanilla.

3 With the mixer on low speed, gradually add the flour, beating just until mixed.

4 Pour the batter into the prepared pan, and bake for 1½ hours.

5 Cool the cake in the pan on a wire rack for 10 minutes. Invert the cake onto a wire rack to cool completely.

White Velvet Cake

One of my most popular cakes, this one sometimes comes out so perfectly you won't even have to level it! Plus the taste is so incomparable I've also used it for wedding cakes.

Tools: *Two 9-inch round cake pans (or one 9-x-13-inch cake pan)*

Preparation time: *20 minutes*

Baking time: *45 minutes*

Yield: *12 servings*

¾ teaspoon salt	*2¼ cups granulated white sugar*
1½ teaspoons baking soda	*3 eggs*
3¾ cups sifted cake flour	*1½ teaspoons pure vanilla extract*
2¼ cups vegetable oil	*1½ cups buttermilk*

1 Preheat the oven to 350 degrees F. Grease and flour the pans, and line them with parchment paper.

2 In a large bowl, sift the salt and baking soda over the cake flour, and then stir the mixture with a balloon whisk.

3 In a large bowl, mix the oil and sugar together, and then add the eggs, one at a time, beating well after each addition. Mix in the vanilla.

4 With the mixer set on low speed, add the flour mixture and the buttermilk, alternately, beginning and ending with the flour. Each addition of flour should be mixed until just combined. Scrape down the sides of the bowl twice during beating.

5 Pour the batter into the prepared pans. Bake for 40 minutes, or until a cake tester inserted into the center comes out with moist crumbs attached.

6 Cool the cakes in their pans on wire racks for 10 minutes. Run a knife around the edges, and then invert the cakes onto racks to cool completely.

Chapter 7

Smoothing the Way for Decorating

*A*fter your cake is out of the oven (I cover baking cakes in Chapter 6), you need to put it in tip-top, level shape to smooth the way for fillings to stack up, frostings and icing to shine, and decorations to sparkle. At that point, you can put your design plan in motion on the cake and feature it attractively for serving as well.

Perhaps the only thing worse than a cake that tastes bad is one that looks bad, and if you don't prepare a baked cake properly, your decorations won't look right no matter how skilled you are or how much time you spend trying to get it just right.

Although your work on decorating starts after the cake comes out of the oven, the best way to ensure an attractive cake is to start the design process before you rev up your mixer. That means planning ahead and thinking through your entire cake design before you make your first move. In Chapter 5, I dole out some ideas and inspiration for drawing up the cake design. In this chapter, you take the first steps of actually implementing those creative stirrings on the cake itself. You also get some ideas for covering the cake board in a way that enhances the overall design of your cake, working with design templates and patterns, and mixing colored frosting that makes your cake look just as good as it tastes.

Devising Your Game Plan

So you know what cake you're baking, you've picked a frosting, and you know exactly what you want your cake to look like just before its served, right?

If you don't, take a breather right now and make some decisions. Before you start baking the cake — and even before you preheat that oven — you have to know how the cake is supposed to look in its final presentation.

Of course something may go amiss, you may have to improvise, a color may not turn out as planned, or you may decide that the design of a star tip looks better than a round one. But, overall, you need to have your blueprint in place. If you don't, you're left to make it up as you go along, and that's certainly not the way to get great results.

Start your planning by considering how much time you have to prepare the cake and how best to use that time. You also need to think through your design plan from start to finish in order to make sure you're not left missing ingredients or wondering how everything will come together.

Timing

With the design in hand, map out a timetable that includes your approximate times for

- ✔ Gathering ingredients and materials for your cake's presentation
- ✔ Baking and cooling the cake layers
- ✔ Preparing the frosting
- ✔ Making the filling
- ✔ Decorating the cake
- ✔ Staging the cake

To ensure accuracy and prevent unwanted delays, assemble all your ingredients before you start mixing anything. (You may not want to set out refrigerated ingredients; just make sure you have what the recipe calls for.)

For example, take a look at this timetable for the Play Ball! Baseball Cake from Chapter 13. Keep in mind that you should read through an entire recipe first to ascertain not just prep time, baking, and decorating, but also cooling and refrigeration. Plus, the recipes will include not only the cake, but also the frosting (and possibly separate filling) you'll have to make. Taking all these aspects into account will help create a successful, entire, and complete cake decorating experience. To make this cake from start to finish, you need this much time:

Initial prep time	At least 30 minutes to gather ingredients and to set up your cake board
Preparing the cake batter	15 minutes
Baking and cooling time	50 minutes, plus 2 hours for cooling

Preparing the frosting	10 minutes
Decorating time	1 hour, plus 2 hours for refrigeration
Staging	At least 30 minutes, to ensure that the cake board is clean and free of crumbs and frosting, and also to set up and decorate the area from which the cake will be served

Adding up the different times involved will give you a realistic timetable. Oftentimes, I'll bake the cake the night before a birthday party, for instance, and crumbcoat it. Then, the day of the event itself I'll concern myself with all the decorating and final staging.

Keeping design in mind

Decorating a cake takes time, but you can save yourself some trouble by having all the elements of your design mapped out and ready to go. Consider these questions regarding design elements that may play roles in your cake design:

- ✔ Will you use a template or stencil? If so, do you have it on hand?

- ✔ Will you have to sketch a design out in the frosting? Do you have a bamboo skewer or toothpick to do so with?

- ✔ Are candies or confections part of the design? Do they need to be separated out, and if so, are they?

- ✔ Do you know what you'll do with colored frostings after they're mixed?

- ✔ Do you have the icing tips you need? Would it save you time during decorating to have extra tips available, and if so, do you have them?

- ✔ Will you be scripting a name or message? Do you know how everything is spelled?

- ✔ Have you composed the entire greeting word for word?

- ✔ Have you measured and blocked out the design on a piece of parchment paper the same size as your finished cake to ensure proper placement and proportion?

Covering Cake Boards

The *cake board,* which is the foundation that holds your stunning creation, is an important element of your presentation. Cake boards are usually made of a hardwood pastry board, Masonite, plywood, foam core, or heavy plastic. Before you're in the throes of mixing, baking, and decorating, get your cake board ready and keep it waiting in the wings until you're ready to place your cake on it. A cake from a bakery may just come on plain, sturdy cardboard, but when you're the one doing the baking and decorating, you can decorate the cake board to reflect the special nature of the event the cake is being featured at.

Wrapping it up in paper and fabric

You don't want the cake board decoration to conflict with the look of the cake or distract attention from the cake with too busy a pattern, but a cake board wrapped in a simple print looks festive and polished. Consider folding a piece of fabric, wrapping paper, or patterned tissue paper over the board to lend color and vibrancy.

After you wrap the cake board in paper or fabric, you need to cover it with heavy cellophane as well. If you don't, the cake and frosting are likely to create unsightly stains on the material.

Using fondant or royal icing

Wrap your cake board with a sheet of colored fondant or spread a smooth layer of white or tinted royal icing on the board and let it dry before resting your cake on top. These options bring a beautiful and understated look to your cake presentation and accent the cake with their clean appearance.

Considering unconventional ideas

Other possibilities for dressing up the cake board may fit in with your cake's design while lending fun or elegance to the presentation through visuals that enhance (but don't overwhelm) the cake. A few unconventional covering ideas include:

- A map
- Sheet music
- A collage of greeting cards
- A collage of mementos
- Scrapbook essentials such as striped paper

With each of these coverings, consider their size. You may need to firmly secure the items on a large piece of paper (particularly if you're forming them into a collage), and wrap heavy cellophane over it.

Position the covering so that the most visual elements are around the cake's perimeter. It would be a shame to create a work of art for the cake board and then cover it up completely with the cake.

Leveling and Torting the Cake

Leveling a cake that didn't bake evenly and has a domed top can be an absolute maddening proposition for some. But you must level a cake so that you can create or place your design on a flat surface. Unleveled cakes just don't look very professional. After you put in all the energy and effort to devise a design, bake, frost, and decorate a cake, you don't want your cake eaters concentrating on the hump in the center of the cake; you want them to notice your amazing artistry! And with torting, you want to separate layers so that, after they're filled, they stack back up evenly.

A few tricks can help you level your cake with ease — and none of them require a visit to the hardware store for a construction level!

Loving to level

I actually prefer leveling the cake before I put it on the cakeboard. With bigger, rectangular cakes (such as those that are 12-x-18-inches), that means leveling the cake on the cooling rack and then flipping it over onto your cakeboard so that you have a nice even surface — that's actually the bottom of the cake — to decorate. Smaller layers can be leveled while they're sitting — preferably, if you have one — on a decorating turntable because they'll be easier to move to the cakeboard (with a large spatula/turner, described in Chapter 2) once they're leveled and decorated.

Before you make your leveling move, make sure that your cake has cooled completely.

Some bakers are perfectly content to take a long serrated knife and lop off the offending cake dome (see Figure 7-1). However, not everyone has such a steady hand, and the last thing you want to do is keep slicing into a cake in a futile attempt to even out the mess you've made. If you keep slicing away in a quest for levelness, you may just end up with a very low-lying cake or one that looks like a bed with a sunken hole in the middle.

Instead, consider picking up a cake leveler. With this handy tool (which looks like a hand saw with a wire instead of a saw blade), you adjust the level to your cake's height and draw a steel wire across the top of the cake, slicing off the dome and leaving you with a flat surface. Figure 7-1 shows you how to use a cake leveler.

Walk around the cake after you level it just to make sure that you've leveled the entire cake top and not just the center. I even suggest bending down on your knees to take in the cake top at eye level.

You may also want to consider employing a couple of available methods to encourage a flatter cake top through even baking. These apparatuses are further explained in Chapter 2.

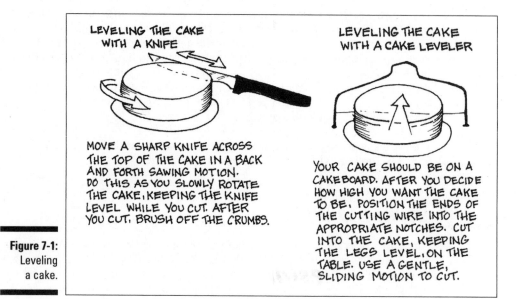

Figure 7-1: Leveling a cake.

Tackling torting

Torting involves splitting each layer of a cake into one or more horizontal layers that you then spread icing or fillings, such as mousse, citrus curd, or jam, on before stacking them back up. Torting a cake makes for a dramatic impact when the cake is sliced because the cake eater gets a peek at layers upon layers of cake and filling.

An adjustable cake leveler, which I explain in the preceding section, works wonderfully to give you a clean cut exactly in the middle of a cake layer. If you want to slice the layers by hand, insert toothpicks halfway into the sides of the cake in the middle of the layer and completely around the circumference. Take the toothpicks out and use the tiny holes they leave as your guide as you slice the layer in half with a sharp, serrated knife (see Figure 7-2).

Accurate torting is important because if you aren't ruthless in evenly slicing the layer in half or into thirds or quarters, you'll have a very difficult time achieving a level cake as the end product. Just one uneven layer can throw your whole cake off-kilter.

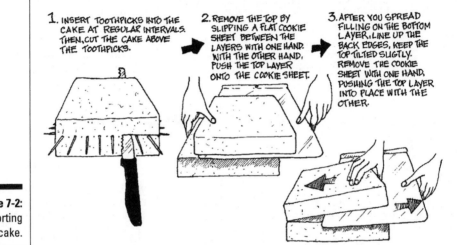

1. INSERT TOOTHPICKS INTO THE CAKE AT REGULAR INTERVALS. THEN, CUT THE CAKE ABOVE THE TOOTHPICKS.

2. REMOVE THE TOP BY SLIPPING A FLAT COOKIE SHEET BETWEEN THE LAYERS WITH ONE HAND. WITH THE OTHER HAND, PUSH THE TOP LAYER ONTO THE COOKIE SHEET.

3. AFTER YOU SPREAD FILLING ON THE BOTTOM LAYER, LINE UP THE BACK EDGES, KEEP THE TOP TILTED SLIGTLY. REMOVE THE COOKIE SHEET WITH ONE HAND, PUSHING THE TOP LAYER INTO PLACE WITH THE OTHER.

Figure 7-2:
Torting
a cake.

Drawing Up Designs

You know what you want your finished cake to look like, but how exactly do you plan to achieve that look? You have several options to go about getting the design you want actually on the cake.

As I explain in Chapter 5, don't feel like you have to be a professional artist with a mastery of paint strokes and who can draw intricate patterns. On the other hand, you don't want your design to look like amateur hour either. Several premade design options are available, including templates that you trace around and patterns you fill in. Still, don't be afraid of freehand drawing or coming up with an original design. For example, flip through a kid's coloring book for a host of easy drawings to mimic. You can break down any illustration into a series of shapes.

Start off simply. Don't try to recreate a Monet the first time out. Instead, start with a tulip or a tree.

Sizing up the cake

For any design or illustration, you have to keep in mind the entire size of your cake. A 6-inch design in the center of a 12-x-18-inch frosting canvas just doesn't look finished. Conversely, and unless you're purposely achieving an all-over design, don't feel like you have to fill up every square inch of the cake's surface and sides. Blank space can have its place too, especially in drawing the eye to your intentional design.

As the cake comes out of the oven, assess your canvas and compare the cake's surface with your design blueprint. Ask yourself these questions:

- ✔ Will everything fit?
- ✔ Do I need to make any adjustments to the design?
- ✔ Did the sides of the cake rise enough to accommodate any piping planned for the perimeter?

If you're creating a three-dimensional cake design, make sure that you have all the pieces you need for the decoration. When your cake comes out of the oven, get your ruler out and make sure that all the pieces will fit as they should and according to your drawing.

Whether your cake will be flat or three-dimensional, make changes to your design before you start decorating. Trust me: You don't want to be midway through decorating and realize that the cake is bigger (or smaller) than you expected, causing your decorations to look askew, awry, or altogether misplaced.

Sketching

If you opt to do a freehand illustration on the cake, use a bamboo skewer to sketch out the design or artwork that you'll fill in later with piped stars, smooth frosting, or some other material.

For the best sketching surface, level the cake, apply a crumb coat of frosting, and refrigerate to seal. Frost the cake and refrigerate it again before you start sketching. It's much easier to carve a sketch into refrigerated frosting because it firms up. If you mess up your sketch, just frost the cake again, refrigerate it, and then have another go at it. (Check out Chapter 8 for tips on smooth frosting techniques.)

Tracing

Tracing a design on your cake is a relatively easy way to decorate with a one-dimensional design. Just cut out the shape or picture of the object you want to have on your cake, lay it on the frosted and refrigerated cake, and trace around it with a bamboo skewer.

If tracing around a paper cutout proves too cumbersome, use the skewer or a toothpick to poke holes around (or even through) the cutout. You can get as detailed as you want by poking holes all over the cake, following the lines and nuances of the design. Tracing in this manner gives you a connect-the-dots design that you can outline by piping over with a pastry bag outfitted with a round tip.

Using templates

Templates are line art that you can blow up or reduce to fit the dimensions of your cake. Follow the tracing process covered in the preceding section to transfer the template design to the cake. Then fill in the template with piped stars or beads, for example.

Templates usually come with color suggestions and tell you what frosting to put where, but the choice really is up to you. I categorize templates more in the free-rein arena of cake decorating because you get the outline but make your own choices about how to complete it.

Following patterns

Patterns are a more regimented approach to cake decorating in that they include suggested frosting colors and placement. Cake decorating patterns usually involve a conventional shape or design or the licensed artwork of a cartoon character.

A pattern for an entire cake usually doesn't come with a template that you trace; rather, you draw the basic design by hand. If you select a specialty pan in a specific shape, like a pineapple, a piano keyboard, or a cartoon character, the pan's packaging is likely to include a photo of the finished cake to show suggested colors and outlines.

Choosing Colors

Color is a key component of the cake design process. Putting together the right contrasting and complementary colors makes your cake visually exciting and appealing and makes your design pop. Unfortunately, no matter how good your cake tastes, the wrong combination of colors can make your cake distracting and uninviting.

Experimenting before proceeding

The key to great cake design colors is experimentation. Working with colored frostings is like working with paints in that your options are unlimited. Particularly if you don't have a lot of experience with tinting frostings, don't be afraid to mix and mess around with colors as you coordinate your design options. You may find colors that you never thought you'd like and fall in love with them when you see them paired with others.

If you mix up colored frosting for your cake and find that the colors just don't go well together after all or aren't what you had in mind, start fresh. Make more frosting and tint another batch, or try mixing a different shade. Just because you make colored frosting doesn't mean you have to use it!

Mixing just the right color

The advice and guidelines in this section apply to working with white frosting, such as buttercream, stiff decorator frosting, or royal icing.

Food coloring gels take a lot of the guesswork out of mixing frosting colors because they come in a variety of shades. The color should be listed and pictured on the squeeze bottle or paste vial of the color, but don't just assume that you'll end up with that color exactly. Test it first. For example, if your buttercream isn't bright white, the resulting hue may be darker than the color on the bottle. Or you may be unable to find the shade of avocado, tangerine, or coral that you need in a tint, so it may be up to you to create it yourself.

Here's some general advice to follow as you mix colored frostings:

- ✔ **Use just a little bit of coloring gel or paste at a time as you're coloring your frosting.** You can always add more, but you can't take it back after it's mixed in!

- ✔ **If you need quite a bit of black frosting, consider adding a black tint to chocolate frosting instead of white frosting.** Because you start with a dark base color, you end up using much less black coloring gel.

✔ **Colored frosting darkens and the color gets richer after it's mixed, so wait an hour before using it on your cake.** The color you see when you first mix a tint with frosting may not be the final color, so make sure that it's the hue you had in mind before you apply it to your cake.

✔ **To make frosting a touch lighter in color, add some white food coloring gel.** To make frosting a little darker in color, add some black gel, but be careful because a tiny bit of black gel goes a very, very long way.

Taking stock of colors

Now's the time to pull out the color wheel you have in your cake decorating kit. Understanding just a few rules about colors will help you mix just the right color for your cake design.

Red, blue, and yellow are *primary colors.* They're considered *stand-alones* because they can't be mixed or created from any other combination of colors . . . no matter how hard you try.

Combining primary colors in equal amounts produces *secondary colors.* For instance, mixing yellow with blue produces green; red with yellow produces orange; and blue with red produces violet. Taking things a step further, mixing one primary with one secondary color yields a *tertiary color.* For example, mixing yellow and green brings, you guessed it, yellow-green, comparable to a chartreuse hue.

If you want to become better versed in the color arena, I suggest setting aside time for a practice and experimentation session. Gather up a bottle each of red, yellow, and blue food coloring gels, and mix up a few batches of butter-cream frosting. With a color wheel nearby, combine colors to your heart's content. Have pen and paper handy so that you can record what your different combinations yield, and use that information for coloring your future cake designs.

Charting different shades

Food coloring gels come in a variety of colors and shades, and to make things even easier for you, manufacturers also provide recommendations for creating even more hues by combining their available colors. In the end, though, you have to mix and decide for yourself, adding in a few drops here and there or electing not to add in as much color to begin with. When you're shopping for food coloring gels, keep the following points in mind:

✔ If you're striving for a vivid hue, check out the gels that have "Super" or "Neon" as a prefix. They tend to offer deeper, richer tones.

✔ The name of a coloring gel may not always be what you expect. For example, I'm partial to the color leaf green, but it's really more of a kelly green. If your design involves leaves on a tree and you want them to be as realistic as possible, you may opt for forest green, pine green, or moss coloring gels (or mix up a color on your own).

Table 7-1 breaks down the combinations for a variety of colors. I developed these color recipes by mixing many batches of frosting and colors, but mixing colors isn't an exact science. Brands of coloring gels differ slightly in the colors they offer (even if the hues share the same name), so use the information in this table as a jumping off point for your coloring endeavors, and then develop your own tried-and-true combinations.

Table 7-1	Mixing Your Own Frosting Colors
Final Color	*Components Colors*
Apricot	2 parts orange plus 1 part golden yellow (or egg yellow)
Aqua	5 parts sky blue plus 1 part leaf green
Avocado	4 parts lemon yellow plus 1 part leaf green plus a dab of black
Burgundy	5 parts rose pink plus 1 part violet
Chartreuse	8 parts lemon yellow plus 1 part leaf green
Copper	1 part golden yellow (or egg yellow) plus 1 part brown plus 1 part bright red
Coral	3 parts rose plus 2 parts lemon yellow
Dusty rose	5 parts rose plus 1 part violet
Gold	10 parts lemon yellow plus 3 parts orange plus 1 part red *or* 4 parts golden yellow (or egg yellow) plus 1 part brown
Gray	a dab of black added to white frosting
Jade	2 parts forest green plus 1 part leaf green
Lavender	5 parts pink plus 1 part violet
Mauve	5 parts rose plus 2 parts orange plus 2 parts red plus 1 part black
Melon	3 parts rose plus 1 part orange
Navy	1 part sky blue plus 1 part violet
Plum	1 part violet plus a dab of bright red
Raspberry	3 parts rose plus 1 part bright red
Rust	8 parts orange plus 2 parts red plus 1 part brown
Teal	9 parts sky blue plus a dab of lemon yellow

Part III
Topping, Filling, and Embellishing Your Creations

The 5th Wave   By Rich Tennant

"Anyone for more caramel upside-down cake?"

In this part . . .

This part lets you in on ideal recipes and easy instructions for mastering the decorating process. You collect pointers on topping the cake with frostings and icings and tucking in fillings for sweet surprises. I also help you decode the language of icing tips with an array of hints and instructions. As for embellishments, I give you the luscious lowdown, from the surprisingly simple and widely used to more artistic endeavors and secret, impressive finds.

Chapter 8

Whipping Up Frostings

*E*veryone's familiar with the kid who decadently draws his finger through some fluffy frosting, samples his stash, and then happily licks his lips. (Or maybe you were once that kid!) If you do your job right, everyone who sees your cakes, adults included, will wish they could act just like that kid.

The frosting on your cake is more than just a sweet covering — it's the first impression your cake eaters get of the creation they're about to indulge in. In this chapter, you find out how to pair a cake with the right frosting for the best effect in both taste and appearance. You also get a handle on some simple frosting recipes that work in an array of decorating situations. I explain how to color frostings and how to frost your cake just so for a clean space on which to create your masterpiece. If you're interested in a simpler design, I cover your options for texturing your frosting, too.

Stirring Through the Rules for Frosting

For any cake, frosting presents two challenges:

✔ It has to win your cake eaters over with its taste.

✔ It has to be smooth, spreadable, and flexible enough to allow you to pipe and otherwise create decorations for the cake.

With those goals in mind, take care in preparing your frostings to perfection. Pay particular attention to the following:

✔ **Sifting:** Sift your dry ingredients, especially confectioner's sugar, when the recipe calls for it. It may seem unnecessary, but if you don't sift the sugar, you'll end up with clumps (small and large) of sugar in your frosting that detract from a smooth finish.

- **Creaming:** Solids like cream cheese and butter should be thoroughly creamed (but not overmixed). Clumps of these solid ingredients make for a sloppy frosting appearance, and they also can wreak havoc with your pastry bag, leaving the frosting stuck in the tip rather than flowing onto your cake.

Some recipes in this chapter refer to using a mixer's paddle attachment. Using a paddle rather than a whisk attachment makes creaming butter, cream cheese, or shortening a faster and easier proposition.

- **Working with clean equipment:** Take care to use clean, grease-free bowls and attachments for mixing frosting. If you have to use the same bowl that you mixed your cake in, wash it with hot, soapy water, and dry it thoroughly before preparing your frosting. The same goes for your whisk or paddle. When your equipment isn't clean, you run the risk of introducing unwanted flavors into your frosting or messing up the mixing with bits of cake batter.

Matching up Frostings and Cakes

Party guests and cake eaters appreciate variety, so don't feel like you always have to pair chocolate cake with chocolate frosting and white cake with white frosting. Those combinations are appropriate for some events, but after you have some frosting basics down, you can be inventive, creative, and experiment a bit with cake and frosting combinations.

Don't lose control of your taste combinations. Some flavors are great on their own but not so great together; this is particularly true with strong-flavored cakes and frostings. For instance, orange-flavored frosting on a peanut butter cake may not go over so well with most cake eaters.

Frosting to the rescue

In medieval times, wedding guests brought small cakes that were stacked on a table, and the bride and groom had to try and kiss over all the stack of cakes. Seeking to avoid a messy, mushy ruckus, a young baker decided to put all the cakes together and cover them with frosting, paving a sweet way for the concept of tiered wedding cakes.

Before you go to all the work to bake and decorate a cake, taste your cake and frosting combination for yourself. Your skills and success depend on sampling, practicing, and being excessively familiar with the taste and mouth feel of frostings such that you can match them up appropriately with the right kind of cake. So, indulge! Getting a handle on the tastes and consistencies of your frostings will bring you greater success in your cake decorating.

The possibilities for cake and frosting pairings are limitless! However, if you're not into experimentation, think about flavor combinations that you like in candy bars, ice cream flavors, or sundaes. These favorites will help you determine what cake and frosting flavors work well together.

The most common pairings (and the safest ones for big crowds) are

- ✔ Chocolate cake with chocolate buttercream frosting
- ✔ Yellow cake with chocolate or vanilla buttercream frosting
- ✔ White cake with vanilla buttercream frosting
- ✔ Carrot cake with cream cheese frosting

Although there are no hard and fast rules for combinations, keep your answers to these questions in mind when making a cake and frosting pairing:

- ✔ Have you tasted this combination before (in a cake, candy bar, or other confection)?
- ✔ Do these flavors "get along," or will one overpower the other one?

Mixing Frostings

The frosting recipes in this section are basic ones that you can tint, flavor, or leave alone for an equally great taste and appearance. All are good for piping designs (covered in Chapter 11) or dressing up with edible or nonedible decorations.

Whichever frosting you choose to make for your confection, work toward a spreadable consistency. The frosting should be thick enough to hold a piped shape but thin enough to pipe with just gentle pressure on the pastry bag.

A little frosting *doesn't* go a long way, so you should always be prepared to make another batch of frosting in case you start decorating and find you're running short. You never want a cake to look — or taste — like you skimped on the frosting.

Following you'll find some suggested guidelines for frosting and its basic equivalencies for some popular cake sizes.

- ✔ 2 cups is enough to fill and frost two 9-inch rounds
- ✔ 2 cups is enough to frost the tops of 24 cupcakes
- ✔ 3 cups is enough to fill and frost two 10-inch squares
- ✔ 2½ cups is enough to frost the top and sides of one 9-x-13-inch rectangle

Buttercream Frosting

The most versatile of the lot, buttercream frosting is sure to be an essential component of your frosting repertoire. It spreads and pipes wonderfully, and because of its lustrous, white appearance, you can tint it to exactly the color you want. As if that weren't enough, this recipe requires no cooking!

Tools: *Electric mixer, paddle attachment*

Preparation time: *10 minutes*

Yield: *2 cups*

1 cup unsalted butter, softened	*3¾ cups confectioners' sugar, sifted*
1 teaspoon pure vanilla extract	*¼ cup milk*

1 In a large bowl, beat the butter and vanilla on medium speed for about 30 seconds.

2 Gradually add half the sugar, beating well.

3 Beat in the milk, and then add the remaining sugar. Continue beating until the frosting is smooth and creamy and reaches the desired consistency.

Tip: *If the frosting is too thick, add milk in 1 teaspoon increments, beating each addition well, until it reaches the desired consistency.*

Vary It!: *For chocolate buttercream, beat in 1 tablespoon unsweetened cocoa powder in Step 1. For almond buttercream, substitute 1 teaspoon almond extract for the vanilla. For orange buttercream, substitute ½ teaspoon orange extract for the vanilla.*

Stiff Decorator Frosting

If you have a lot of ground to cover decorating-wise on your cake, or if the intricacy of the design will require time and patience, this frosting is an excellent choice because it holds its shape for a long time, without hardening immediately, allowing you the latitude to futz with the decorating without it "melting."

Tools: *Electric mixer, paddle attachment*

Preparation time: *10 minutes*

Yield: *4 cups*

7 cups sifted confectioners' sugar

¾ cup all-vegetable shortening

⅓ cup whole milk

¼ teaspoon almond extract

1 Combine the sugar and shortening in the bowl of an electric mixer. Beat on low speed until the ingredients start to come together. Beat in the almond extract.

2 Gradually add the whole milk as you increase the mixing speed until the frosting is smooth and creamy. If necessary, beat in a few more drops of milk until you reach the desired consistency, which should be holding firm but pliable peaks.

Cream Cheese Frosting

This frosting pairs exceptionally well with a host of cakes, including the Best Carrot Cake Ever (Chapter 6), Red Velvet Cake (Chapter 17), Piña Colada Cake (Chapter 14), and Key Lime Cake (Chapter 15) . With a consistency and color similar to buttercream, it's also an ideal frosting for piping. ***Note:*** For optimal flavor and texture, don't use reduced fat cream cheese or Neufchatel cheese in this recipe.

Tools: *Electric mixer, paddle attachment*

Preparation time: *10 minutes*

Yield: *2 cups*

8-ounce package cream cheese, softened	*3¾ cup confectioner's sugar, sifted*
½ cup unsalted butter, softened	*1 teaspoon pure vanilla extract*

1 In a large bowl, cream the butter and cream cheese on medium speed until combined and fluffy.

2 Set the mixer on low speed, and add the confectioner's sugar to the creamed mixture in batches. After all the sugar is incorporated, increase to medium speed to thoroughly mix the ingredients.

3 Add the vanilla, and continue beating until combined.

Tip: *If the frosting doesn't completely combine in your mixer, scrape down sides of the bowl with a rubber spatula and continue beating.*

Vary It: *For a peppermint cream cheese frosting, substitute ½ teaspoon peppermint flavoring for the vanilla. For a lemon cream cheese frosting, substitute ½ teaspoon lemon flavoring for the vanilla.*

Chocolate Ganache

This simple recipe for a rich, dense, and delicious chocolate frosting speeds up the process with an assist from your microwave. You can't tint ganache, but its deep brown color is more than delightful.

Tools: 2-quart glass measuring cup

Preparation time: 5 minutes plus 1 hour for refrigeration

Yield: 3 cups

3 cups (18 ounces) semisweet chocolate chips

1½ cups heavy cream

2 tablespoons unsalted butter

1 In the glass measuring cup, combine the chocolate chips and heavy cream. Microwave on high for 1½ minutes, or until the chips melt. Stir the mixture with a rubber spatula until smooth and evenly combined; no chunks of chocolate should remain.

2 Add the butter to the warm chocolate mixture, and stir until melted. (The butter gives the ganache a glossy sheen.)

3 Cover the measuring cup with plastic wrap and refrigerate it for about 1 hour, until the ganache holds its shape such that it's thick enough that you could frost a cake with it. You can test it by spooning out a bit to see how it stands up on a spoon, or tilt the measuring cup back to make sure the ganache doesn't jiggle. Stir the ganache again when you're ready to frost the cake.

Tip: To pipe ganache, divide it up before you refrigerate it. If it gets too stiff in the refrigerator, put it in a heatproof bowl over a saucepan of hot water, and stir it until it warms up enough to pipe.

Milk Chocolate Frosting

This versatile frosting adds a nice (and decadent) depth to the Cocoa Chocolate Cake (Chapter 6) and White Chocolate Cake (Chapter 17), and it amps up the flavor as a filling for the Delicious Yellow Cake (Chapter 6) and A Most Excellent White Cake (Chapter 6). Whatever cake you decide to pair it with, know that it's always a hit with candy bar connosseurs.

Tools: *Electric mixer, paddle attachment*

Preparation time: *10 minutes*

Yield: *About 2 cups*

½ cup unsalted butter, softened

¼ cup sifted unsweetened cocoa powder

2 cups sifted confectioners' sugar

3 tablespoons heavy whipping cream

1 In the bowl of an electric mixer, beat the butter until fluffy.

2 Add the cocoa powder and sugar, and beat on medium speed to combine.

3 Gradually add in the whipping cream, beating until the frosting is creamy. If necessary, beat in additional cream one drop at a time until the frosting reaches the desired consistency to be perfectly spreadable.

Tinting Frostings

Part of the beauty of frostings such as buttercream and cream cheese is their ability to take on strikingly beautiful colors that enhance your decorating adventure.

To tint frosting, you need to pick up some food coloring paste or gels from your local craft store or a cake decorating supply house. The colors widely available on grocery store shelves don't produce the brilliant, deep hues that pastes or gels do. In addition, gels and pastes come in an amazing variety of colors, so you may be able to buy a more unusual color like lavender, chartreuse, aqua, or magenta rather than mix it up yourself.

In tinting frosting, the key is to add just a little coloring at a time. If you dump in a whole bunch at once, you have no recourse in correcting the color if it's too deep, too bright, or just plain wrong.

I've found that the best tool for coloring is a toothpick. Follow these steps for tinting:

1. **Insert the toothpick into the gel, and scoop out a bit of coloring.**

2. **Shake a drop or two of coloring into the frosting, and stir it in with a spoon, evenly distributing the shade. Evaluate the result and decide whether or not you need to add more coloring.**

3. **Repeat Steps 1 and 2 until you have the color you want.**

4. **Stir your frosting completely so that you don't have white streaks zooming through your perfectly tinted frosting.**

If you're using a squeeze gel container of coloring, you can squeeze a few drops into the frosting. However, until you're comfortable with the coloring process, stick with the toothpick method. You'll have more control over your color's outcome that way.

The longer the frosting sits, the deeper the hue becomes, so don't be surprised when your perfect shade of leaf green gets a little dark. Instead, compensate for the change during the coloring process by going a little easy on the green gel.

Don't flavor your frosting and then throw off your cake eaters with a different color. For example, a lemon-flavored frosting should be yellow, not pink, just as an orange-flavored one should be orange and not green. People expect certain colors to taste a certain way, and mixing up colors and flavors distracts them from taking in the full beauty and impressiveness of your brilliant creation!

Frosting with Finesse

Frosting a cake is more than just slapping on a layer of sweet confection and calling it a day. Frosting the right way requires time, tools, and attention to detail. The most important tools you should have on hand are different sized icing spatulas, a pastry brush, and a decorating turntable. Check out Chapter 2 for more information on these.

When you have your plain or colored frosting ready to apply to your cake, check its consistency. If the frosting is too thick, you'll tear the cake as you attempt to spread the frosting. To thin out your frosting, return it to the mixer and add some milk (a teaspoon at a time) until it's the right, spreadable consistency. If the frosting is too thin, it will run or puddle, leaving you with incomplete and unattractive coverage. If it was once the right consistency, it probably has just gotten too warm, so put it in the refrigerator for a few minutes to allow it to thicken.

Keep your frosting from crusting and drying out by covering the bowl with a damp paper towel until you're ready to frost. If you won't be using the frosting soon, cover the bowl with an airtight lid and place in the refrigerator.

Follow these steps, which are illustrated in Figure 8-1, to frost a two-layer, 9-inch round cake. These guidelines are easily adaptable to other cake sizes:

1. **Gather all the tools you'll need to frost: wax paper, offset icing spatula, frosting knife, silicone brush, and (preferably) a pedestal that has a rotating round top.**

2. **Place four 2-x-8-inch strips of wax paper around the board your cake will sit on for presentation. Place the first layer of the leveled cake on the board, and then put the board on the pedestal.**

3. **With the silicone brush, sweep all excess crumbs off your cake layer.**

4. **Use the frosting knife to scoop about ½ cup of frosting onto the cake layer. With the offset icing spatula, spread the frosting evenly and smoothly on the top of the cake only. The initial crumb coat (which I discuss a little later) will be a scant, thin layer of frosting; think of it as providing a "protective seal" for your cake. The subsequent coat will be quite thicker, about ¼-inch to ⅜-inch thick.**

   A frosting knife is a specialty tool with a generous blade that allows you to heap frosting onto your cake layers easily. You can also use a rubber spatula to scoop frosting out onto your cake.

   The way to use an icing spatula depends on what's best for you. Spreading icing from the front edge of the spatula may be more comfortable than holding the back edge, so practice to see which method you prefer.

5. **Place the second cake layer — flat side up — on top of the first. Again, sweep any excess crumbs off the top and sides of cake.**

6. **Use the frosting knife to scoop ½ cup of frosting on top of the cake, and use the offset spatula to spread it out in even strokes to be a thin seal for the crumb coat, and a ¼ to ⅜-inch thickness for the second coat. Use excess frosting from the top of the cake to frost the sides of the cake, rotating the pedestal as you use the flat edge of the spatula for a smooth, even finish. Add more frosting from the bowl as necessary to cover the sides with a thin layer of frosting.**

   This first layer of frosting is the *crumb coat* (which I explain in the next section). The cake needs to be refrigerated for at least 1 hour before you apply the final frosting coat.

7. **For the final coat of frosting on the cake's top and sides, repeat Step 6 but with a thicker layer of frosting. Keep adding and subtracting frosting until you have the smooth, finished look that you desire.**

Taking care to crumb coat

Have you ever noticed that some cakes have bits of crumbs in the frosting? Unless you're going for the speckled look, applying a *crumb coat* to your cake will stop those crumbs in their tracks. The thin layer of frosting provides protection to keep crumbs out of your decorations and the frosting layer that your partygoers see. This one simple step ensures professional-looking results for your frosted cake. Follow these steps to crumb coat your cake:

1. **After your cake has cooled completely, level it and brush off any excess crumbs.**

2. **Using a wide icing spatula, spread a thin layer of frosting over the top and all sides of the cake.**

3. **Refrigerate the cake for a least 1 hour.**

   Chilling the cake allows the frosting to crust and seal in any crumbs that may still be left on your prepared cake.

Thanks to the crumb coat, when you apply the second coat of frosting to the cake, you don't have to worry about any crumbs mixing in with the frosting. You're guaranteed to get a clean, polished presentation.

Figure 8-1:
Frosting
a cake.

1. PLACE A LARGE BLOB OF FROSTING IN THE MIDDLE OF THE CAKE. USE A SPATULA TO SPREAD IT TO THE EDGES. *PUSH, DON'T SCRAPE THE ICING WITH THE SPATULA.*

2. TO REMOVE EXCESS FROSTING AND LEVEL IT, HOLD THE SPATULA AT A 45° ANGLE TO THE CAKE. START AT THE EDGE FAR-THEST FROM YOU AND DRAG THE SPATULA TO YOU. TURN THE CAKE SLIGHTLY AND REPEAT A FEW TIMES TO LEVEL THE FROSTING.

YOU MAY SLIDE A SECOND LAYER ON HERE...

3. ADD A THICK COAT OF ICING TO THE TOP AND SIDES. FOLLOW THE 1st TWO STEPS. MAKE SURE THE ICING IS SMOOTH AND EVEN. MAKE SURE TO ADD ENOUGH ICING TO THE SIDES FOR A NICE THICK COAT. CONCEAL THE CAKE ROUND. * DIP YOUR SPATULA IN "HOT" WATER TO MAKE A SMOOTH COAT!

Smoothing out the frosting

Some cake designs benefit from a textured coat of frosting, which I discuss in the next section. But many bakers and cake decorators crave the smooth look that wedding and other elaborate cakes tend to sport.

Make the process of frosting your cake a bit easier by setting your cake board on a sturdy surface. If necessary, place it on damp kitchen towels to keep it from shifting as you work. If you're frosting a round cake, consider putting it on a turntable that you can spin as you frost.

You have a few options to go about getting a smooth coat of frosting on your cake.

- ✔ **Use an icing spatula.** Perhaps you grew up watching a parent or grandmother frost cakes using a butter knife. That was fine then, but for best results, bring in an icing spatula! The spatula flattens out the frosting and creates sharp edges, particularly at the corners of a square or rectangular cake.

  Put some frosting on your cake and then slide the spatula's flat edge across the top of the cake in an even, continuous motion. Then run the spatula over each side of the cake, working your way around.

- ✔ **Use a piece of parchment paper or a paper towel.** Press the paper onto the frosting and then lift it off, or carefully pull it across the surface of the cake. Work on the top of the cake first, and then the sides.

- ✔ **Use the straight edge of a ruler or strip of stiff, clean cardboard or poster board.** Draw the straight edge across the cake, collecting the excess frosting and leaving a smooth surface in your wake. Perform this method on the top of the cake first, then repeat on the sides.

If you try these methods and still don't achieve the smooth results you want, refrigerate your cake to let the frosting harden a bit. Then try using the icing spatula again or a bench scraper to even out the frosting.

Going the Textured Route

Cake decorators love to use embellishments, but you may find that the most appropriate cake decoration for an event, gathering, or party is a simple textured frosting. With just a few simple tools — a spoon, an icing spatula, and a decorator's comb — you can create a number of different textures in your frosting.

Ridges

For this texture, drag a decorator's comb through the cake's frosting, creating evenly spaced lines that run vertically or horizontally across the top of the cake. Create the same effect on all four sides of a square or rectangular cake.

In using a decorator's comb, I usually position it at a 45-degree angle. However, you can produce more distinct lines by holding the comb perpendicular (at a 90-degree angle) to the cake.

To create the ridge effect, you have a choice among several kinds of combs, with different spaced-teeth and also line effects that include waves, shallow-and-deep lines, alternating widths, and thick grooves. Take advantage of that variety for the look and impression you're trying to achieve.

This texture looks particularly good on a round cake. Combing the side of the cake as well as the top creates a dramatic look because the lines circle the cake.

Hobnails

For this look, make sure that you spread a lot of fluffy frosting on the top and all sides of your cake. Press the back of a soup spoon into the frosting and then give the spoon a twist to swirl the frosting, and lift the spoon off the cake (see Figure 8-2).

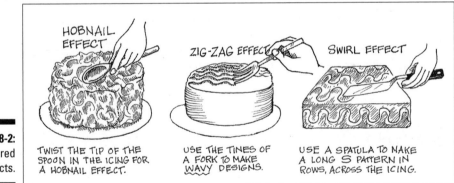

Figure 8-2: Textured effects.

Zigzags

To create a zigzag texture, use your decorator's comb or a fork to make rows of Ws. First draw the comb down to the right, and then draw it up to the right (see Figure 8-2). Repeat the process across the cake's surface and sides.

Swirls

For a whimsically swirly appearance (see Figure 8-2), pull the decorator's comb through the frosting in a wave-like motion. Or for more texture, draw an icing spatula through the frosting in a series of S shapes all over the cake.

Petals

This look takes the hobnail a step further. With a soup spoon, gently press the back of the spoon into the frosting, and then lift up the spoon in an arc, causing the impression to look like a tear-shaped flower petal.

Chapter 9

Dusting and Glazing: It's Icing on the Cake

*I*n addition to using frostings (which I cover in Chapter 8), you can dress up cakes in all sorts of sweet — and often easy — ways. Icing, dusting, and glazing are all ways to not only decorate a cake but also add flavor (and even seal in flavor!).

In this chapter, you get a handle on cake toppings and coverings that delight in both taste and eye-appeal and many of which are fun, simple methods to top off a cake. In addition to icing recipes that are certain to become fixtures in your decorating repertoire, you also delve into preparing glazes, stenciling with confections, and making fondant (which, as I explain, can be either an icing or a covering).

Sweetening Up Your Cake with Icing

Like frostings, icings offer a wealth of taste and flavor options. But unlike frostings, which are generally thicker in content, taste, and structure, icings are thinner and often pourable (although you can also spread many icings, too). Over time, they harden up.

Sugar is the major component of icing (and, actually, glazes too; see the section "Putting the Shine on with Glazes" later in this chapter), and the two main types of icing are

- **Confectioners' sugar icing:** This icing basically consists of confectioners' sugar (also referred to as *powdered sugar*) and some type of liquid. You can thin it out with additional liquid and flavorings in order to make it easier to pour or spoon over a cake for a quick finish.

- **Royal icing:** You make this icing with confectioners' sugar and egg whites, and its consistency is ideal for piping (see Chapter 11).

Be mindful that — as with frostings — you want the icing to complement the taste of your cake, not overpower it. So although a chocolate icing would be delicious on a chocolate or cinnamon cake, I wouldn't put it on a lemon or rhubarb one. Instead, I'd decorate those cakes with a simple confectioners' sugar icing, which goes with just about any flavor you can think of.

With most of the icing recipes in this chapter, don't skip the step of sifting confectioners' sugar. If you don't sift, you're likely to end up with little clumps of powdered sugar on the top of your cake. The clumps are harmless, but they're unsightly and detract from a cake's polished presence.

Starting with basic confectioners' sugar icing

Basic confectioners' sugar icing consists of confectioners' sugar (big surprise) and some kind of liquid or liquid flavoring. The beauty of these simple icings is that you don't need a mixer to make them; you can whisk them up by hand.

Consistency is an important concern with basic confectioners' sugar icing. If it's too thick, you have a gloppy mess on your cake. If the icing's too thin, it slides right down the cake and forms an icing river at the base.

Icing a cake with this type of icing is relatively simple in that you have two basic options:

✔ **Drizzling:** With this technique, you partially cover the cake with an icing design; you can decorate the cake with a striped or circular effect, for example. To drizzle basic powdered sugar icing on your cake, follow these steps:

1. **For easy clean-up, place waxed paper on your counter or work surface.**

2. **Set a wire rack on the waxed paper, and place the cake to be iced on the rack.**

   Alternately, you can place the cake directly on a cake plate: First lay strips of wax paper on the plate where the cake will sit, and then place the cake on top. You'll remove the paper strips after you've finished drizzling.

3. **Dip a large spoon, a ball whisk, or even a fork (different tools give you different looks) into the icing, hold it approximately 1 inch above the cake, and move the utensil in a circular or rectangular direction (depending on your cake's shape), letting the icing drizzle across the cake (and, if you like, over the sides).**

   Pay attention to how the icing lays on the cake as you drizzle. If you find that it's pooling at the bottom of your cake, the icing is too thin and you need to whisk in more (sifted) confectioners' sugar to thicken it.

4. **If your cake's not already on a cake plate or serving platter, use a large spatula to move the cake from the wire rack to the serving plate.**

✔ **Pouring:** With this technique, you cover the cake completely with icing. For a quick covering of icing, follow these steps, which are illustrated in Figure 9-1:

1. **Place the icing in a container that has a spout, like a large glass measuring cup.**

2. **Place wax paper on your counter or work surface. Set a wire rack on the wax paper, and place the cake to be iced on the rack.**

3. **Pour the icing over the cake to cover, working for even coverage. For a rectangular cake, pour the icing in rows. For cakes in other shapes, pour in a circular fashion.**

4. **Carefully tip the wire rack back and forth to let excess icing drip off, ensuring smooth, even coverage. Run a spatula around the sides of the cake for a smooth finish.**

5. **Use a large spatula to move the cake from the wire rack to its serving platter or cake plate.**

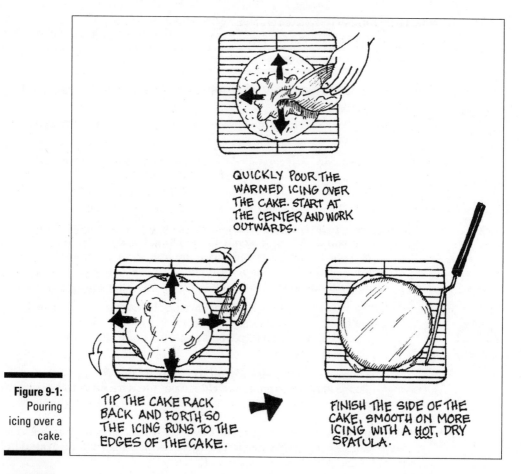

QUICKLY POUR THE
WARMED ICING OVER
THE CAKE. START AT
THE CENTER AND WORK
OUTWARDS.

Figure 9-1:
Pouring
icing over a
cake.

TIP THE CAKE RACK
BACK AND FORTH SO
THE ICING RUNS TO THE
EDGES OF THE CAKE.

FINISH THE SIDE OF THE
CAKE, SMOOTH ON MORE
ICING WITH A HOT, DRY
SPATULA.

Although basic confectioners' sugar icings aren't ideal for piping because of
their thinness, you can tint them with colors for a fun effect. (An icing that *is*
a good candidate for piping is royal icing, which I cover in the next section.)

Simple Confectioners' Sugar Icing

You'll find yourself calling on this versatile recipe again and again. It's a particularly tasty way to dress up a pound cake! This icing is best used for drizzling over cakes.

Preparation time: *5 minutes*

Yield: *1 cup*

2 cups sifted confectioners' sugar

½ teaspoon pure vanilla extract

2 tablespoons plus 4 teaspoons whole milk (use more as needed)

1 In a medium bowl, whisk together the sugar, vanilla, and 1 tablespoon milk.

2 Whisk in the additional milk 1 teaspoon at a time until the icing is of drizzling consistency (that is, it's lustrous and opaque and coats the back of a spoon).

Vary It! *Give this icing a citrus twist by substituting ¼ teaspoon lemon extract or ½ teaspoon orange extract for the vanilla. For a nutty, almond-flavored icing, substitute ¼ teaspoon almond extract for the vanilla.*

A fun way to jazz up the basic vanilla confectioners' sugar icing is to create a tie-dye effect on your cake. Tweens and teens especially love the groovy colors and design. The great thing about this technique is that you can't mess it up, I promise! Just let your creativity take over. (This tie-dye effect looks particularly great on the Rich Pound Cake recipe in Chapter 6.) Follow these steps to give your cake a tie-dye look:

1. **Gather a variety of food coloring gels.**

   I like to use green, blue, pink, green, and orange for this decorating technique.

2. **Divide the confectioners' sugar icing into small bowls — one for each color you're using.**

3. **Add each coloring gel to its own bowl of icing until you achieve the desired color. Start with just a bit of the gel — a little goes a long way — and add more as needed.**

4. **Use a teaspoon to drizzle each icing color separately around the top of the cooled cake, letting them run together to produce the tie-dye effect.**

   You can also draw the colors into each other using the tip of a bamboo skewer.

Simple Chocolate Confectioners' Sugar Icing

To please chocolate lovers in a jiffy, drizzle this icing over a one-layer Cocoa Chocolate Cake (refer to Chapter 6) or Lori's Chocolatey Chippity Cake (refer to Chapter 19).

Preparation time: *5 minutes*

Yield: *½ cup*

1 cup sifted confectioners' sugar

2 tablespoons cocoa powder

1 tablespoon plus 2 teaspoons whole milk (use more as needed)

1 In a medium bowl, whisk together the sugar, cocoa powder, and 1 tablespoon of milk.

2 Whisk in the additional milk 1 teaspoon at a time until the icing is of drizzling consistency (that is, it's lustrous, and coats the back of a spoon).

Sunshine Cupcake Icing

With this very easy, citrus-flavored icing, you can quickly decorate a multitude of white or yellow cupcakes. After the dipping part, top each one with a candied orange or lemon peel to indicate the icing flavor, or add a beach-themed cupcake pick for decoration.

Preparation time: *5 minutes*

Yield: *2¼ cups (enough to top 4 dozen cupcakes)*

⅛ cup fresh-squeezed lemon juice

½ cup fresh-squeezed tangerine juice

6 cups sifted confectioners' sugar

1 In a medium bowl, whisk together all the ingredients.

2 Dip the top of each cupcake into the icing, and then set it upright on a wire rack until the icing hardens.

Getting versatile with royal icing

One of the most popular icings is royal icing. Typically made with confectioners' sugar and egg whites, royal icing is a cake decorating favorite because it can be used in a variety of applications.

Royal icing differs from basic confectioners' sugar icing (see the preceding section) in that it's often used in piping decorations. When prepared correctly, royal icing hardens in such a way that allows you either to keep it as is on your cake or to use other forms and colors to embellish a design made with it. You can even use royal icing to cover the board that a cake sits on as a way to surround the cake with a smooth, white base.

How you want to use royal icing determines its consistency. You use a thicker royal icing to coat a cake; you use a slightly thinner version for intricate lettering or details.

For any task, if the royal icing's not the right consistency, your cake, decorations, or both, won't look right. Like basic confectioners' sugar icing, if your royal icing is too thick, add more liquid; if it's too thin, add more sugar. When working with royal icing, it's important to cover what you're not using at the moment with a damp cloth or paper towel to ensure that it doesn't dry up and crust over.

For decorating, royal icing tints beautifully because the base color is such a bright white. Use food coloring paste or gel to achieve the desired color (you may need to use more than you would to color frosting).

One of royal icing's prime components is egg whites, but you shouldn't use raw egg whites to make the icing. Although raw eggs yield the same results in the following recipes, they may cause food poisoning and shouldn't be consumed by pregnant women, young children, or the elderly. Instead, use meringue powder or pasteurized egg whites. (I prefer pasteurized egg whites because you don't have to mix anything, whereas meringue powder must be mixed with water.)

Royal Icing

I like to use this icing for drawing, filling in, and accenting designs and forms on cakes. (It also works well for decorating cookies.)

Preparation time: *5 minutes*

Yield: *2 cups*

4 cups sifted confectioners' sugar

¾ cup pasteurized egg whites

1 tablespoon fresh-squeezed lemon juice

1 In a large bowl, combine all the ingredients.

2 Beat the mixture with a stand or a hand-mixer until the icing holds its shape and isn't runny. If it's too thin for piping, add more sugar 1 tablespoon at a time and continue mixing until it reaches the desired consistency.

Tip: *To tint the icing several different colors, pour the icing into separate bowls, and then add and adjust coloring gels with a toothpick or by squeezing a few drops of color at a time into the icing.*

Giving Fondant a Try

You may not know what *fondant* is, but chances are you've seen it on cakes or sweet treats at some point. Fondant is an icing comprised of confectioners' sugar and gelatin (among other ingredients). In its most common incarnation for cakes, fondant is kneaded into the form of soft dough and rolled out to form a smooth covering that seals in freshness and adds a perfect-looking, smooth, hard coating to cakes. However, it's something of a multiutility player in the world of cake decorating because it can take many forms: rolled or poured, for coverings, trims, and even shapes, figures, and a variety of edible decorations. And no matter how you plan to use it, the natural white color of fondant not only looks great as is but also tints beautifully.

Fondant is often preferred for cakes appearing at outdoor events because it tends to hold up in hot or humid conditions. However, as with all cake creations, don't plan on keeping your fondant-covered cake out for a long time in the heat.

Working with rolled fondant

In its rolled form, fondant is like a chewy, creamy sugar paste. Most likely you've seen it as that smooth-as-silk covering on a wedding cake. This kind of fondant's dough-like consistency allows you to roll it out, drape it over the cake's surface, and form it around the cake. As such, it gives the cake a finished, polished look.

I include a recipe for rolled fondant in this section, but you have easier and less time-consuming options at your disposal. Many baking supply stores (and even national craft store chains) offer ready-to-use fondant as well as fondant mix. In tackling the all-encompassing responsibilities of cake decorating (think planning, designing, baking, and crafting decorations), mess-free, ready-made fondant gives you at least a little breathing space time-wise. And although you sacrifice the "completely homemade" moniker by taking a fondant shortcut, you don't sacrifice taste or texture.

Rolled Fondant

Preparation time: *30 minutes*

Yield: *1 pound*

¼-ounce package unflavored gelatin

3 tablespoons cold water

½ cup corn syrup

1 tablespoon glycerin

2 tablespoons vegetable shortening

1 teaspoon clear pure vanilla extract

8 cups sifted confectioners' sugar

1 In a medium bowl, stir together the gelatin and the cold water; let the mixture stand until it thickens. Then place the gelatin mixture in the top part of a double boiler and heat it over medium heat, stirring continuously until the gelatin is dissolved.

2 Add the corn syrup and glycerin to the gelatin mixture, and mix well. Stir in the shortening, and just before it's completely melted, remove the mixture from the heat and stir in the vanilla. Let the mixture cool until it's lukewarm (about 90 degrees F on a candy thermometer).

3 Place 4 cups of confectioners' sugar in a large bowl. Make a well in the center, place all the lukewarm gelatin mixture in the well, and then use a wooden spoon to draw the sugar from the edges into the liquid.

4 Mix in some of the remaining sugar ½ cup at a time until the stickiness disappears.

5 Transfer the fondant from the bowl to your work surface, and knead in the remaining confectioners' sugar. Knead until the fondant is smooth, pliable, and doesn't stick to your hands. (If it's too soft, add more sugar. If it's too stiff, add water one drop at a time.)

6 Use the fondant immediately, or store it in the refrigerator in an airtight container. When you're ready to use it, bring it to room temperature, and knead it until it's soft again.

Tip: *If you don't have a double boiler, you can make your own: Fill a heavy, medium-sized saucepan with water about ⅓ of the way up the sides of the pan. Bring the water to a boil, and set a medium, heat-proof bowl snugly on the top of the saucepan.*

Preparing a cake for a fondant cover

Before being covered in rolled fondant, a cake typically is frosted with buttercream or royal icing. The buttercream or royal icing acts as glue for the fondant to neatly stick onto the cake. (You can find out more about buttercream — including a recipe — in Chapter 8. A Royal Icing recipe appears in the section "Getting versatile with royal icing" earlier in this chapter.)

For a nice sticky surface for rolled fondant to adhere to, you also can cover the cake in a glaze first. For more on glazes and glaze recipes, see the section "Putting the Shine on with Glazes" later in this chapter.

Placing fondant on a cake

Placing fondant on your cake isn't too tricky a proposition with an able assist from a rolling pin. You also need an offset spatula, a pizza wheel cutter, and *cake smoothers,* which are handy, flat-handled plastic squares that you use to flatten the fondant. When you have your tools assembled and your cake is ready and waiting (see the preceding section), follow these steps, which you can see in Figure 9-2, to cover the cake:

1. **Sprinkle cornstarch on your work surface, and roll the fondant to a thickness of ¼ inch and a circle that's slightly bigger than the size needed to completely cover the top and sides of your cake.**

2. **Gently roll the fondant onto your rolling pin. Place the fondant-rolled pin at one edge of your cake, letting the fondant drape down that side of the cake. Roll the pin away from the edge where you started so that the fondant rolls off your pin and onto the cake top.**

   The fondant should cover the top and drape the sides of your cake.

3. **Using your hands, gently press the fondant into the sides of the cake.**

   You should have excess fondant all around the base of your cake.

4. Use a pizza wheel cutter to trim the excess fondant from the base of the cake. With the back edge of an icing spatula, flatten the fondant into the base all around the cake.

5. Use a cake smoother to gently press the top and sides of the cake for a finished, flat effect.

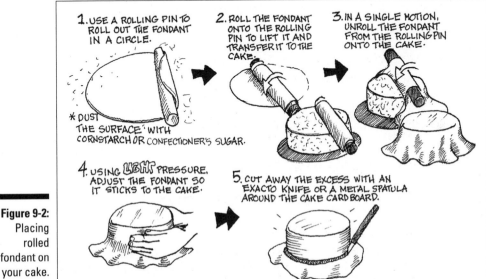

Figure 9-2:
Placing rolled fondant on your cake.

Pouring fondant

Poured fondant is — as its name suggests — fondant that you pour over your cake for a hard, shiny, smooth coating. Poured fondant is most commonly used on *petit fours,* those dainty, bite-sized and usually elaborately decorated cakes you often see at wedding receptions and baby showers.

As with rolled fondant, you can find more-than-adequate premade possibilities when it comes to poured fondant. Options include powdered fondant mix that you add ingredients to and heat over a double boiler to reach the right pourable consistency and fondant that you simply have to melt.

Poured Fondant

You can use this poured fondant to cover petit fours or even to cover an entire cake. This is one of two recipes for swift, pourable fondant; the other is 2EZ Petit Fours Quick Fondant. Which one you use is a matter of your preference for taste and appearance. This fondant imparts a sweet, vanilla flavor and creates a thicker fondant shell on the confection.

Preparation time: *5 minutes*

Yield: *4 cups*

6 cups sifted confectioners' sugar	*2 tablespoons light corn syrup*
½ cup water	*1 teaspoon clear pure vanilla extract*

1 Combine all the ingredients in a large, heavy saucepan.

2 Cook over low heat, stirring constantly, until the mixture reaches a temperature of 110 degrees F on a candy thermometer. Remove from the heat and pour over your cake.

If you're taking on icing small cakes, such as petit fours, follow these steps to minimize the mess and make the most efficient use of your poured fondant:

1. **Set the petit four on a multitined chocolate fork or angel food cake slicer. Hold the fork or slicer in one hand over a bowl of warm poured fondant.**

2. **With a large spoon in your other hand, spoon the fondant over the petit four, covering the top and all sides. Spoon additional fondant until the petit four is complete covered. As you work, let the excess fondant drip back into the bowl.**

3. **Use the flat edge of a knife to slide the petit four off the fork or slicer onto a cooling rack so that the fondant can harden completely.**

2EZ Petit Fours Quick Fondant

This recipe is very easy to double, triple, or even quadruple depending on how many petit fours you need to decorate. Its almond flavor sets it apart from the Poured Fondant in the preceding recipe.

Preparation time: *5 minutes*

Yield: *1 cup*

2 cups sifted confectioners' sugar	2 tablespoons light corn syrup
2 tablespoons water	½ teaspoon almond extract

1 In a medium bowl, whisk together all the ingredients until smooth.

2 Transfer the mixture to a saucepan and heat over low heat until warm, about 100 degrees F on a candy thermometer. Remove from the heat.

3 If necessary, add hot water, drop by drop, as you stir the fondant until it reaches the proper consistency (thick but pourable).

4 Place the saucepan containing the icing over another saucepan or bowl of hot water to prevent it from thickening as you use it.

Tip: *If the poured fondant starts to become gloppy and unmanageably thick, mix in a few drops of a simple sugar syrup (1 cup of sugar dissolved in 1 cup of water).*

As you keep your poured fondant warm while you use it, don't leave it on the stove to continue cooking and run the risk of burning. Keep the icing at around 100 degrees F on a candy thermometer or it will thicken, crust-up, and otherwise be too hard to work with.

Dusting for a Different Look

Dusting refers to lightly sprinkling an ingredient over your cake for a finished look that doesn't interfere with your cake's flavor. Dusting can be done in a jiffy, and it's a sound choice for a cake that's rich and dense on its own. Dusting also is a great way to decorate cakes that you're trying to keep on the lighter side and may be serving only with some fresh fruit, for example.

In addition to being quick and easy, dusting allows you to create lots of different designs on your cakes. For instance, stencils (that you buy or make) can produce many pretty patterns — from scattered snowflakes and stars to rows of clowns and ballerinas. Just think about the variety of cookie cutters out there, and you get an idea of the various sizes and shapes you can festoon a cake with.

Deciding what to dust with

With a couple of primary ingredients that you can probably find in your pantry, you're well on your way to executing some stunning cake-top creations in mere minutes.

Confectioners' sugar and cocoa

For dusting's easiest incarnation, place confectioners' sugar or cocoa powder in a sieve and shake it over the top of a cake for a beautiful sprinkling.

Before you start dusting, make sure that the top of your cake is dry (not in taste, but to the touch!). If you've just removed your cake from the refrigerator or the top is otherwise too moist, the cake will absorb the sugar or cocoa and you'll be left with a blotted mess. So bring the cake to room temperature before proceeding.

Items with different flavors and textures

The great thing about dusting is that you can use practically anything! Ingredients such as sanding sugar, nonpareils (little chocolate discs covered in sugar sprinkles), and even finely-crushed cookies and peppermints not only look spectacular but also taste fantastic!

For these heartier dusting ingredients, you need to frost your cake with a medium such as buttercream frosting (see Chapter 8) that the decorations can easily adhere to. If you were to sprinkle jimmies or nonpareils on a dry cake, most of them would slide right off and you'd be right back where you started!

Using stencils

Combining the dusting technique with stencils opens a world of creativity for your cake decorating endeavors. Although stenciling looks best when it's done with confectioners' sugar or cocoa powder, design options abound. Although you can use stencils in repetitive patterns, I've also used separate ones with confectioners' sugar to create a snowy winter scene and even a performance of *The Nutcracker!* I've also used nonpareils in various colors to fill in a rainbow stencil and placed blue and pink jimmies in different sizes of circles for a child's "Playing with Bubbles" party.

A stencil sits on top of your cake, so you may want to coat the underside of it with a thin layer of vegetable shortening for ease in lifting it off after you're done dusting your design.

To use a stencil for dusting your cake top, follow these steps, which are illustrated in Figure 9-3:

1. **If the shape of your stencil allows it, stick two small loops of masking tape on the facing side of the stencil at opposite edges (like at the positions of 3 o'clock and 9 o'clock).**

2. **Gently set the stencil on the cake.**

3. **Put confectioners' sugar or cocoa powder in a sieve, and shake the sieve over the open portions of the stencil, using a gentle tapping motion with the heel of your hand for a light, controlled sprinkle.**

4. **When the open portions are completely dusted, gently lift the stencil off by the handles you created with the masking tape, taking care to hold the stencil level.**

   If you slant the stencil at all, you may wind up with sugar or cocoa in unwanted spaces on your cake.

Figure 9-3:
A sieve, a stencil, and confectioners' sugar or cocoa powder are all you need for a quick show-stopping decoration.

1. MAKE HANDLES FOR YOUR STENCIL WITH MASKING TAPE. FOLD 2 PIECES BACK ONTO THEMSELVES, PINCHING THE MIDDLES TOGETHER, STICKING THEM TO THE TOP AND BOTTOM ON 2 SIDES.

2. PLACE THE STENCIL ON THE CAKE AND DUST OVER IT WITH CONFECTIONER'S SUGAR OR COCOA POWDER.

3. USE THE TAPE 'HANDLES' TO LIFT THE STENCIL UP OFF THE CAKE.

Creating your own stencils

You can find a variety of cake decorating stencils in baking supply stores and even national craft store chains, but you also shouldn't be shy about creating your own. Children's coloring books and clip art available on the Web and in books both provide excellent images for homemade stencils.

Using scissors or a razor blade knife, cleanly cut out any image you want to use on your cake and cut out the open space that will be dusted. If you want a sturdier stencil, just trace the image onto cardboard and cut it out again.

If you like an image but it's too small or too large for your cake top, enlarge or reduce it on a photocopier to the desired size. Cut it out of the paper, trace it onto cardboard, and cut it out again to get your stencil.

Filling in cookie cutters

In addition to buying or making your own stencils, cookie cutters offer a vast array of shapes, forms, and sizes that you can also use to dust designs on your cake. You can use just one — like a dolphin or seashell shape — or create a scene with several cookie cutters. For instance, you may group the shapes of a Christmas tree, stockings, and a Santa Claus on the top of a holiday cake.

To use a cookie cutter as a stencil, simply lay it gently on the cake top, use a sieve to dust on confectioners' sugar or cocoa (or sprinkle another dusting ingredient by hand, if you like) either in the open space or around the outside of the cutter depending on the type of cutter you're using and the design you prefer. Carefully remove the cutter to reveal your design. If necessary, use your fingers to gently pack in any jimmies or crushed candies that may have strayed from the outline.

Putting the Shine on with Glazes

With their glossy sheen, glazes literally highlight the cake that you set on a table. Besides their sweet taste, glazes actually add to a cake's appearance, giving the cake top or topping — such as sliced or whole fruits — a shiny, glassine look. Glazes also seal in moisture and prevent any fruits on the top of your cake from browning.

Typically, glazes consist of confectioners' sugar, water, and such additions as melted chocolate, citrus zest, extracts, or fruit juice. However, some glazes are simply fruit jams melted over low heat. Whatever the ingredients, a glaze tends to be more liquid than icing *and* has a perked-up flavor.

Unlike frosting or icing, most glazes aren't intended to cover an entire cake. The desired look is a glaze-covered cake top with drips of glaze down the sides.

The glazes that I supply recipes for in this section pair nicely with sponge cakes that soak up flavor as well as pound, butter, angel food, and plain chocolate cakes. While I supply recommendations for glaze and cake flavor combinations in each of the glaze recipes, keep in mind that Bundt-shaped cakes are often ideal for glazes, which particularly flatter that shape and make for an eye-catching confection.

To glaze your cake, follow these easy steps:

1. **Set the cake on a cooling rack, and place the cooling rack over a cookie sheet lined with parchment paper.**

   Conversely, you can set your cake on a wax paper–lined cake plate and just remove the wax paper after you're done glazing.

2. **Use a spoon to heap a portion of the glaze onto your cake, and let the excess drip down the sides. Continue spooning glaze over the entire surface of the cake until the top is covered.**

   For thicker glazes, use a pastry brush to distribute the glaze more evenly.

Buttery Vanilla Glaze

Pour this glaze over your cake shortly after you remove the cake from the oven. You want the cake to soak up the glaze while it's still warm.

Preparation time: 12 minutes

Yield: 2 cups

1 cup granulated white sugar

½ cup buttermilk

1 tablespoon light corn syrup

½ cup unsalted butter

1 teaspoon pure vanilla extract

1 In a medium saucepan, heat the sugar, buttermilk, corn syrup, and butter over medium heat, stirring constantly, until it reaches a boil.

2 Boil for 2 minutes, stirring the mixture continuously.

3 Remove the pan from the heat, and stir in the vanilla. Let the glaze cool a few minutes before applying it to your warm cake.

Chocolate Glaze

This glaze is a sweet, shiny addition to any cake. And in my opinion, practically anything tastes better with a smooth chocolate coating!

Preparation time: *5 minutes*

Yield: *1 cup*

½ cup granulated white sugar

½ cup unsweetened cocoa powder

½ cup heavy cream

2 teaspoons light corn syrup

1 tablespoon butter, cut into small pieces

1 teaspoon pure vanilla extract

1 In a medium bowl, whisk together the sugar and cocoa powder with a balloon whisk.

2 In a 4-cup glass measuring cup, combine the cream and corn syrup.

3 Add the sugar mixture gradually into the cream mixture, whisking until smooth. Add in the butter, and stir to combine.

4 Microwave on high for 2 minutes until the mixture is completely smooth. Then stir in the vanilla. Let the glaze cool for a few minutes before spooning onto the cake.

Mocha Glaze

I think coffee and chocolate make a delicious, unbeatable combination, and this glaze is perfect for chocolate cakes, butter cakes, pound cakes, and — of course — coffee-flavored cake. (The recipe for Coffee-Flavored Cake, which is a modified version of my Delicious Yellow Cake, appears in Chapter 17.)

Preparation time: *5 minutes*

Yield: *1 cup*

⅔ cup heavy cream

2 tablespoons light corn syrup

1½ teaspoons instant espresso powder

12 ounces semisweet chocolate, chopped

1 In a medium saucepan over medium heat, combine the cream, corn syrup, and espresso powder. Bring to a simmer (which should take about 2 minutes), and stir to make sure the espresso powder dissolves.

2 Remove from the heat, and mix in the chocolate. Stir until smooth.

Caramel Glaze

This glaze is one of my favorites. Its richness pairs exceptionally well with a host of cakes, such as nutty ones (such as almond and walnut), basic varieties (such as chocolate and yellow cake), and the complementary Brown Sugar Cake (turn to Chapter 17 for the recipe). Not surprisingly, it's a hit over apple and banana cakes as well.

Preparation time: *5 minutes*

Yield: *1 cup*

4 tablespoons unsalted butter

¼ cup granulated white sugar

¼ cup light brown sugar

½ cup heavy cream

1 In a medium saucepan over medium-low heat, melt the butter.

2 Add the granulated and light brown sugars to the melted butter. Cook the mixture, stirring frequently until the sugar dissolves, about 2 minutes.

3 Stir in the cream (be careful of splattering), and bring to a boil.

4 Stir constantly as the mixture boils for 2 minutes. Then remove it from the heat. Let the glaze cool for a few minutes before you pour it on your cake.

Lemon Glaze

This quick glaze's lemon kick makes it light and refreshing. Try it served over citrus, poppy seed, and even cherry cakes. For best results, pour this warm glaze over a warm cake.

Preparation time: *5 minutes*

Yield: *1 cup*

½ cup fresh-squeezed lemon juice   *1½ cups sifted confectioners' sugar*

1 In a medium saucepan over low heat, combine the lemon juice and sugar. Stir frequently until the sugar dissolves.

Fruit Glaze

You brush this glaze on fruit to give it an attractive, glossy appearance, both on top of a cake and in a fruit filling. For best results, bring this glaze to room temperature before putting it on the fruit.

Preparation time: *5 minutes*

Yield: *¼ cup*

2 tablespoons light brown sugar   *2 tablespoons water*
1 tablespoon light corn syrup

1 In a small saucepan over medium heat, combine all the ingredients.

2 Bring the mixture to a boil, and let it boil for 2 minutes, stirring frequently.

Chapter 10

Amping Up the Flavor: Spreading Fillings

*F*or some cakes, the frosting is also the *filling* — the sweet confection you find in between the cake layers. But for other cakes, you can take flavor to new heights by introducing another layer of taste: Use a filling between the layers that differs from — but complements — the frosting.

Fillings can take on any number of textures and tastes; smooth, creamy, chunky, fruity, nutty, and chocolatey are just the tip of the iceberg. With so many options, how's a cake baker to choose? In this chapter, I give you the lowdown on selecting the perfect filling for your cake and follow up with recipes that tackle both traditional and unique flavors. And, I fill you in on adding flavor to layers another way — with sweet syrups ideal for cakes.

Picking the Best Filling for Your Cake

You may associate fillings with wedding cakes, but it's time to move past the formal ceremony and consider all the delicious possibilities where fillings are concerned. With the right filling, you can give a cake for any occasion an entirely different personality. As you consider your cake creation, think about adding a filling that complements your cake and frosting to add depth and interest.

When deciding on the kind of cake you'll make, give some thought to how the flavors and tastes will coalesce. The following list offers recommendations for tasty cake and filling combinations:

- **Chocolate cake** pairs well with caramel filling, peanut butter filling, mocha filling, and pecan filling.

- **White chocolate cake** pairs well with raspberry filling, cherry filling, and dark chocolate filling.

- **Yellow cake** pairs well with chocolate or fudge filling, tropical fruit (mango, passion fruit) filling, summer fruit (peach, blueberry) filling, and spicy fillings such as cinnamon, fig, or raisin-nut.

- **White cake** pairs well with strawberry filling, lemon curd filling, and coconut filling.

Be aware that not all cake and filling combinations make taste buds happy. For example, I usually avoid pairing chocolate cake with fruit fillings and carrot cake with chocolate fillings.

You aren't obligated to use a different filling than the frosting on your cake. Just make it a consideration in your cake creation and design. Particularly with a white cake, you have a virtually wide open playing field because white cake provides such an impartial, subtle flavor. But whenever you're baking a cake that has a strong taste and scent, like fudgy chocolate, pineapple, mocha, or red velvet, you're best sticking with a simple, basic frosting and bypassing fillings altogether.

Taking Care with Fillings

Spreading a filling on your cake isn't much different from frosting your cake. Follow these basic steps:

1. **Make sure that your cake has sufficiently cooled down before you begin filling it.**

2. **Anchor the bottom layer to your cake pedestal or cake board with a dab of frosting.**

3. **To hold your filling in place and prevent oozing, pipe a thick ridge of frosting around the outside edge of your layer, as shown in Figure 10-1.**

   For best results you'll want to put about a ½ cup of frosting into a pastry bag that's been outfitted with a #11 or #18 tip to pipe a ridge that's thick enough to hold in the filling but not be obtrusive.

4. **To place the filling inside the frosting border, either spoon or pour it carefully.**

Then use an offset spatula to spread the filling around, getting as close to the frosting border as possible.

Figure 10-1:
Piping a ring
of frosting
around
the layer
keeps your
filling from
escaping.

USE A #18 STAR PIPING TIP TO PIPE ICING AROUND THE CIRCUMFERENCE OF THE CAKE. THIS CREATES A DAM FOR THE FILLING.

As with frosting, don't skimp on the filling; make sure you have plenty to work with. But also, don't overfill your cake layers: You don't want the filling running off and down the sides of your cake, mixing in unwantedly with your frosting and ruining all your hard decorating work.

Indulging in Creaminess: Smooth Fillings

With smooth fillings, the flavor is the star. With just a few basic ingredients, you can create light, flavorful fillings that add a special decadence to your already delicious cakes.

In addition to whipped cream fillings, I'm also very fond of filling cakes with mousses, which have whipped cream folded into them to make them light and fluffy. The recipes for creamy fillings in this chapter range from tasty variations on whipped cream, to the thicker, candy-like flavors — like chocolate and caramel — that work so well with many cakes, and both a traditional (chocolate again!) and nontraditional (key lime) take on irresistible mousses.

For these fillings, you'll want to use a hand or stand mixer (instead of trying to do the work by hand) to achieve the best results in both taste and consistency — and to save you time. While I prefer using a stand mixer, a hand mixer will do the trick.

The filling recipes in this chapter that call for whipped cream require it to be whipped until *stiff peaks* form. What exactly are stiff peaks? That's when the cream has reached a point that it stands up on its own. (However, pay attention to the process: If you beat beyond that point for too long, you'll end up with butter!) When you're done whipping the cream (that is, you've achieved stiff peaks and added any flavorings or sugar), fill your cake as soon as possible. Timing is everything: If you're using whipped cream, whip it close to serving time, and plan on keeping it refrigerated. If not, the whipped cream loses its volume and starts puddling.

For recipes that tell you to whip cream into stiff peaks, it's essential to start out with cold whipping cream. Absolutely don't use whipping cream that's been sitting out of the refrigerator and collecting drops of moisture for any amount of time. You need to use very cold (but not frozen) cream to achieve the desired result.

Put your empty mixing bowl and beater into the freezer for 30 minutes before you begin whipping cream to help your cause.

Basic Whipped Cream

Whipped cream is a popular choice for fillings, particularly with fruit flavored cakes, because it imparts a subtle, sweet flavor that both highlights virtually any kind of cake and spotlights stronger flavorings. Its texture also makes it a nice, lighter alternative to consider for buttercream frostings. While it's not a good choice for covering the outside of your cake, you can also have this available to be served with your cake as a cake condiment.

Preparation time: *5 minutes*

Yield: *4 cups*

2 cups heavy whipping cream   *¼ cup confectioners' sugar*

1 In a large bowl, beat the cream on medium speed until it starts to firm up a bit, and gradually add in the confectioners' sugar.

2 Beat on high speed until stiff peaks form.

Chocolate Whipped Cream

This is another popular filling that, like Basic Whipped Cream, can also be served on the side with your cake. Depending on your frosting choices, this is a wonderful filling for white, yellow, and chocolate cakes.

Preparation time: *5 minutes*

Yield: *3 cups*

1½ cups heavy whipping cream

1¼ cups confectioners' sugar

⅓ cup cocoa

½ teaspoon pure vanilla extract

1 In a large bowl, combine all ingredients and beat on high speed until stiff peaks form.

Coffee Cream

This coffee-flavored filling is a deliciously different take on whipped cream that makes an excellent filling in chocolate cakes. Just don't substitute regular instant coffee for the espresso powder. The taste won't be the same, and the instant coffee crystals don't dissolve as well in the filling as espresso does.

Preparation time: *5 minutes plus 1 hour for refrigeration*

Yield: *4 cups*

2 cups whipping cream

¼ cup confectioners' sugar

3 teaspoons instant espresso powder

1 teaspoon pure vanilla extract

1 In a large bowl, combine all ingredients and beat on high speed until stiff peaks form.

2 Fill the cake immediately, and refrigerate it for at least 1 hour, or until you're ready to serve it.

Some smooth fillings, like the Caramel Filling that follows, require cooking, which means that you need to get your hands on a candy thermometer. The candy thermometer sits in the saucepan while the mixture cooks and allows you to easily monitor the temperature of your filling to ensure that it reaches the proper temperature.

A candy thermometer is a must-have when you're making a filling recipe that requires you to boil a mixture to the *soft-ball stage,* which happens around 238 degrees F. The soft-ball stage means that, if you were to drop a hot glob of filling in cold water, it would form a soft ball.

Caramel Filling

This filling is particularly delicious with yellow cakes, chocolate cakes, and the Brown Sugar Cake (see Chapter 17), and it pairs well with a variety of chocolate frostings. I've often called on this to create cake versions of candy bars because its sweet, rich taste is so satisfying.

Preparation time: *30 minutes (includes cooling)*

Yield: *2 cups*

1 cup firmly packed light brown sugar	*½ cup whole milk*
1 cup granulated white sugar	*1 teaspoon pure vanilla extract*
½ cup unsalted butter	

1 In a large saucepan, combine all ingredients and bring to a boil, stirring to dissolve the sugar completely. Remove the filling from the heat when it reaches 238 degrees F on a candy thermometer (soft-ball stage), which should take about 8 minutes.

2 Transfer the filling to a medium bowl, and let it cool to room temperature (about 20 minutes). Beat on medium speed until the filling reaches a spreadable consistency.

Amazing Chocolate Filling

This delicious filling is smooth and chocolatey but not too sweet to be paired with a chocolate cake.

Preparation time: *45 minutes (includes cooling)*

Yield: *2 cups*

1 cup cocoa	*1 cup evaporated milk*
1 cup granulated white sugar	

1 In a medium bowl, sift together the cocoa and sugar.

2 In a medium saucepan, stir to combine the dry mixture with the milk over medium-low heat.

3 Stirring frequently, cook until the mixture thickens to a spreadable consistency (about 20 minutes).

4 Transfer the filling to a medium bowl, and let it cool to room temperature (about 20 minutes) before using it on your cake.

Chocolate Mousse

Here's a delectable take on chocolate mousse that makes a beautiful inside surprise to several kinds of cakes, including (obviously) chocolate, but also white chocolate, marble, and, in a deconstructed twist on a German chocolate cake, coconut.

Preparation time: *15 minutes plus 1 hour for refrigeration*

Yield: *3 cups*

1 cup semisweet chocolate chips

1½ cups cold heavy cream, plus ½ cup heavy cream

½ cup confectioners' sugar

¼ cup granulated white sugar

2 teaspoons pure vanilla extract

1 In a medium saucepan, combine the confectioners' sugar and ½ cup heavy cream, stirring over low heat.

2 Add the chocolate chips, stirring frequently as they melt and the mixture becomes well blended.

3 Remove from heat, stir in the vanilla, and set this chocolate mixture aside.

4 In a large bowl, beat 1½ cups of heavy cream on medium speed, and gradually add in the granulated sugar. When all the sugar has been incorporated, beat the mixture on high speed until stiff peaks form.

5 Fold the whipped cream into the chocolate mixture, taking care not to overmix. Refrigerate for at least 1 hour before using on your cake.

Key Lime Mousse

This tart and refreshing mousse is a great filling for white, coconut, or citrus cakes. You can use the juice of other limes, but key limes give it a distinctive taste that cake eaters love and comment upon.

Preparation time: *20 minutes plus 2 hours to overnight for refrigeration*

Yield: *3 cups*

½ cup fresh key lime juice (from about 15 key limes)

⅔ cup granulated white sugar

2 eggs

2 egg yolks

½ cup unsalted butter, cut into ½-inch pieces

¼ cup cold whipping cream

1 In a medium saucepan, combine the key lime juice and sugar, stirring over medium heat for 2 to 3 minutes until the sugar dissolves. Then remove from the heat.

2 In a medium bowl, whisk together the eggs and egg yolks.

3 Gradually add the key lime syrup to the eggs, and then return the custard to the saucepan over medium-low heat, stirring constantly for 2 to 3 minutes until it coats the back of the spoon. Be careful not to let the custard boil.

4 Remove the key lime custard from the heat, and add the butter, stirring until the butter dissolves. Refrigerate the custard for at least 2 hours. (If possible, refrigerate the custard overnight for best results.)

5 In a large bowl, beat the cream on high speed until stiff peaks form. Mix a small amount of cream into the refrigerated key lime custard, and then fold the remaining cream into the custard, gently drawing the two together without overmixing. Refrigerate the mousse until you're ready to use it on your cake.

Dulce de Leche Filling

A popular dessert in Latin American countries, *dulce de leche,* which is essentially carmelized sugar in milk, has quickly found a following in cake decorating circles. This recipe is an easy way to turn dulce de leche into a fabulous filling.

Preparation time: *1 to 1¼ hours*

Yield: *3 cups*

2 14-ounce cans sweetened condensed milk

1 Preheat the oven to 425 degrees F.

2 Pour the milk into an 8-x-8-x-2-inch clear glass baking dish that fits into a larger, deeper cake pan. Cover the glass dish with aluminum foil.

3 Place the large cake pan on the oven rack, and set the glass dish inside it. Fill the larger pan with boiling water until the water reaches two-thirds of the way up the sides of the glass dish.

4 Bake for 1 to 1¼ hours, or until the milk turns a caramel color.

5 Use a rubber spatula to scrape the filling into a large bowl. Beat the filling on medium speed until it reaches a spreadable, smooth consistency (about 1 minute).

Crunching Things Up: Chunky Fillings

Chunkier fillings add a depth of texture to your cake. As with smooth fillings, you have to be mindful of what fillings you pair with what cakes. For example, if your decoration plan includes several crunchy decorations on your cake, you may not want to overdo it with a chunky filling, too. Take the whole cake — and each bite — into account.

Pink Cherry Filling

This cherry filling is a nice soft one for white birthday cakes, and the color contrast of pink filling against white cake is particularly pleasing to the eye.

Preparation time: 10 minutes

Yield: 4 cups

2 cups whipping cream

¼ cup sifted confectioners' sugar

½ cup chopped maraschino cherries

2 tablespoons maraschino cherry juice

1 In a large bowl, beat the cream on medium speed, and gradually add in the confectioners' sugar. When all the sugar has been incorporated, beat on high speed until stiff peaks form.

2 Stir in the cherries and cherry juice.

Crazy Crunchy Filling

With candy bits and chocolate syrup, this filling is a fun and tasty crowd-pleaser in kids' cakes.

Preparation time: 10 minutes

Yield: 4 cups

2 cups whipping cream

¼ cup sifted confectioners' sugar

½ cup chocolate-covered toffee bits (two 1.4-ounce bars)

2 tablespoons chocolate syrup

1 In a large bowl, beat the cream on medium speed, and gradually add in the confectioners' sugar. When all the sugar has been incorporated, beat on high speed until stiff peaks form.

2 Stir in the toffee bits and chocolate syrup.

Peanut Butter Filling

If you're a peanut butter lover (or you know someone who is), this filling will be an instant hit. It goes especially well with chocolate, peanut butter, and even yellow cakes.

Preparation time: 10 minutes

Yield: 2 cups

½ cup unsalted butter

1 cup confectioners' sugar

1 tablespoon whole milk

½ teaspoon pure vanilla extract

½ cup chunky peanut butter

1 In a medium bowl, beat the butter on medium speed until smooth. Gradually add the confectioners' sugar, beating until smooth.

2 Add the milk and vanilla, and beat on high speed until fluffy.

3 Stir in the peanut butter by hand.

Vary It!: Not into chunky peanut butter? You can substitute smooth peanut butter for the same taste with a smooth texture.

Coconut Filling

Any time you're looking to add a tropical twist to a white cake, yellow cake, or even carrot cake, look no further than this zesty and creamy addition.

Preparation time: *15 minutes*

Yield: *2 cups*

1 cup sweetened condensed milk	8 tablespoons unsalted butter
1 cup granulated white sugar	1½ cups shredded coconut
3 egg yolks	1 cup chopped walnuts

1 In a medium saucepan, combine the milk, sugar, egg yolks, and butter. Bring to a simmer, and continue cooking until thickened (about 10 minutes), stirring occasionally.

2 Transfer the mixture to a large bowl, and stir in the coconut and nuts. Let the filling cool to room temperature before using it on your cake.

Raspberry Filling

Raspberry is a popular filling for wedding cakes, but you're certainly not limited to that usage. This simple, unadorned filling spreads sweetly and vibrantly and tastes especially great on white chocolate cake.

Preparation time: *10 minutes*

Yield: *1½ cups*

1 cup granulated white sugar	2 tablespoons unsalted butter
¼ cup cornstarch	3 cups fresh raspberries
½ cup water	

1 In a medium saucepan, combine the sugar and cornstarch over medium heat. Gradually add the water, and stir to dissolve.

2 Add the butter and raspberries, and bring the mixture to a boil. Boil the filling, stirring constantly, until it thickens to a spreadable consistency.

3 Let the filling cool to room temperature before spreading it on your cake.

Summoning Syrups

Certain cakes, like the Sponge Cake (Chapter 6), and heavier denser cakes, such as the Honey Cake (Chapter 17), practically scream to be moistened with a flavorful syrup for ultimate deliciousness. Syrups are usually made with a ratio of confectioners' sugar and water, with some flavoring added, and they're brushed on cakes that will readily soak them up.

The ratio of sugar to water that you choose dictates a heavy or light syrup. For instance, after being heated, a 1 cup sugar to 1 cup water ratio produces a thicker syrup than one in which ⅓ cup of sugar is dissolved in 1 cup of water.

If you're interested in checking out how different syrups complement or detract from different kinds of cake, you can pick up bottles of fruit-flavored syrups at some specialty markets, online retailers, and restaurant supply stores.

Orange Syrup

This syrup really livens up a cake with its citrus zip and would be nice on a Sponge Cake that has a fruity filling. The sugar-liquid ratio will produce a thin syrup with a highly-concentrated taste.

Preparation time: *10 minutes*

Yield: *1 cup*

1 cup granulated white sugar

2 cups fresh-squeezed orange juice

½ cup orange liqueur

1 In a medium saucepan, stir to combine all the ingredients.

2 Bring the mixture to a simmer over medium-high heat, stirring occasionally. Simmer for about 10 minutes until the mixture thickens and reduces slightly.

3 Remove the syrup from the heat, and let it cool partially before using it.

Your Choice Fruit Syrup

This recipe couldn't be easier — or produce a tastier result. All you have to do is pick up your favorite fruit preserves, jam, or jelly, or you can explore your grocery's jelly aisle and branch out with a new flavor. For instance, mango or papaya preserves add an exotic, tasty flavor to the layers of a tropically themed coconut cake. Apricot jam brings a wonderfully complementary flavor to vanilla-flavored or honey cake. (This recipe makes ¼ cup but is easily doubled or tripled.)

Preparation time: *5 minutes*

Yield: *¼ cup*

½ cup fruit preserves, jam, or jelly (your choice)

1 In a small saucepan over medium-low heat, simmer the preserves until they liquefy and stir easily.

2 Strain the partially cooled mixture through a sieve before using it.

Tip: *You can also spread this syrup over fruit on a cake.*

Chapter 11

Tip Talk

In This Chapter

▶ Getting to know icing tips

▶ Working with piping tools

▶ Taking on piping techniques

For some, icing tips can be an intimidating aspect of cake decorating. The thought of filling and operating a pastry bag with these tiny metal cones attached may seem cumbersome, unwieldy, and difficult. And the idea that they produce stars, flowers, and even words can seem downright inconceivable.

But cake decorating that ventures beyond a basic coat of frosting usually involves tips — with their vast varieties and amazing effects — so it's an area you should get comfortable with. In this chapter, I help you sort out the tips available for your artful creations and tell you which tips produce which designs. I also offer instructions on using tips to create popular designs such as shells, stars, swags, and basket weaves as well as flooded and filled in outlines, and frozen frosting transfers.

Decoding Tip Numbers

You may have taken a look at icing tips before and thought: How can there possibly be so many? How will I ever know what to do with each of them? Aren't they like a pencil . . . can't one sort of do everything?

Tips are marvelous because, after you master the mechanics of filling and holding a pastry bag, they put a staggering number of decorating possibilities at your disposal. Don't be put off by the number of tips there are to choose from or think of the preparation part as drudgery. Think of yourself as a painter lining up brushes and tools to accomplish a masterpiece.

When you first get started using tips, you're likely to rely on a few tips for most of your designs and projects. When you get comfortable with those, it's easier than ever to branch out into more tips and add more designs to your repertoire.

A tip-tionary

Although you probably know what *scripting* means, you may not have heard some of the other common terms that relate to a tip's form and function. (The next section tells you which tips create which result.) The following are standard tip techniques:

- **Basket weave:** With a basket weave, you replicate in frosting the look of a woven basket. Traditional basket weave tips are grooved, creating depth and dimension for rows and rows of straight lines that run alternately horizontally and vertically, usually around the sides of a cake.

- **Borders:** Borders can be straight lines, stars, rosettes, shells, or many other forms and frills. They provide a finished look along the top and bottom edges of the cake.

- **Drop flowers:** Drop flowers are usually more representative than realistic in their design. You use any number of tips to create a quick flower.

- **Fill in:** When you *fill in,* you complete an artwork outline using lines or stars in a repeating pattern, compacting those lines and stars as close as possible so that the background frosting doesn't show through. Fill in is similar to the paint-by-number process or coloring in a coloring book.

- **Fleur-de-lis:** This pretty cake adornment is a stylized version of the iris flower. It makes a dramatic repeated design.

- **Garlands and swags:** These designs consist of strands of icing that can resemble ribbons, vines, or swinging banners. You can embellish them further with frosting shells, dots, or rosettes. They create interest around the circumference of the cake.

- **Lace:** Tight, skinny lines and curls of frosting create this look, which is especially popular on shower and wedding cakes.

- **Lattice work:** Much like a trellis you'd find as part of a landscape design, lattice work on a cake makes a realistic backdrop for climbing designs. Lattice work is kind of like a basket weave but features more space in between the piped lines.

- **Lettering:** You use the most basic round tips to create block letters on a cake.

- **Outlines:** If you're trying to set off part or all of your decorating work, you may opt to define it with a fine or thick outline of icing in a darker color.

- **Rosettes:** Resembling mini-roses, rosettes are a pretty addition to a cake's rim, base, or surface design. Like drop flowers, they're more representative than realistic.

- **Ruffles:** These wavy, thick bands of frosting make a luxurious border.

- **Scripting:** This technique refers to writing words on the cake in cursive.

- **Shells:** Another popular border choice, shells may take a bit of practice to get right. The icing tip's groove marks create indentations like you'd find on a seashell. You can leave shells plain or embellish them for more dramatic effect.

- **Stars:** A very popular decoration for borders and a feature in a multitude of designs, stars fit in with many themes and color schemes. Besides being simple to pipe, rows and rows of stars can fill in sections of a bigger design for a textured and impressive (but easy to complete) look.

The most popular tips

Icing tips are numbered according to their sizes and shapes, and as you can see in Table 11-1, you have (literally) hundreds of tips to choose from. The table covers the basic icing tip groups, lists the tip numbers in those groups, and tells you what designs you can produce using those tips. Many of the tips and designs are shown in Figure 11-1.

Table 11-1		An Icing Tip Primer	
Tip	*Description*	*Numbers*	*Uses*
Round	Smooth and circular	00, 000, 1–12, 260, 800–809	Writing, borders, lace, outlines, fill-ins, lattice, lines, dots, strings, stems
Open star	Star-shaped	13–22, 262, 820–829	Stars, rosettes, borders, lines, lace, fleur-de-lis, fill ins
Fine star and open shell border	More-detailed star shape	32, 172, 199, 362–364, 800–869	Stars, rosettes, borders, outlines, lines, drop flowers, fill-ins, shells
Closed and deep closed star	Compact star shape	23–31, 33–35, 132, 195, 232, 233, 501, 502, 504, 506, 508, 840–849, 852–858	Borders, stars, rosettes, drop flowers, shells

(continued)

Table 11-1 *(continued)*

Tip	Description	Numbers	Uses
Multihole	More than one opening	41–43, 133, 134, 221, 234, 889, 2010	Borders, drop flowers, grass, garlands, hair
Basket weave	Typically one smooth side and one serrated side	44–48, 46a–48a, 789, 790, 895, 897, 898	Basket weave, lattice, straight lines, borders
Leaf	V-shaped	65–76, 94, 95, 112–115, 263, 349, 350, 352	Leaves, borders, garlands
Rose and flower	Sharp, rounded ends that are teardrop-shaped	101–104, 124–128, 180, 264	Roses, flowers, borders, garlands, swags
Drop flower	Usually a thin round piece attached to the center inside the tip	105–109, 129, 131, 135–140, 146, 171, 177, 190, 191, 193, 194, 217, 220, 223–225	Drop flowers, filler flowers, specialty flowers
Petal	Fluted edges	59–61, 59a, 97, 116–119, 120–123, 155, 159–162	Borders, roses, flowers, garlands, swags

Note: Basket weave tips #895, #897, and #898 are large tips that create thick rows great for quickly frosting a cake. Also, drop flower tips create a flower with no center, so you can fill in the center with a single dot or several dots (using a small round tip) to form a stamen in any other color you choose.

The cake decorating recipes in Part IV give you an idea of how to use the most popular and common tips. A beginner's cake decorating kit typically has just a couple of round tips (#3 and #12), star tips (#16 and #21), the rose (#104), and the leaf (#352), but you have a plethora of other options available. Experimenting with all the tips that you can get your hands on will make your cakes even more impressive.

The next time you're in a bakeshop or at your grocery store's bakery department, take a look at the cakes to see if you can tell which tip was used for which design element. Take particular note of effects you'd like to put on your own cakes. If you have trouble figuring it out, just ask the bakers behind the counter; they usually love answering questions about their work. Seeing and learning about others' decoration work can influence yours for the better.

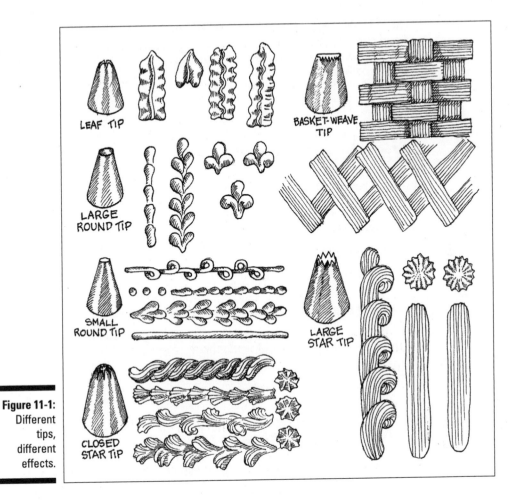

LEAF TIP

LARGE ROUND TIP

SMALL ROUND TIP

CLOSED STAR TIP

BASKET-WEAVE TIP

LARGE STAR TIP

Figure 11-1: Different tips, different effects.

Preparing to Pipe

You have many choices for pastry bags: featherweight, reusable plastic ones; cone-shaped bags; and even 15-inch parchment paper triangles that you roll into cones. But for me, there's only one choice: clear, plastic disposable bags. They're widely available in grocery stores, craft stores, and cake decorating shops, which is evidence that cake decorators everywhere love the convenience they offer. Disposable piping bags offer these advantages:

- ✔ They make cleanup a snap.
- ✔ You can keep track of the frosting colors and easily grab the one you need because the bags are transparent.
- ✔ You can quickly gauge how much frosting you have left in a bag.

Initially, I tried using the featherweight, reusable plastic bags, but aside from having trouble telling which color was in which bag, I could never get them as clean as I wanted. When you're working with rich buttercream and ganache, you have to contend with residue that takes lots of hot water and scrubbing to get rid of. It's my guess that what I spend on disposable items I probably save in hot water!

Gathering the goods

As you prepare to master tip techniques, in addition to pastry bags and tips, you need the following equipment:

- **Couplers:** To hold the tip in place in the pastry bag
- **Coupler rings:** To screw tips onto couplers
- **Large icing spatula:** To transfer frosting from the tinting bowl to the pastry bag
- **Locking bag clips:** To keep the pastry bag sealed as you work
- **Tall cups:** To hold the frosting-filled pastry bags upright while you fill them and when you're not using them
- **Moist paper towels:** To place inside the tall cups to keep tips from drying out while you work

Outfitting a pastry bag

Follow these instructions (and check out Figure 11-2) to outfit a pastry bag with the proper hardware and your beautifully tinted frosting:

1. **Prepare one tall plastic cup (16 ounces or so) for each pastry bag you plan to fill. For each cup, moisten a paper towel, fold it into a square, and place it in the bottom of the cup.**

2. **Drop a cone-shaped coupler into a pastry bag and position it so that the small end of the coupler fits into the point of the bag. Snip off the end of the bag only to the point that the cone is flush with the opening.**

3. **Insert an icing tip into the coupler ring, and screw the coupler ring onto the pastry bag.**

4. **Fold down the wide end of the bag to make a 2-inch cuff. Set the bag upright in the tall cup, and fold the cuff over the rim of the cup.**

   The cuff keeps the bag neat.

5. **Using the large icing spatula, transfer ½ cup to ⅔ cup of frosting to the bag.**

   These amounts are great for practicing. When you're decorating a cake, you want to fill the bag half-full. Any more than that and frosting will ooze out as you pipe.

6. **Roll the cuff back up, and secure the bag with a locking bag clip.**

   A bag clip is similar to a chip bag clip that snaps into place.

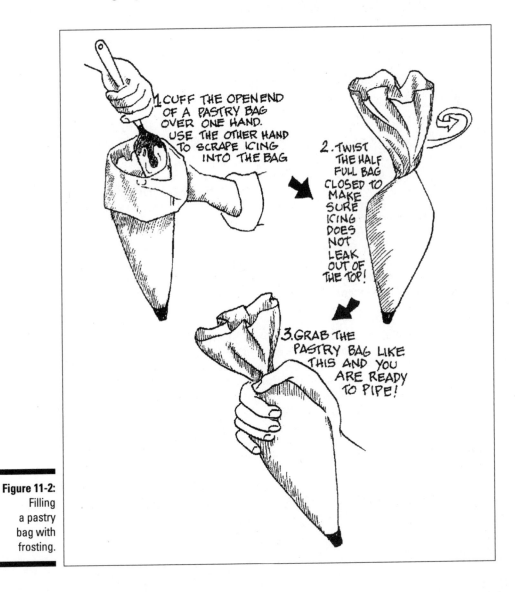

Figure 11-2:
Filling a pastry bag with frosting.

Holding the bag

Before you begin piping, remove the bag clip that you affixed to the bag. As you work, you'll keep the bag sealed with your guiding hand loosely gripped around it.

When piping, you apply pressure to the bag with your dominant hand and guide the bag with your other hand. To hold the bag while decorating, curl four fingers of your nondominant hand around the top of the bag, and apply even pressure with your dominant hand at the tip end to squeeze frosting through the tip. The frosting will continue coming out until you stop squeezing. As you decorate, periodically squeeze frosting from the top of the bag down toward the tip so that you get a steady flow of frosting and therefore a neater execution of your design.

Practicing Tipping Points and Techniques

There's no secret to mastering tip techniques for cake decorating. Succeeding in piping boils down to one word: practice. Fortunately, setting up a practice station is incredibly easy, and working with the tips to experiment and craft creations is fun, too.

To practice, you need some frosting to work with, such as the stiff decorator frosting recipe in Chapter 8. I prefer to practice with actual frosting, but you also may use shortening, which has a similar consistency to frosting and is more convenient because it doesn't involve any preparation. The medium you use is your choice.

To set up a practice station, place sheets of wax or parchment paper down on a smooth work surface or an inverted cookie sheet. Follow the directions for outfitting a pastry bag provided in the section "Preparing to Pipe" earlier in this chapter, line up the tips you want to practice with, and pipe away. When you're comfortable with one tip and design, switch it out for another tip and continue practicing.

To keep track of your tip studies, write the tip number on the wax or parchment paper in permanent marker, and then pipe next to it. Study the tip as well as the frosting that comes out, examining the tip's features from all angles. For example, tip #67 makes leaves from one direction but, if you flip the tip over and pipe, you get attractive ruffles.

Lining up dots, rosettes, shells, stars, and leaves

All dots, rosettes, shells, stars, and leaves are not created equal. Different tips turn these designs out in all different sizes, making it easy to create variations on these popular decorations. For instance, dots — the easiest shapes to pipe — can be as small as the #1 tip or as big as the #809 tip. More than likely, you'll stay in the #1 to #12 range. (You can find descriptions of these designs in the section "A tip-tionary" earlier in this chapter.)

To pipe a dot, you simply hold your bag at a 90-degree angle, squeeze the frosting out, stop squeezing, lift up your tip, and move on. If tips intimidate you, start with the open round tips in the #1 to #11 range, which are easy to maneuver.

When you feel confident in a simple dot, try enhancing your dots. For instance, with a #10 round tip, you can form a heart by piping two inverted teardrops side by side. A teardrop is just a modified dot in that, instead of lifting the tip up immediately, you draw it away from the dot before lifting up.

Rosettes, shells, stars, and leaves may take a bit more practice and patience than dots, but you'll be crafting them in no time as well. Just be sure that you outfit your pastry bag with the right type and number of tip; refer to Table 11-1 for guidance.

For rosettes:

1. **Hold the bag at a 90-degree angle to the surface, about ⅛ inch above it.**

2. **Squeeze the pastry bag and hold the tip in place briefly before moving the tip around to the right in a short circular motion.**

3. **Stop squeezing just before you reach the original starting point, and pull the tip away.**

To make shells:

1. **Hold the bag at a 45-degree angle to the surface, slightly above the surface.**

2. **Squeeze the pastry bag until the frosting builds up and fans out into a base as you lift the tip up slightly.**

3. **Relax pressure as you lower the tip, just until it touches the surface.**

4. **Release the pressure on the bag. Pull the tip away without lifting it off the surface, drawing the shell to a point.**

For a row of shells, place the head of one shell on the tail of the shell that precedes it. For larger shells, increase your piping pressure. For smaller shells, use less pressure.

To create stars:

1. **Hold the bag at a 90-degree angle to the surface, about ⅛ inch above it.**

2. **Squeeze the pastry bag until a star forms. Release the pressure, and pull the tip away at a 90-degree angle. To get a well-defined star, make sure that you stop squeezing before you pull the tip away.**

To make leaves:

1. **Hold the pastry bag at a 45-degree angle to the surface, touching the tip to the surface.**

2. **Squeeze the pastry bag, drawing the tip into a leaf shape, lessening pressure as you move to the leaf's point.**

3. **Release pressure on the bag, and bring the leaf out to a point.**

Guiding lines, garlands, and swags

For outlining, you guide your tip around an illustration already present on your cake's surface. To practice outlining, draw a design on paper in permanent marker and lay it underneath the wax or parchment paper on your practice surface so that the design is visible. Then follow these steps:

1. **Hold the bag at a 45-degree angle to the surface, touching the tip to the surface.**

2. **Pick a starting point, and squeeze the pastry bag with the tip on the surface so that the icing sticks. Raise the tip slightly as you squeeze and move the tip along the design, guiding the tip above the surface.**

3. **To end the outline, stop squeezing the bag, touch the tip to the surface, and pull the tip away.**

When you're done practicing and ready to attempt curved lines, garlands, or swags around a cake's diameter, a plastic lid comes in exceptionally handy. Just press it lightly all around the sides of the frosted cake so that part of the lid forms either the bottom-half of a circle or a downward-facing arc, depending on your desired design. The indentations serve as your piping guide.

Piping borders

A succession of dots, rosettes, shells, or stars makes for an interesting, multi-dimensional border. For variety, you can stagger the effects or pipe them out in contrasting directions.

Also, you can combine these designs for borders. For instance, a vine looks even sweeter with rosettes at points along it. Rosettes also may be separated by leaves, and swags can join shells together. Enliven combinations even more with tiny accent dots, stars, or thin ruffles, or join spaced-out decorative groupings together with frosting strings.

 You can add a lot to borders to make them appealing and attractive, but don't overdo it or you'll end up with a gloppy frosting mess of overlapping, indistinguishable shapes. Spend some time sketching out your ideas beforehand, taking note of which embellishments fit where, which complement each other, which are the focal points, and which work best as accents.

Make some practice time to perfect your border design . . . particularly if it's a technique that you haven't tried before or you're combining two (or more) techniques for the first time.

Basket weaving without becoming a basket case

The basket weave design makes for an elegant allover covering for a cake, but it's also sometimes referred to as the ultimate border because, for full effect, it must cover the entire perimeter of a cake, from top to bottom edges. As a border design, the basket weave works on cakes of any shape.

After you master the specifics of basket weaving, you'll realize that you can use many different tips to accomplish the look — even those that aren't specifically designated for basket weaving. It's all a matter of preference for the size and style of the cake you're decorating. Just remember to keep your lines crisp and your weaving orderly.

Follow these directions to execute the basket weave design, and refer to Figure 11-3:

1. **Position your pastry bag perpendicular to the side of the cake. Starting at the top edge, and with the ridged side of the tip facing up and the tip just touching the surface, squeeze the bag as you lift the tip just**

barely away from the side of the cake and move it down slowly in a vertical line, applying even pressure as you go from top to bottom. At the bottom edge of the cake, touch the tip to the surface of the cake again, stop squeezing, and lift the bag completely away.

2. Hold the bag perpendicular to the side of the cake, and position it at the top of the vertical column from Step 1, ½ inch to one side of it. The ridged side of the tip should face away from the cake. Pipe a bar that extends ½ inch to either side of the vertical column.

3. Right underneath the horizontal bar in Step 2, press the edge of your tip into the cake to make a slight indentation. Underneath that indentation, pipe another bar the same size as the first one. Repeat the indentation and piping all the way down the vertical column.

4. Pipe the next vertical column from the top edge of the cake to the bottom, covering the ends of the horizontal bars.

5. Pipe horizontal bars over the column from Step 4, spacing them so that they fill in the gaps left by the previous horizontal bars.

6. Repeat Steps 4 and 5 around the perimeter of the cake.

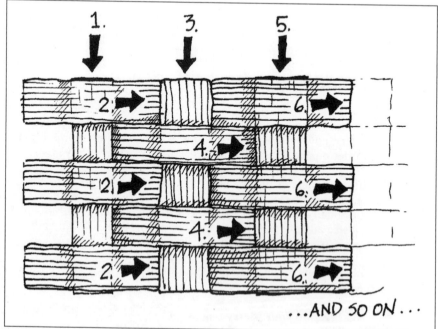

Figure 11-3: Creating a basket weave design.

Flooding, Filling, and Other Fun Design Techniques

As you become familiar with a host of tips, you'll undoubtedly appreciate their use and ease in some simpler applications that can feature small illustrations on your cake or ones that cover the entire surface.

Tips afford you the chance to decorate and accentuate your cakes with a range of designs, including filled outlines and scripted letters and messages. Another interesting technique, the frozen buttercream transfer, is a fun and somewhat unconventional way to add dimension to your cake in an eye-catching way.

Flooding a design

Flooding a design is a common way of decorating cookies, and it works for cake decorating, too. To begin, you need a cake that's already been crumb coated, frosted, and refrigerated to form a crust.

With this decorative method, you use royal icing (refer to Chapter 9 for a recipe) to outline an image, and then, with a large round tip on a pastry bag (or even a squeeze bottle), you fill in the outline with a solid color of frosting. You should squeeze out enough royal icing to flood or completely fill the outline.

Depending on the consistency of the royal icing, you may need to smooth it out with an icing spatula after you flood the outline.

If you want to add different-colored accents to a flooded design, you have to let the icing set and dry for several hours first.

Filling a design

Flooding is just one way to fill a design; other methods add dimension and texture to the design. For example, cake pans in the shapes of teddy bears, beach balls, or cartoon characters usually come with guidelines that tell you what icing tips and frosting colors to use to fill in the designs in a paint-by-number fashion. You also have the option of coming up with your own tip and color designs to add color, character, and dimension to cakes in interesting shapes.

The easiest and most effective way to fill a design is to use a #16 star tip with multiple frosting colors. Follow these instructions:

1. **Frost your cake with a neutral-colored base frosting and refrigerate it for 1 hour so that the frosting hardens into a crust.**

2. **Use a toothpick to section off or sketch out the different areas or shapes that you plan to fill in.**

3. **With a #3 icing tip, outline those areas in the color frosting for that particular graphic component.**

4. **Pipe stars, each one right next to the other, to fill in the design area. The base frosting in the design area should be completely covered with stars.**

   For a star how-to, refer to the section "Lining up dots, rosettes, shells, stars, and leaves" earlier in this chapter.

To complete the design, you may choose to pipe straight lines or ruffles around the cake's perimeter for additional dimension. Outlining your star-filled creation gives it a finished look.

Lettering and scripting

Sometimes, a simple message can really make (and take) the cake. When you've mastered letters in different styles, you can take your cake lettering and scripting to new heights. Writing on a cake can be as simple as fashioning initials or as detailed as using a sheet cake's rectangular shape as a page in a book, complete with the text you'd find in a fairy tale, for example. For most, lettering on a cake is a way to express a snappy, happy greeting or warm wishes.

Granted, you're at an advantage if you already have good penmanship. If your regular handwriting is messy or unattractive, practice your technique to get a feel for how to mold, shape, and guide letters and also the best way to hold and guide your pastry bag.

Practice is very important when it comes to lettering and scripting in frosting. Use the different sizes of round tips, like #1 to #12, to get a feel for the size and thickness of letters they produce. When you practice, don't be afraid to play around a bit and try block letters and cursive. If you're feeling particularly adventurous, tip #44 is a great choice for calligraphy-style scripting. If you're struggling with different writing styles, surf the Internet for calligraphy examples or pick up an instructional book on calligraphy at your local library and practice writing in different ways before you try piping. (On more than one occasion, I've literally drawn on the techniques I learned in a calligraphy class.)

When you feel comfortable enough to try writing on a cake, decide what you're going to write before you take the tip to the surface! Don't wait until you have frosting coming out of your pastry bag to choose your words — you're likely to end up with a squiggly mess or misspelled words. Also, the number of letters or words you're putting on a cake dictates the size of the tip you use; if you're just scripting initials or a short message, you can use a large tip, but if you have a lot of words to fit on the cake, a small tip is best.

Follow these guidelines for turning your words into a frosting message:

- ✔ For scripting, use buttercream or stiff decorator frosting (see Chapter 8 for recipes). Both are smooth and firm enough to produce crisp letters.

- ✔ On a cake that has been crumb coated, frosted, and refrigerated, use a toothpick or bamboo skewer to sketch out the message. Don't bear down too hard; you're just blocking out where your letters will appear. If you make a mistake, frost the cake again, refrigerate it, and start over.

- ✔ Don't put too much frosting in the pastry bag — stick with about ⅔ cup. And before you start scripting on the cake, test the frosting's consistency by piping a few letters or words on a piece of wax paper.

- ✔ Make sure that the cake you're scripting on is placed straight on the table or work surface. If it's slanted, your writing may end up slanted, too.

- ✔ If you're unhappy with the way your writing looks, lift it off the surface of the cake delicately with a toothpick or bamboo skewer, and begin again. (It's particularly easy to lift your lettering off the cake if the cake has been refrigerated and the frosting is cold.)

When you make frosting for lettering and scripting, it's important to sift the confectioners' sugar thoroughly. Little balls of sugar in the frosting can clog up the pastry bag as you pipe, and although you can usually remove or break up the clog with a toothpick, the flow of your scripting will have already been interrupted. Unlike some decorations, it's hard to hide mistakes in writing.

Creating a frozen buttercream transfer

With a frozen buttercream transfer, you create a graphic image off the cake, freeze it for permanence, and then adhere it to the cake. This technique draws on some of the tip techniques discussed in this chapter, but it allows you to cheat a bit in the sense that you create artwork that looks as if it were applied directly to the cake. For this process, you need:

- ✔ Buttercream frosting
- ✔ Pastry bags and round icing tips
- ✔ Wax paper
- ✔ A graphic image printed in reverse
- ✔ Tape
- ✔ A flat, portable surface (preferably a large wooden cake board)

Follow these steps to create a frozen buttercream transfer:

1. **Tape the image to the cake board, and then tape a piece of wax paper over the image.**

   The wax paper, which serves as tracing paper, will hold your finished design.

2. **Use your choice of outline color to pipe an outline of the picture with fresh, firm buttercream frosting.**

   Follow the bold lines on your image. This step is similar to outlining a fill-in design on the cake itself, which I cover earlier in this chapter.

3. **Much like you would for a paint-by-number picture, fill in the outline by piping the different colors you desire. Use round tips to fill the design with solid frosting.**

   Think about the layers of your colors, and color the parts of your image that stand out first. For example, if you're filling in a flower arrangement of flowers and leaves in a vase, you do the flowers first, then the leaves, and finally the vase. (Think about a real flower arrangement: The flowers cover up the leaves, which cover up the top of the vase.)

4. **When you finish coloring the graphic by filling in the outlined areas, smooth out the frosting by gently pressing it down with an icing spatula. Take care not to blend the colors underneath.**

   Smoothing settles your frosting into the grooves to create a clean and complete finished product.

5. **Place the creation into the freezer for at least 1½ hours.**

6. **Remove the transfer from the freezer, unfasten the tape from the cake board, and turn the design resting on the wax paper over onto your frosted cake.**

7. **Gently peel off the wax paper.**

   Your reverse image should be a colorful, layered piece of artwork on top of your cake.

Chapter 12

Enhancing with Embellishments

. . . .

In This Chapter

▶ Starting out with fruit, flowers, and nuts

▶ Crafting marzipan

▶ Modeling gum paste

▶ Piping roses

▶ Selecting treats and candies

▶ Exploring inedible decorations

. . . .

Recipes in This Chapter

▶ Tropical Fruit Panorama Cake

▶ Marzipan

▶ Gum Paste

As cake decorating increases in popularity, now more than ever before you have a host of accoutrements, accessories, trimmings, frills, and figures to choose from when decorating your cake. Some require a bit of know-how to master, like modeling marzipan and gum paste or making roses, whereas others just call for a keen eye for fun detail.

This chapter welcomes you to a world of creativity as you explore and pick up the skills involved in transforming your cake into a celebratory, theme-appropriate vision with a plethora of enhancements.

Easing into Enhancements

The beauty of cake decorating is that sometimes a simple, fresh, and natural approach is best. You don't always have to undertake a huge, monumental task; the occasion or the time available to decorate may force you to go with a simpler and quicker — although still impressive — design.

The great thing about starting out simply is that you get a strong handle on fundamentals of placement and design in your cake decorating endeavors. These opportunities provide you with the chance to show off basic skills while dressing up a cake beautifully at the same time.

Adding zip with fresh fruit

Cakes topped with fresh fruits look spectacular. Just wander down the produce aisle of your local grocer and imagine the possibilities. Consider the beauty — and simplicity — of a cake topped with a concentric arrangement of glazed whole cherries, raspberries, strawberries, sliced peaches, or halved apricots. (Flip to Chapter 9 for glaze recipes.) If you're planning a cake that will feature fruit as a prime component, take these guidelines into account:

- In choosing fruit to put on top of the cake, keep in mind the flavor of your cake. Choose fruits that will complement it, not overpower or work against it. For instance, raspberries pair well with white and dark chocolate, but mangoes would make for an odd pairing with any kind of chocolate. However, they're delicious with white and yellow cakes.

- Certain fruits, such as sliced bananas and apples, brown quickly, so they won't look as appealing as other options. For that reason, I advise that you avoid glazing these fruits on cakes.

- Consider the fruit's appearance. For example, lemon and orange slices look nice and shiny, but quartered wedges of these fruits are too bulky and don't present them in such a flattering light.

- Stick with fresh fruits. Although frozen fruits are convenient and a great ingredient in some recipes, they tend to get mushy when they're defrosted and also may bleed juice onto your cake if they're not completely defrosted and drained before you arrange them.

- Quality control is a must. Make sure that any fruits you plan to decorate with are clean and free of brown or moldy spots.

The following fruits all make particularly colorful additions to a cake:

- Strawberries (whole or sliced)
- Raspberries
- Blueberries
- Mango slices
- Kiwi slices
- Pineapple chunks
- Star fruit slices

Tropical Fruit Panorama Cake

Here's a tropical cake take on a fruit tart that includes luscious fruits on top of white cake. It's pretty, simple, and makes for a beautiful presentation.

Tools: *Two 9-inch round pans*

Preparation time: *15 minutes plus 1 hour for refrigeration*

Yield: *12 servings*

One batch Most Excellent White Cake batter (see Chapter 6)

One batch Buttercream Frosting (see Chapter 8)

½ cup guava jelly

2 kiwis, skinned and sliced

½ pint blueberries

½ pint strawberries

Mango, pitted, skinned, and sliced

1 Bake the cake according to the recipe in Chapter 6. After the layers have cooled, level them, and stack them with a layer of buttercream in between.

2 Apply a crumb coat (thin layer) of buttercream frosting to the cake, and refrigerate it for 1 hour. Then frost it again.

3 In a small saucepan, heat the guava jelly over low heat, stirring occasionally, until it liquefies.

4 Arrange the fruit in concentric circles on top of the cake. Begin with the kiwi slices in the center of the cake, fanning them out; circle the blueberries around the kiwi; circle the strawberries around the blueberries; and add the sliced mango around the strawberries.

5 Brush the fruit with guava glaze.

Smelling the fresh flowers

Edible flower decorations can range from a simple marigold, zinnia, or chrysanthemum popping out of the middle of a Bundt cake to mounds of roses and violets climbing trellis-like up a five-tier wedding cake.

Although some flowers are edible, I recommend that you use them only for decoration.

Regardless of whether guests will be munching on floral decorations or just admiring them, the flowers you use on a cake should always be pesticide-free. To be safe, you should either buy them from a trusted source or use ones that you or someone you know has grown personally so that you know firsthand that they're safe. You don't want anyone getting sick from the residue left on the cake by the flowers you selected. Fortunately, if you don't have the time or space to grow them yourself, it's fairly easy to find organic flowers that fit the bill.

Considering floral options

You have a wide range of "safe" flowers to consider for your cake, including:

- Apple blossoms
- Carnations
- Cornflowers
- Daisies
- Gardenias
- Gladioli
- Hibiscuses
- Honeysuckle
- Lavender
- Lilacs
- Marigolds
- Nasturtiums
- Pansies
- Passionflowers
- Petunias
- Roses
- Sunflowers
- Violets

If you know of a flower that you really want on your cake, do some research on it first to determine whether it's food-safe. For instance, lily of the valley is beautiful and has a lovely scent, but it's also poisonous.

Poisonous (though beautiful) flowers include:

- Hyacinths
- Hydrangeas
- Lilies of the valley
- Morning glories
- Sweet peas
- Wisteria

If you're determined to have poisonous flowers play a starring role on your cake, recreate them in frosting, gum paste, or marzipan. They'll be more awesome than the real thing because they'll be safe!

Keeping flowers perky

You may need to keep the flowers on your cake hydrated, especially if your cake will be on display for a while before it's eaten. You have two options:

- ✓ Cut a 3-inch piece of a drinking straw, and tape one end closed. Fill the straw with water, and then place the flower's stem inside.
- ✓ Purchase flower holders or spikes from a floral or cake decorating supply company. You fill these holders with water and insert the flower stems.

With both options, you can press the hydration station into the cake and then insert flowers, or you may choose to insert flowers into the holders and then lay them on the surface of the cake, arranging them so that blooms artfully cover the holders.

Use flowers in tiered cakes that feature separators. Fill the space between the layers with flowers, arranging them so that the blooms are all you see.

Getting a bit nutty

Decorating with fruits and flowers means that you have to follow a few rules, but you don't have to be quite as picky with nuts. No matter the presentation, nuts add both flavor and presence. If you're not familiar with different nutty tastes, spend some time conducting a taste test to sample and appreciate the myriad possibilities you have.

Pair nuts with flavored cakes. Macadamia nuts taste delicious with banana cake, walnuts and carrot cake make a great team, and pecans and bourbon cake are a natural combination. As for peanuts, they're great with brownie cake, but their strong flavor means they don't work well with other flavored cakes such as lemon, mint, or spice.

Some kinds of nuts that you're sure to find in multiple ready-to-use forms (shelled, whole, sliced, chopped, and even slivered) include

- ✓ Almonds
- ✓ Cashews
- ✓ Hazelnuts (also known as *filberts*)
- ✓ Macadamia nuts
- ✓ Peanuts

- ✔ Pecans
- ✔ Walnuts

Whole, sliced, chopped, or slivered?

Whether you're working with whole or sliced nuts, you can fan them out on the top of a cake or apply them to the sides. With chopped nuts, you can sprinkle them in a pattern on the top of a cake (for example, you may place them inside a stencil or cookie cutter) or press them onto the sides. You can use slivered nuts similarly. The most commonly found slivered nuts are almonds, which are usually blanched and slivered. If you want to use slivered almonds, buy them that way; preparing them would be difficult and time-consuming.

If you're using whole nuts, such as pecans or walnuts, make sure that they're in good, unblemished shape, and aren't chipped or streaked in some way. Similarly, if you're decorating with sliced or slivered nuts (such as almonds), only use full, complete slices or slivers; keep those that are chipped or broken out of your design.

If you decide to use chopped nuts and opt to do the chopping yourself rather than buy them ready-to-use, prepare them in a consistent size. When you're working with a lot of nuts, it's best to chop them in batches. Make sure that the size matches throughout each nut batch, and don't combine your chopped batches until you're happy with the size of the nuts in each batch. Pick out any bigger pieces while the quantities are still small.

Go easy on yourself

Don't add to your cake decorating work by using nuts that have to be cracked, skinned, shelled, or otherwise prepared. Find ones that are ready to place on your cake or that need only to be chopped. When you have to spend time roasting and rubbing skins off hazelnuts, for example, your prep time increases, taking away from the time you have to decorate.

Modeling with Marzipan

Marzipan is an almond paste that you can use to cover entire cakes, but generally, it's more commonly formed into embellishments and decorations. I love working with marzipan: I find it fun, rewarding, and even therapeutic to mold it into all sorts of fascinating shapes and decorations.

Made from ground almonds, marzipan also has a great taste. It's an embellishment cake eaters enjoy diving into. You can make your own marzipan, but it's readily available at most grocery stores on the baking aisle. (It's usually sold in 7-ounce tubes.)

Marzipan

This recipe for homemade marzipan requires you to get your hands dirty, so roll up your sleeves. Plus, if you like, you can get kids to join in on the marzipan merriment.

Preparation time: *15 minutes*

Yield: *2 pounds*

16 ounces almond paste	*½ teaspoon almond extract*
⅓ cup pasteurized egg white	*4 cups confectioners' sugar*

1 In a large bowl, use your fingers to break up the almond paste into small chunks.

2 In a separate bowl, sift the confectioners' sugar; set aside ¾ cup for use when kneading the marzipan.

3 Stir the almond paste into the sugar, and make a well in the center of the mixture.

4 In a small bowl, combine the egg white and almond extract; pour into the well in the almond paste and sugar mixture. Stir until well mixed.

5 Sprinkle your work surface with a little of the reserved confectioners' sugar, and turn out the almond mixture. Knead the mixture, adding more sugar as needed to prevent sticking, until the marzipan is smooth and pliable.

Simple techniques: Coloring and cutting

With just a few drops of a coloring gel or paste, it's easy to tint the neutral color of marzipan. The best way to color marzipan's neutral shade is to break off a chunk of marzipan to work with, dip a clean toothpick into your coloring gel or paste, and poke the toothpick into the marzipan. Roll the marzipan between your fingertips and against your palm, kneading it to evenly distribute the color.

When kneading color into marzipan, spread a little vegetable shortening on your fingertips if you find that the marzipan is sticking to your fingers too much.

Easy ways to decorate with colored marzipan (or uncolored, for that matter), are rolling it into balls (all the same size, or different sizes for interest) or flattening it out and cutting out different shapes.

To cut shapes from marzipan, use a nonstick rolling pin on a clean work surface and roll the marzipan out to a thickness of ⅛ inch. Press cookie cutters into the marzipan just as you would into cookie dough. If the cookie cutters stick to the marzipan, rub their insides with a little vegetable oil. In a sense, marzipan is much like cookie dough in that you can make the most out of it by gathering the scraps and rolling them out over and over.

Advanced techniques: Modeling

After you play around with marzipan a bit and become comfortable with its texture, working with it becomes increasingly easier. Marzipan is particularly easy to sculpt because it's soft enough to shape and pieces of it stick together very easily.

You can sculpt many shapes and figures simply with your fingers. My favorite — and probably the most common — are marzipan fruits and vegetables. But once you have the hang of it, no shape is off-limits! I've seen marzipan Easter eggs, Halloween ghosts, Christmas stockings, and even golf balls and gift-wrapped boxes. One of my favorite marzipan creations is an avocado!

When you start modeling marzipan, have the actual object you're trying to recreate in front of you (or a picture of it, if you can't get your hands on the real thing). For example, if you want to make a marzipan strawberry, have a real strawberry in front of you to refer to and examine as you work. Your effort will be so much better for it! Although you undoubtedly know what an orange or pumpkin or rose looks like, you'll look at it differently when you have to recreate it through food sculpting.

Several tools can help you in your marzipan modeling. What you use really depends on how fancy, intricate, or detailed you want your creations to be, but here are some of the most basic tools:

- **Coloring pastes or gels**
- **Deviled egg plate:** Use it as your palette if you're working with several different colors
- **Nonstick rolling pin**
- **Metal (preferably) or plastic cutters in round or leaf shapes**
- **Veining tool:** Has curved, sharp ends that allow you to both sculpt and craft detail work on an object's surface
- **Umbrella tool:** Has a rocket tail–shaped point to make lifelike impressions at the top of certain fruits and vegetables, like where leaves would come out of an apple, for example
- **Craft knife:** Scores the surface of vegetable shapes
- **Small grater:** Leaves fine imprints on the surface of a shape

If you think you're not ready to take on marzipan but would like to work on your shapes, practice with a very accessible — and very unintimidating — substance: kids' modeling clay.

The following instructions for creating vegetables and fruits allow you to transform marzipan into stunning cake decorations. Remember: Many of these shapes begin simply with a small ball of colored marzipan.

Tomato

Roll a piece of red marzipan into a ball, squash the ball slightly to give it a plump, oval shape, and score the sides, as shown in Figure 12-1. For the top of the tomato, roll out some green marzipan. Use a small star-shaped cutter or cut a star with a craft knife or paring knife, and affix the piece to the top of the tomato.

Carrot

Roll a piece of orange marzipan into a tapered cone shape. Use the craft knife to make hash marks on the sides of the carrot. Roll out a piece of green marzipan, and cut out a large leaf shape (see Figure 12-1). Use the knife to make cuts all around the leaf's perimeter to resemble the dainty fronds that top a carrot.

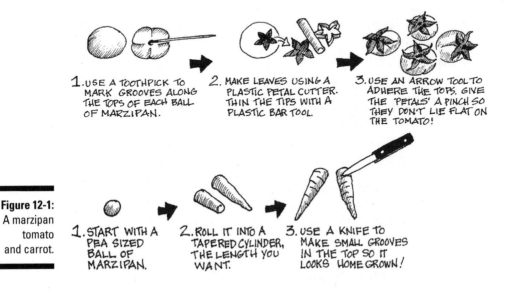

1. USE A TOOTHPICK TO MARK GROOVES ALONG THE TOPS OF EACH BALL OF MARZIPAN.

2. MAKE LEAVES USING A PLASTIC PETAL CUTTER. THIN THE TIPS WITH A PLASTIC BAR TOOL.

3. USE AN ARROW TOOL TO ADHERE THE TOPS. GIVE THE 'PETALS' A PINCH SO THEY DON'T LIE FLAT ON THE TOMATO!

1. START WITH A PEA SIZED BALL OF MARZIPAN.

2. ROLL IT INTO A TAPERED CYLINDER, THE LENGTH YOU WANT.

3. USE A KNIFE TO MAKE SMALL GROOVES IN THE TOP SO IT LOOKS HOME GROWN!

Figure 12-1: A marzipan tomato and carrot.

Pumpkin

Roll out a ball of orange marzipan, and score the sides with a craft knife. Create a pumpkin vine by rolling green marzipan into a spaghetti strand thickness and coil it around a bamboo skewer that's been dusted with confectioners' sugar to prevent sticking. You can also add leaves to the vine by pinching small balls of green marzipan into tiny leaf shapes and affixing them to the vine and to the top of the pumpkin.

Lettuce head

Begin with a pea-sized ball of green marzipan. Roll out another piece of green marzipan and cut out several small pieces in the shape of small rose petals. One at a time, wrap the petal-shaped pieces around the ball to create a layered effect.

Strawberry

Roll a ball of red marzipan between your hands to form a strawberry shape — wide at one end tapering to a rounded point at the other end. Press the sides of the strawberry into a small food grater to give it the look of seeds. For the strawberry cap, cut three small triangles out of green marzipan, and affix them to the top.

Blackberry

Roll out a ball of deep purple marzipan, and break off little pieces one at a time to make several tiny balls. Press them together gently into a berry shape. Make a stem out of a tiny rectangle of green marzipan, and press it into the blackberry's top.

Working with Gum Paste

Gum paste is a malleable substance that can be crafted into a variety of decorations. Most likely, you've seen gum paste in the form of flowers on top of wedding cakes. Although edible, unlike marzipan, gum paste doesn't taste very good at all, so it's definitely the sort of decoration that should be admired but not consumed. Gum paste can be stored indefinitely, so decorations can be kept as mementos to commemorate an event.

You can make gum paste from scratch with only a few specialty ingredients, but most cake decorators opt to purchase ready-made gum paste from baking supply and craft stores.

Although you can transform gum paste into any number of objects, flowers are the most popular gum paste creation. Though difficult to master, gum paste gives you complete control over the kinds of flowers you can decorate your cake with as well as the colors of those flowers. So although you can't put the poisonous lily of the valley on a cake, you can use gum paste stems of them. Or if real dogwood blossoms aren't available in your area, you can still decorate with them through the magic of gum paste.

To be honest, gum paste can present quite a challenge for cake decorators. Although the end product looks intricate, beautiful, and life-like, getting there takes a lot of practice, patience, and dedication to perfection. Working with gum paste is time-intensive, so unless you've become highly proficient, don't expect to whip up an entire cake's worth of flowers quickly.

Some of the more popular gum paste floras used in cake decorating include:

- Calla lilies
- Carnations
- Daisies
- Ferns
- Forget-me-nots
- Freesia
- Gardenias
- Ivy
- Leaves
- Lilies of the valley
- Lisianthus
- Orchids
- Roses
- Stargazer lilies
- Stephanotis
- Sweet peas

Gum Paste

Whether you just want to play around and get some flower-making practice in or you're ready to tackle decorations for a special cake, try this recipe for homemade gum paste. It calls for a specialty ingredient, gum tragacanth, that's widely available in some outlets of national craft store chains as well as cake decorating supply stores and Web sites.

Preparation time: *15 minutes plus overnight for the paste to mature*

Yield: *1 pound*

1 tablespoon corn syrup

¼ cup warm water

1 tablespoon gum tragacanth (also known by the brand name Gum-Tex)

4 cups sifted confectioners' sugar, divided

1 In a medium saucepan, heat the corn syrup and water over low heat until just warm.

2 In a medium bowl, combine the gum tragacanth with 1 cup of confectioners' sugar. Remove the corn syrup mixture from the heat, and stir in the sugar mixture.

3 Turn the contents out onto your work surface. Gradually knead in the remaining confectioners' sugar until your paste is pliable and not sticky.

4 Store the gum paste in a plastic bag overnight to let it mature to the right consistency before you work with it.

If gum paste intrigues you but you're not ready to commit to working with it just yet, you can purchase many kinds of gum paste flowers at bakeries and baking supply stores. Select some premade flowers, examine and inspect them close-up, and note the detail on petals, stamens, and leaves. Then figure out the best way to place them to dress up a cake, and see if you like the look and aura.

Tooling around with gum paste

Whether you've made your own gum paste or bought some ready-made, you have a variety of tools at your disposal to craft flowers out of. (Keep in mind that many of these also come in handy for marzipan molding.)

- ✔ **Food coloring gels or pastes:** You use these to tint the gum paste to a desired shade.
- ✔ **Cutters:** You can rely on a wide range of plastic or metal cutters to help you achieve a realistic look and design. Some cutters are the actual shapes of flowers whereas others are petal-shaped.

✔ **Tools:** Five tools come in handy for a host of shaping techniques. They're all about 6 inches long and are usually plastic, pencil-shaped, and easy to grip (see Figure 12-2). They are

- **Dogbone:** Pressing this tool, which has a rounded hook on the end, into gum paste makes a petal look open.

- **Ball:** This tool has a small, hard ball on the end that you can use to cup or smooth out a petal.

- **Veining:** This tool, which tapers off to sharp points on each end, works nicely for drawing a leaf's veins.

- **Shell:** This tool has a scalloped end with which to imprint lines on flowers.

- **Umbrella:** You can insert this sharp-pointed tool into the gum paste for scoring, forming buds, and imprinting veins.

✔ **Foam mat:** You set your gum paste on a foam mat to make it easier to sculpt with the tools. (You can even use a gardener's kneeling pad or a computer mouse pad.)

✔ **Adhesive:** Although you have a number of adhesive options for holding gum paste designs together, pasteurized egg white is a good choice. For another adhesive, dissolve ¼ teaspoon gum paste in 1 tablespoon water.

✔ **Heavy-gauge wire:** Wire allows you to spear the bud you're working on to attach petals to the flower.

✔ **Petal dusts:** These are highly concentrated powdered colors that you can apply to your gum paste flowers after they're dry. Dusts make flowers look more realistic.

✔ **Paint brushes:** You need one brush to apply adhesive to gum paste pieces. In addition, craft paintbrushes in a range of sizes help you in applying petal dust in both large and small spaces.

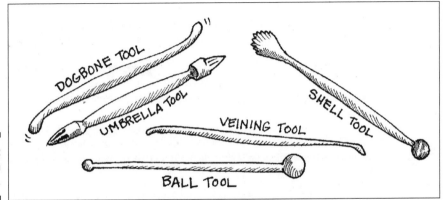

Figure 12-2:
Gum
paste tools.

Assembling and coloring gum paste flowers

Some cake decorators adamantly steer clear of gum paste, always opting for fresh flowers instead and arguing that those made of gum paste are too artificial. Although I understand their point, it's easy to marvel at flowers that look so real but have been sculpted out of a foodstuff.

To make a wide variety of different kinds of gum paste flowers, you start with the same basic steps. For almost every kind of flower, follow these steps:

1. **Dust your work surface with cornstarch.**

2. **Tint a small amount of gum paste if you want the flower to be a certain color.**

   Use a toothpick to dab the color into the gum paste. Then knead the color in (drop by drop) until you achieve your desired shade.

3. **Using a (preferably) nonstick roller, roll out the gum paste to a paper-thin (¹⁄₁₆ inch) thickness.**

   Have a large glass bowl turned over and standing by so that you can put gum paste you're not working with at the moment underneath it to keep the gum paste from drying out.

4. **Using the appropriate cutter, cut the entire flower (such as a daisy or dogwood blossom) or the petals (such as for a rose or carnation) that you need to form the bloom. Simply press the cutter down hard, and lift it straight up; don't twist it back and forth to release the shape.**

5. **Place your shape(s) on a foam pad.**

6. **With the appropriate tools (refer to the preceding section), shape the flower's petals or leaves.**

7. **Set the shape on a piece of parchment paper to dry and harden.**

8. **When dry, use a brush to dust the shapes with petal dusts — if desired — to accent their details and make them look more realistic.**

If you're adding stamens, sepals (the little green bits under the petals), stems, or other greenery, prepare those items out of gum paste just as you do the petals and leaves and then apply them with adhesive (usually pasteurized egg white).

Lilies and roses are two flower varieties that require some special work to grow out of gum paste. The following sections walk you through the specifics of crafting these flowers.

A dreamy confection that draws raves, "The Ballerina Stage Cake" stars pink accents and a strawberry buttercream filling. Another delightful choice for a girl's birthday party, the "Real Doll" cake shows off a colorful dress that's easy

Rev up tastebuds with the "Have a Good Year Race Car Cake," as partygoers love sampling the many delectable treats

Different colors and shapes of rock candy become a girl's best friend with this pink velvet "Jewelry Cake," certain to impress ladies of all ages. To amuse the men in your life, make tee time delicious with the "Golf Game Cake," which

At a wedding shower, the "'Tasteful' Registry Cake" honors the bride and groom with an edible china setting and gifts. For a baby shower, the "Cupcake Tower" lets grown-ups in on the fun with key lime cupcakes and giant swirls of fluffy

Fondant circles spotlight the "Anniversary Bubbledot Cake," which is easily adaptable for other celebrations.

A simple yet impressive wedding cake, the "Italian Chocolate Wedding Cake" offers up deconstructed layers of the

This Halloween, carve a Jack-O'-Lantern out of lip-smacking brown sugar cake with this easy-to-assemble treat. Or serve this spooky showstopper, the fudgy "Haunted Mansion Cake," which calls on seasonal sweets for decorations.

"**The Christmas Tree Cake**" brings merry revelry with its frosting tree, candy ornaments, and a moist red velvet cake
tucked inside. On Valentine's Day love is even sweeter with the "Heart O' Mine Cake."

Lilies

Although it may look complicated, this flower is surprisingly easy to make with gum paste. Just follow these steps, and check out Figure 12-3:

1. **Tint the gum paste to your desired shade (or buy some already colored).**

2. **Roll the gum paste out to a thickness of 1/16 inch. With a cutter or small paring knife, cut out five leaf-shaped petals that are 2¼ inches long, ¾ inch wide at the center, and taper at the ends.**

3. **Wad up a small piece of aluminum foil into a tall cone shape. Sprinkle cornstarch on the foil (so that the finished lily doesn't stick to it), and place a small ball of colored gum paste (the same color as the lily) at the top of the cone. Use a pastry brush to cover the ball with pasteurized egg white.**

4. **Affix the petals to the ball one at a time, overlapping them slightly and making sure that they stick to the ball. In the overlapping, use a bit of egg white to make the petals unfurl from each other. Bend the petals slightly outward at the bottom of the cone so that it looks like the flower is opening when it is inverted.**

5. **Let the lily dry on the aluminum cone for 24 hours before gently twisting it off.**

6. **Adhere artificial stamens, which are available at craft stores, to the ball inside the lily, or sculpt some out of thin white ropes of gum paste with tiny yellow or brown spheres attached to one end.**

7. **Attach the stamens to the ball either by inserting them into a few dots of royal icing piped onto the ball or by lightly brushing the ball with egg white and sticking them to it.**

Roses

The most popular gum paste cake flower is also probably the most difficult to make, so be patient with the process. Your persistence will pay off, I promise!

For a single rose, you need the following materials: gum paste, four sizes of petal cutters (small, medium, large, and extra large), a dogbone tool, pasteurized egg white, and a 6-inch length of 24-gauge wire. The following steps and Figure 12-4 outline the procedure:

1. **Tint the gum paste as desired.**

2. **Shape a small ball of paste into a miniature cone that's approximately 1½ inches wide at its base and ¼ inch wide at its top point.**

3. **Make a hook at one end of the 6-inch length of wire, and insert it into the base of the gum paste cone, driving it up almost to the tip. Let this dry and harden for 24 hours.**

4. **Roll out a small piece of gum paste, and cut two petals out of it with a small cutter. Soften their edges with a dogbone tool.**

5. **With a little egg white, attach the first petal to one side of the cone, wrapping it halfway around the cone. Holding the wire, twist the cone to your right (if you're right-handed; work the other way if you're left-handed), and attach the second petal so that it's slightly higher than the first petal and overlaps the first petal's edge. Molding these two petals around the tip of the cone creates the center of the rose.**

6. **Cut three medium size petals out of the gum paste, and soften their edges. Attach each one to the first layer of petals with some egg white, overlapping them slightly on the sides such that the first petal is tucked inside the second petal and the second inside the third. Pinch the tops of the petal outward a bit to resemble a rose in full bloom.**

7. **Repeat Step 6 with four large petals, then with five extra large petals, and finally with five more extra large petals. When you're done, five layers of petals should surround the cone.**

8. **Dry the entire rose overnight.**

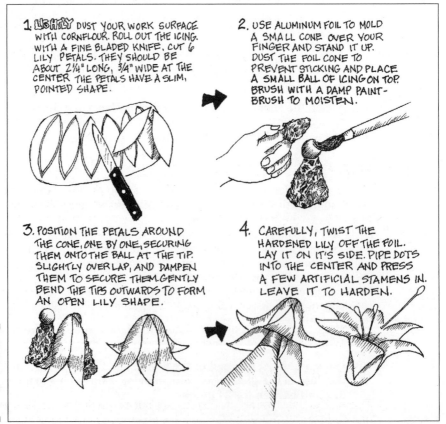

Figure 12-3:
Molding and constructing a gum paste lily.

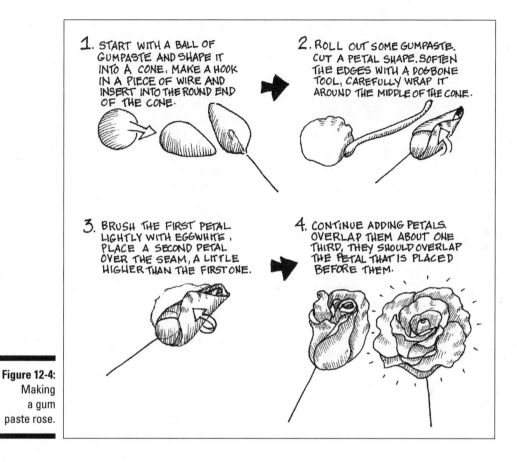

1. START WITH A BALL OF GUMPASTE AND SHAPE IT INTO A CONE. MAKE A HOOK IN A PIECE OF WIRE AND INSERT INTO THE ROUND END OF THE CONE.

2. ROLL OUT SOME GUMPASTE. CUT A PETAL SHAPE. SOFTEN THE EDGES WITH A DOGBONE TOOL, CAREFULLY WRAP IT AROUND THE MIDDLE OF THE CONE.

3. BRUSH THE FIRST PETAL LIGHTLY WITH EGGWHITE, PLACE A SECOND PETAL OVER THE SEAM, A LITTLE HIGHER THAN THE FIRST ONE.

4. CONTINUE ADDING PETALS. OVERLAP THEM ABOUT ONE THIRD, THEY SHOULD OVERLAP THE PETAL THAT IS PLACED BEFORE THEM.

Figure 12-4:
Making
a gum
paste rose.

Tending to Frosting Roses

Making roses with frosting requires a certain level of comfort in handling a pastry bag, which I cover in Chapter 11. However, with just a bit of practice, you'll get the hang of it and be well on your way to making beautiful roses for your cakes.

I always encourage aspiring cake decorators to take a close look at a real rose before they begin piping one. Even though a frosting rose isn't the most life-like representation of the actual thing, getting an idea of a rose's natural form will help you create a sweet replica.

Nailing the form

The easiest way to start crafting a rose out of frosting is to affix a small marzipan cone onto a *flower nail,* which basically looks like a long nail with a large, flat head. Outfit a pastry bag with frosting (tinted to the color of rose you want) and a #104 icing tip, which has a big, curved end that tapers to a point at the bottom, follow these steps and check out Figure 12-5.

1. **Hold your pastry bag in your right hand so that the thin end of the icing tip faces upwards at a 45-degree angle, and hold the flower nail in your left hand.**

   If you're left-handed, hold the pastry bag in your left hand and the flower nail in your right.

2. **Mound some frosting at the top of the marzipan cone, and rotate the nail as you pipe around the cone to form the center of the rose.**

3. **Begin the petals by piping just below the rose's center, turning the nail as you make horseshoe-shaped motions with the pastry bag. Make three petals in this manner.**

4. **Add petals in odd numbers for succeeding rows. Make sure to begin each row in the middle of one of the existing petals to create an overlapping, blooming effect, and start each new row of petals below the preceding row.**

5. **When you've achieved the size and fullness you want, insert the nail into a piece of foam to keep it upright while the frosting dries and hardens, about 1 hour.**

Figure 12-5:
Piping a
frosting
rose.

If your rose looks smashed or flat, your initial cone may not have been high enough to accommodate the layers of petals. If the petals are too skinny, you may have held your frosting bag too close to the rose as you piped your petals, creating a more vertical look. If your petals are squiggly, you may have squeezed the bag too hard. Make the necessary adjustments when piping your next rose.

If you don't want your rose to have a marzipan center or you simply don't have any marzipan, put a 2-x-2-inch piece of wax paper on the nail head. Using the #104 icing tip and holding the pastry bag at a 90-degree angle, mound a cone of frosting on the wax paper, and then follow the regular steps covered in this section. After the rose hardens, you can lift it off the wax paper and place on your cake.

Skipping the nail and going straight for the cake

When you feel confident in your ability to maneuver a pastry bag to create a frosting rose, you can pipe roses directly on the cake. Start by piping a mound of frosting with the #104 tip. Then follow the steps in the preceding section for making a rose on a marzipan cone or wax paper.

Consider piping other kinds of flowers directly onto the cake, too. For instance, piping a sunflower or daisy on a cake is fairly easy. For a large daisy, use a #69 icing tip, which is curved. With the curved end facing up, start in the center of the cake and draw the frosting petal outward, releasing pressure on the pastry bag so that the petal narrows to a point. Repeat this all around the cake. With a #3 icing tip and frosting in a contrasting color, pipe small dots in the center of the daisy to resemble a stamen.

Make the process of piping flowers onto the cake easier by putting your cake on a turntable. It allows you to pipe the petals more fluidly and also spin the cake easily when determining the best placement for flowers.

Dipping into the Candy Jar

Whether your goal is to fashion a totally edible experience for your guests or simply to get creative with your decorating, candies and other edible foodstuffs provide limitless possibilities for making everything from a tile mosaic to train wheels, from jewels in a treasure chest to picnic paraphernalia on the beach.

I enjoy conceiving a design and then trying to figure out how to make it work using different and often unexpected edibles. For instance, I discovered a completely sweet and edible way to make a rose out of a lollipop surrounded by chewing gum petals. And sometimes I see a new kind of candy and find myself inspired to build a cake around that!

Try to look at candy and foodstuffs differently. You never know what could become the shape or foundation for a cake design you're working on!

Simple but sublime options

The easiest and most common decorations are sparkles, nonpareils, and jimmies. They jazz up a cake in a jiffy. But rather than just scatter them on top, give some form and function to your decoration by placing them inside a cookie cutter, pressing them into the sides of the cake, or using them to fill in a design. You also can use them to highlight or outline other designs.

Candies

In addition to adding color and interest to your cake, candies are great for spelling out numbers and names, or you can reinvent them as all sorts of objects and object parts. Consider these different applications of easy-to-find candies:

- **Peppermints** can be pinwheels.

- **Gumdrops** can be little caps and hats, blinking lights, or the centers of flowers. You can also roll them out and cut or form them into different shapes.

- **Necco wafers** can be a mermaid's scales or roof tiles on house.

- **Jawbreakers** can be beach balls.

- **Whips or shoestring licorice** can be animal whiskers, railroad tracks, or eyelashes.

- **Jelly beans** can be jewelry. They look especially good as the gemstone in a frosting ring or pendants on a necklace.

Online vendors such as www.groovycandies.com and www.candyware house.com offer an amazing variety of specialty candies; if you have an idea for a decoration but aren't sure what candy to use, they may have just the kind, color, and shape of candy you're looking for.

For a lot of cake designs, you don't need much candy to get the right look. If that's the case for your design, visit a bulk candy store to get just a few pieces of a favorite treat or just pick up the small packages or boxes of candy in a grocery store's check-out aisle.

Confections

In addition to candy, a plethora of other sweets offer a variety of options for your cake decorating adventures. Consider these possibilities for a scene or object you're trying to create:

- **Marshmallows** can be pillows or soapsuds.
- **Squares of gum** can be floor tiles or bases on a baseball field.
- **Wafer rolls** can be fences.
- **Doughnuts** can be tires or inner tubes.
- **Cotton candy** can be clouds or a ballerina's tutu.
- **Crushed cookies** can be dirt, sand, a racetrack, or a ball field.
- **Coconut** can be unruly hair (if it's tinted) or snow (if it's not).
- **Fruit-striped gum** can be fashioned into surfboards, snowboards, skis, pennants, and license plates.

Other treats

Don't stop at the stuff you find only in the sweet shop. The supermarket is overflowing with opportunities to craft and create. Consider these ideas:

- **Ice cream cones** can be castles, princess hats, or cornucopia shapes.
- **Pretzel sticks** can be ladders or flag poles.
- **Graham teddy bears, animal crackers, and gummi bears** add a lively animal presence to a scene.
- **Raw sugar or brown sugar** can be a beach shore.
- **Flavored gelatin** can be pool water (blue) or lava running down the side of a mountain (red).
- **Fruit tape** can be fashioned into a pet's collar, a necklace, or leather straps on a treasure chest.

Choosing Inedible Features

When it comes to outfitting a cake for an event, by no means are you limited to the packaged offerings of cake decorating supply companies. For some events, parties, and celebrations, you may find that the most appropriate cake decorations aren't edible — and that's okay. The great thing about cake decorating is that you're free to expand your horizons occasionally or often and include cake decorations that are for show rather than taste.

When you're working with inedible decorations, make sure that you clean them thoroughly before placing them on the cake. Also, if you know that children will be at the party or event, make sure that you (or the party's host or hostess) remove all inedible features before cutting and serving the cake.

Toy stores and toy departments at chain stores are brimming with items that make excellent cake toppers. For example, if your cake is for an aspiring action hero's birthday, check out action figures, which can serve double-duty as decorations and gifts. For one aquarium-themed cake I made, I was hard-pressed to find edible sea animal decorations. When I thought outside the box, I went to a toy store and found a large plastic tube filled with a variety of plastic whales, seals, octopuses, and fish.

Don't forget to check the Internet and flea markets for unconventional cake decorations. Consider wedding cakes: Some engaged couples insist on vintage cake toppers and won't settle for reproductions; the Internet is one of the best resources for such items. In another example, I was hired to make a cake with a 1960s-era home theme for a housewarming party, and the thought of creating furniture out of gum paste or frosting seemed tedious. Plus, I wasn't sure that the results would sparkle with a sense of fun. Instead, I found mod, colorful dollhouse furniture on the Internet, which turned the dessert into a conversation piece!

The only limit to embellishing your cake is your imagination: Gather inspiration from shapes, sizes, foods, treats, themes, and nature as you turn your creation into a one-of-a-kind design.

Part IV
Sweetening Life's Special Occasions

The 5th Wave   By Rich Tennant

"I was going to do a basketweave, but I know the bride and I think a chain link fence would be more appropriate."

In this part . . .

1t's always a wonderful time for cake, but this part looks at some of cake's most important starring roles: at birthdays, weddings, holidays, and showers . . . just to name a few. Fun-filled recipes and lip-smacking results are sure to have you celebrating before, during, and after the cake is served.

Chapter 13

Festive Cakes for Kids

A kid's birthday presents one of the most creative, exciting, and fulfilling occasions for designing and making a celebratory cake. A kid's face — along with those of friends and relatives — is sure to light up with happiness at the sight of a cake dedicated to the big event.

The cakes in this chapter begin with a simple, standard dimension. With shaping, embellishments, or both, I tell you how to amp up the architecture to take on the look of elaborate construction.

Conceiving the Perfect Birthday Cake

When you're faced with creating a cake for a child's or teen's birthday, it's important to remember that your cake becomes more special when it truly takes into account the personality of the birthday boy or girl. If the child is turning 1 or 2, it's likely that you're the one deciding the cake's theme. But an older child usually has a definite idea about the flavor and look of the cake he or she wants you to create.

In thinking about baking and decorating the perfect cake for the occasion, consider answers to these questions:

- ✔ What does the child like?
- ✔ What are his or her current interests, hobbies, or obsessions?
- ✔ What are his or her favorite colors?
- ✔ What is his or her favorite cake flavor?

Realistically, carving a cake into the shape of a favorite video game character, a football helmet, a train, a floral teapot, or a cheerleading pom-pom seems a bit intimidating. But you can always use a kid's current likes as a great jumping-off point. With a little ingenuity and a few common ingredients, you can turn the top of a cake into a computer screen or make a pom-pom out of icing.

Kids' cakes, more than any other themed cakes, challenge you to look at traditional circular and rectangular cake shapes in new and different ways.

Carving Cakes into the Shape of Numbers and Letters

One of the simplest ways to personalize a birthday cake is to carve the cake (or cakes) into the shape of

- ✔ **Numbers,** to announce the age of a birthday celebrant
- ✔ **Letters,** to form initials or entire names

With a sharp knife and a diagram to follow, you're on your way. Do assess the cake prior to taking your knife to it, though. For instance, you may want to use a toothpick or bamboo skewer to lightly mark your cutting lines. Figures 13-1 and 13-2 show how you can easily carve a cake up to be a number or a letter of the alphabet.

Use a long, sharp knife to make the cuts, and have a tall glass or pitcher of warm water nearby to dip your knife into if the cuts aren't coming out cleanly.

If the letters you're cutting have spaces such as the triangle in an A or the horseshoe-shaped ovals in a B, P, or R, don't worry about cutting out the space if you feel like you'll make a mess of it. You can insert all kinds of decorations in the space instead, such as little candies, squares of chocolate, or even real flower blooms.

You can personalize both number and letter cakes even more by

 ✔ Decorating them with favorite candies

 ✔ Sprinkling them with edible confetti

 ✔ Adding symbols of favorite hobbies or characters

 ✔ Creating special scenes with edible and inedible features

 ✔ Dressing them up with fresh flowers, fruits, or nuts

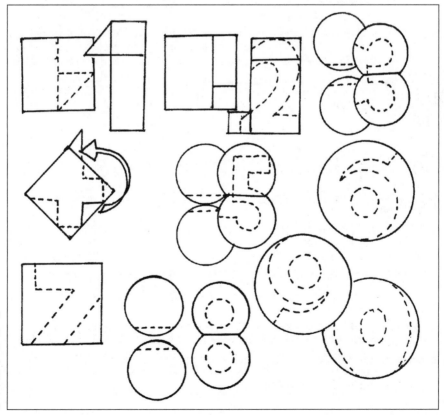

Figure 13-1:
Carve cakes into numbers 0 through 9.

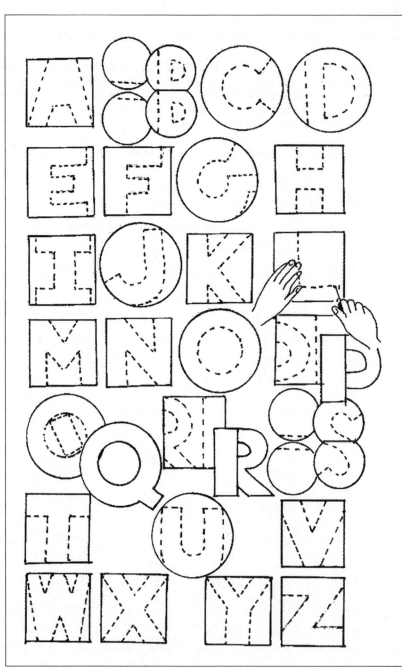

Figure 13-2:
Create
initials or
even spell
out a name
by cutting
cakes into
letters A
through Z.

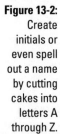

Theme Cakes Boys Go Nuts Over

In my experience making cakes for kids' birthday parties, I've noticed that boys tend to be partial to the same sorts of cake designs: Action heroes, moving vehicles like race cars, trucks, tractors, and motorcycles, and sports of all kinds usually get the greatest reactions from boys.

Following are two of my most favorite designs to make for boys' birthday parties.

Play Ball! Baseball Cake

A sheet cake provides the perfect playing field for several sports. In this recipe, with the help of some frosting "grass," chocolate candies, crushed graham crackers, and some action figures, you can transform an everyday cake into a baseball fan's paradise.

Note: Creating the grass and the blue ball trim around the base of the cake requires a great deal of frosting, so have a few batches ready for coloring.

Tools: 12-x-18-inch cake pan, #3 icing tip, #5 icing tip, #11 icing tip, #133 icing tip

Preparation time: 30 minutes

Baking time: 50 minutes plus 2 hours for cooling

Decoration time: 1 hour plus 2 hours for refrigeration

Yield: 32 servings

For the cake (recipe follows):

2 batches Cocoa Chocolate Cake batter (see Chapter 6)

1½ cups miniature chocolate chips

For the frosting:

3 batches Buttercream Frosting (see Chapter 8)

For the decorations:

Leaf green food coloring gel

Royal blue food coloring gel

Brown food coloring gel

½ cup graham cracker crumbs

40 foil-wrapped milk chocolate baseballs

5 baseball figurines (batter, fielder, pitcher, catcher, and umpire)

Making the Chocolate-Chocolate Chip Cake

1 Preheat the oven to 350 degrees F. Grease the cake pan and line the bottom with parchment paper. Set the pan aside.

2 Prepare the Cocoa Chocolate Cake batters as described in Chapter 6, and combine in large bowl. Stir in the miniature chocolate chips.

3 Pour the batter into the prepared pan. Bake for 50 minutes, or until a cake tester inserted in the center comes out with moist crumbs attached.

4 Let the cake cool in the pan for 20 minutes. Run a knife around the edges, and invert the cake onto a cooling rack to cool completely.

5 Level the top of the cake (see Chapter 7 for leveling instructions).

Decorating the cake

1 Cover the cake with a crumb coat (thin layer) of frosting, and refrigerate it for 1 hour.

2 Add a second coat of frosting, and refrigerate the cake again for 1 hour.

3 Divide and tint the remaining frosting as follows: 3 cups leaf green, 2 cups royal blue, and ½ cup brown. Leave the remaining frosting — approximately ¼ cup — untinted to use to pipe the bases.

4 On the cake's top surface, use a toothpick to make a wide V: Start in the top left-hand corner, draw a diagonal to the center of the bottom edge, and continue the line up to end in the top right-hand corner of the cake. (The inside of the V will be the bottom half of a baseball diamond; the area outside the V will be grassy areas.)

5 Use the #3 tip to outline the V with brown frosting.

6 Inside the V, use your smallest icing spatula to spread a very thin layer of untinted frosting. Sprinkle the graham cracker crumbs on this layer of frosting to form the infield, and pat them down.

7 If desired, pipe "Happy Birthday" or the boy's name inside the baseball half-diamond with the #5 tip. If you mess up, gently scrape off the piped frosting, sprinkle more graham cracker crumbs, and try again.

8 Outside the V, use the #133 tip to pipe grass. Starting in the top left-hand corner of the cake, pipe a giant L, moving the tip in a circular motion as you pipe. Pipe a smaller L inside the first L, and repeat the process until you've filled in that side of the baseball diamond. Repeat on the right-hand side of the V.

9 At the top two corners of the graham cracker infield and at the bottom of the V, use the #11 tip to pipe 1½-x-1½-inch white squares to mark first base, third base, and home plate.

10 Use the #11 tip to pipe little royal blue "balls" around the outside edge of the cake top, and around the base of the cake. (See Chapter 11 for tips on piping dots and ball shapes.)

11 Press the foil-wrapped chocolate baseballs into the vertical sides of the cake. If they don't stick, dab a little frosting on them before placing them on the cake.

12 Dab some of the remaining frosting on the undersides of the baseball figurines, and arrange them on the cake to create a winning scene like the one shown in Figure 13-3.

Figure 13-3: Your young baseball player is going to love the Play Ball! Baseball Cake.

Other ideas for boys

Trains, rockets, pirate ships, bugs, and dinosaurs are just a few other theme possibilities for cakes guaranteed to please boys.

Don't worry — you don't have to create a 3-D masterpiece. You can start out simply. Use miniature loaf pans to create the perfect size cakes for train cars, and affix cookies to the bottom edge of each miniature cake to look like wheels. If you're going for a bug theme, cover the top of a cake with crushed chocolate cookies to look like dirt, and scatter gummi bugs and worms for the full effect. You can even stick the worms into the cake so that they look like they're crawling out!

"Have a Good Year" Race Car Cake

Boys in particular always seem to appreciate a car that zooms. I've found this race car cake to be a favorite of boys from 5 to 15 years old — and piping the boy's age on the cake as the car's number makes it even more memorable! Before kids dive in, they're sure to linger and appreciate all the different treats that make up the wheels, spoiler, steering wheel, tailpipe, and headlights. This cake is shown on the second page of the color section.

Tools: *Two 9-x-13-inch cake pans, #5 icing tip, #7 icing tip, 8 toothpicks, 10-inch bamboo skewer, long serrated knife, ruler*

Preparation time: *30 minutes*

Baking time: *30 minutes plus 2 hours for cooling*

Decoration time: *90 minutes plus 2 hours for refrigeration*

Yield: *32 servings*

For the cake:

2 batches Delicious Yellow Cake batter (see Chapter 6)

For the frosting:

2 batches Buttercream Frosting (see Chapter 8)

For the decorations:

Royal blue food coloring gel

Electric blue food coloring gel

Red food coloring gel

7 strips striped sour fruit tape

4 chocolate doughnuts

5 small, vanilla yogurt–covered pretzels

4 chocolate kiss candies, wrapped

3 teaspoons honey

Lengthwise half of a 7-ounce chocolate bar

5 gumdrop candies (two yellow, two red, one green)

2 red licorice whips

12 miniature marshmallows

1 Prepare two Delicious Yellow Cakes following the recipe in Chapter 6. After the cakes are completely cool, level them (see Chapter 7). Apply a crumb coat (thin layer) of frosting to one of the cakes, and refrigerate it for 1 hour.

2 Place the second cake squarely on top of the first cake.

3 Create the raised area for the spoiler and the slanted top of the race car. On one of the short sides of the cake, measure 3½ inches in from the edge, and lightly score the top of the cake with a toothpick at that measurement. Measure ½ inch down from that point on each side of the cake, and insert a toothpick on each side of the cake at that measurement. With another toothpick, lightly score the cake diagonally from the first toothpick to the bottom of the top layer of cake. Repeat on the other side of the cake. Using the lines and toothpicks as your guide, use a serrated knife to cut away the top part of the cake. Discard the cake that comes off with the diagonal cut.

4 Apply a crumb coat of frosting to the cake's top layer and sides, and refrigerate the cake for at least 1 hour. (If possible, refrigerate the cake overnight for best results.)

5 Tint 2 cups of frosting with equal parts royal blue and electric blue food coloring gel. Frost the entire cake with the blue frosting.

6 Tint 1½ cups of frosting with red food coloring gel. Use the #7 tip to outline the lines and right angles of the car (the car's base, the rectangles of the car's sides, and the spoiler's resting place) with red frosting. Pipe a square in the center of the top of the car for the driver's seat. In front of the driver's seat, pipe a big red circle for the car's number to rest on.

7 Affix two fruit tape strips to the sides of the car. Affix two more strips so that they run down the top of the car. With red frosting, outline the strips on the top of the car.

8 Stick three toothpicks, evenly spaced, into each doughnut, and press them into the sides of the cake to look like wheels. Dab some white frosting on 4 yogurt pretzels and place them on the doughnuts to look like hubcaps.

9 Place the chocolate kisses — bottom-side out — side by side on the front end of the car so that the bottoms of the kisses form double headlights. With the #5 tip, pipe a red rectangle frame around each pair of headlights.

10 For the spoiler, spread honey on the back of 3 fruit tape strips and place them on the half chocolate bar. Trim the strips to size. Cut two 3-inch pieces of red licorice, and place a toothpick inside each piece. Gently push each toothpick into each side of the chocolate bar. Affix the spoiler to the back end of the car, where you cut away a portion of the cake in Step 3.

11 Decorate the ½-inch strip below the spoiler with the gumdrop candies.

12 For the tailpipe, cut a 2-inch piece of red licorice. Thread it onto the bamboo skewer, followed by the miniature marshmallows. Stick the bamboo skewer into the back of the race car, licorice end first.

13 For the steering wheel, gently press a yogurt-covered pretzel into the center square at the top of the cake.

14 Either pipe the birthday boy's age into the red circle made in Step 6, or gently press a number-shaped candle into the red frosting circle on the top of the car.

Theme Cakes for Little Ladies

As with cakes for boys, I've been struck by how girls tend to gravitate toward similar cake themes: Princesses, ballerinas, and dolls all make regular appearances on birthday party cake tables when girls are running the show.

Ballerina Stage Cake

Give a girl a birthday stage to dream on with this ballerina scene. You can even redress this stage for other themes; for example, use the same basic structure but showcase a doll show or a Broadway hit. This cake is shown on the first page of the color section.

Tools: *Three 9-inch round cake pans, #5 icing tip, #18 icing tip, 3½-inch round plastic lid, 3-inch round plastic lid*

Preparation time: *30 minutes*

Baking time: *40 minutes plus 2 hours for cooling*

Decoration time: *1 hour plus 2 hours for refrigeration*

Yield: *20 servings*

For the cake:

1½ batches Most Excellent White Cake batter (see Chapter 6)

For the frosting:

2 batches Buttercream Frosting (see Chapter 8)

¼ cup unsalted butter

2 cups sifted confectioners' sugar

1 teaspoon pure vanilla extract

¼ cup seedless strawberry preserves

2 tablespoons whole milk

For the decorations:

Soft pink food coloring gel

Burgundy food coloring gel

8 pink hard-shelled candies or jelly beans

10 plastic ballerina figurines

Making the cake

1 Preheat the oven to 350 degrees F. Grease and flour three 9-inch cake pans.

2 Prepare the Most Excellent White Cake batter according to the recipe in Chapter 6. Evenly distribute the batter among the three pans.

3 Place the pans in the oven, making sure that they have at least 1 inch of space in between them. Rotate them once during baking to make sure they bake evenly. Bake for 30 minutes, or until a cake tester inserted in the center comes out with moist crumbs attached.

4 Let the cakes cool in their pans for 15 minutes. Run a knife around the edges, and invert them onto cooling racks to cool completely.

5 After the cakes are completely cool, level them (see Chapter 7).

Preparing the Strawberry Buttercream Frosting

1 Combine the butter, confectioners' sugar, vanilla extract, and strawberry preserves in the bowl of an electric mixer. Beat on low speed until the mixture starts to come together.

2 Gradually add the milk, continuing to beat on low speed, until the frosting takes on a creamy consistency.

Decorating the cake

1 Cut one layer in half to form two semicircles. Line up the semicircles to form a semicircle of double thickness. Trim the cut sides to make them equal and uniform, if necessary. Sandwich the two semicircles together with strawberry buttercream frosting, and set the cake aside.

2 Spread strawberry frosting on the top of one of the other cake layers, and place the third cake layer on top.

3 Spread strawberry buttercream on half of the top of the double-layer cake. Place the semicircular cake on that frosting, arranging the semi-circular cake so that the rounded side aligns with the rounded edge of the two-layer cake. This forms the stage backdrop.

4 Spread a crumb coat (thin layer) of white buttercream frosting over the cake and the backdrop. Refrigerate for 1 hour.

5 Spread a second, thicker layer of white buttercream over the entire cake and backdrop. Refrigerate for 1 hour.

6 Divide and tint the remaining white buttercream as follows: 2 cups soft pink and 1½ cups burgundy.

7 Outfit a pastry bag with a #18 tip and pink buttercream, pipe pink stars around the base of the cake, the front edge of the stage, and the top of the backdrop. (Refer to Chapter 11 for further information on piping stars.)

8 Make the curtains on either side of the backdrop. On the left side of the backdrop, use a toothpick to mark where the drapes would fall on each side (refer to the photograph in the color insert); your mark should look like a letter K that begins three-quarters of the way down from the top of the backdrop. Using the #5 tip and the burgundy frosting, hold the pastry bag at a 45-degree angle and pipe curved thick lines along your mark to resemble the curtains' folds going inward and then curving down to the base of the stage. Pipe a band where the upper and lower arcs meet to resemble a tieback. Repeat the whole process on the right side of the backdrop (the shape on this side is a backwards K).

9 Make the cornice of curtains at the top of the stage. Divide the area into thirds and mark each point with a toothpick. Using the #5 tip and the burgundy frosting, pipe a large semicircle between the first and second marks, making the swag as low as you want the curtain to hang. Fill in the swag with increasingly smaller semicircles. Repeat in the other two thirds of the curtain area.

10 Using half of a 3½-inch round plastic lid as a guide, imprint semicircles around the vertical surface of the two-layer cake to form swags around the circumference of the cake.

Repeat with half of a 3-inch plastic lid, setting the smaller semicircles inside the bigger semicircles.

11 Use the #5 tip and burgundy icing to pipe along both sets of swag markings.

12 Press a pink hard-shelled candy or jelly bean into the meeting place of each set of swags.

13 Dab white frosting on the underside of the ballerina figurines. Arrange them in rows on the stage in front of the backdrop.

"You're a Real Doll" Cake

This cake never fails to impress kids and adults alike because the cake actually forms the dress of a fashion doll. You may find other versions of this recipe that call for shaving the cake in a certain way to form the dress or baking a cake in a round bowl (which I find makes for a hard cake to cut!) to get the right shape. I've found that a Bundt pan and two 9-inch round pans work beautifully to give me the shape I need.

Other than the doll, you don't need any other accoutrements to make this cake special — just lots of frosting. And be prepared to go through lots of it! Because it takes a bit of time to create all the rows of frosting that decorate the dress, this recipe calls for stiff buttercream frosting. After all, you don't want the dress pattern to droop while you work! This cake is shown on the first page of the color section.

Tools: *Two 9-inch round cake pans, 12-cup traditional Bundt pan, #30 icing tip, #35 icing tip, plastic wrap, long serrated knife*

Preparation time: *30 minutes*

Baking time: *45 minutes plus 2 hours for cooling*

Decoration time: *2 hours plus 2 hours for refrigeration*

Yield: *32 servings*

For the cake:

2 batches Delicious Yellow Cake batter (see Chapter 6)

For the frosting:

4 batches Stiff Decorator Frosting (see Chapter 8)

For the decorations:

11-inch tall fashion doll   *Orange food coloring gel*

Deep pink food coloring gel

1 Preheat the oven to 350 degrees. Grease and flour two 9-inch pans and the Bundt pan, and set aside.

2 Prepare two batches of Delicious Yellow Cake following the recipe in Chapter 6. Put one batch in the Bundt cake pan, and divide the other batch into the two 9-inch round pans.

3 Bake the two rounds according to the recipe, and bake the Bundt cake for 50 minutes. After the rounds are completely cool, level them (see Chapter 7). Let the Bundt cake cool completely, but don't level it.

4 Sandwich the two round layers together with a layer of frosting, and spread a layer of frosting on the top layer. Then place the Bundt cake on top. Apply a crumb coat (thin layer) of frosting to the entire cake, and refrigerate it for at least 1 hour. (If possible, refrigerate the cake overnight for best results.)

5 Using the open circle of the Bundt cake as your guide, cut a circle out of the center of the layered cake below. Pull this cake out (you may need to use a serving spoon). Reserve the scraps.

6 Frost the cake again with a thin layer of frosting, and refrigerate for 1 hour

7 Raise the doll's arms and wrap plastic around her arms and hair. Place the doll into the center hole of the cake. To keep her centered and in place, insert cut-up scraps from Step 5 in the open space. Frost around the doll to create a smooth, complete surface for your decorating.

8 Divide and tint the remaining frosting as follows: 4 cups deep pink and 4 cups orange.

9 Outfit a pastry bag with a #35 tip and pink frosting. Starting at the front of the doll, pipe three rows of pink stars (see Chapter 11) down the front of the cake dress. I like to pipe the rows at a diagonal to make it look like the dress is swirling, but if it's easier (or more preferable) for you, you can simply pipe in straight lines down the front of the dress.

10 Outfit a pastry bag with a #30 tip and orange frosting. Pipe three rows of orange stars on either side of the pink stripe. Continue piping three-row stripes around the dress, alternating the frosting color with each row.

11 Using the #30 tip, pipe a band of orange frosting around the doll's waistline.

12 Using the #35 tip and pink frosting, create the ruffled layers of the dress's bodice by piping horizontally around the doll, moving the tip up and down as you go. Finish by frosting pink straps over the doll's shoulders.

13 Remove the plastic wrap from the doll's head and arms.

14 To finish the dress, pipe a ring of orange stars or waves around the base of the cake.

Vary It!: Definitely play into your celebrant's favorite colors by selecting whichever color combination most appeals to her, or use colors that fit the party's theme. If you're not sure or have many favorite colors to choose from, play around with different combinations to determine which ones look best together.

Pleasing the Whole Gang: Cakes for Boys and Girls

Some cake ideas appeal to both boys and girls, so they're great for parties of mixed company. They also really come in handy when the birthday boy or girl is too young to have a say in what he or she wants the cake to look like!

Down on the Farm Cake

This darling cake is sure to be a hit with both city and country folk. (And the farm figurines make quick work of the decoration.)

Tools: *Two 9-inch round cake pans, decorating comb, #32 icing tip*

Preparation time: *30 minutes*

Baking time: *30 minutes plus 2 hours for cooling*

Decoration time: *40 minutes plus 1 hour for refrigeration*

Yield: *12 servings*

For the cake (recipe follows):

1 batch Most Excellent White Cake batter (see Chapter 6)

4 ounces semisweet chocolate squares, melted and cooled

For the frosting:

1 batch Chocolate Buttercream Frosting (see Chapter 8 for the variation on traditional buttercream)

For the decorations:

1 cup crushed chocolate graham sticks or crackers

¼ cup green jimmies

Plastic farm animals, tractor, barn, fence, trees

Making the Marble Cake

1 Preheat the oven to 350 degrees F. Grease and flour two 9-inch round pans and set aside.

2 Pour half the white cake batter into a medium bowl. Spoon all the melted chocolate into the batter, and gently swirl the two together with a rubber spatula. (Don't overmix or you'll end up with a chocolate batter and no marbling.)

3 Divide the remaining white batter evenly between the two pans. Then divide the marbled batter evenly over the white batter. Don't stir them together; the marbled batter will settle into the white batter.

4 Place the pans in the oven, making sure that they have at least 1 inch of space in between them. Rotate them once during baking to make sure they bake evenly. Bake for 30 minutes, or until a cake tester inserted in the center of each cake comes out with moist crumbs attached.

5 Let the cakes cool in their pans for 10 minutes. Run a knife around the edges, and invert them onto cooling racks to cool completely.

6 After the cakes are completely cool, level them (see Chapter 7).

Decorating the cake

1 Apply a crumb coat (thin layer) of frosting to the entire cake, and refrigerate it for 1 hour. Then apply a second coat of frosting to the cake.

2 Using a #32 tip and the chocolate buttercream, pipe shells (see Chapter 11) around the top rim of the cake. (The shells keep the chocolate crumb and jimmie decorations from falling off the edge.)

3 On the top of the cake, use a toothpick to mark a wavy line that divides the surface in half. On one side of the line, scatter the crushed chocolate pieces and press them down gently. On the other side of the line, sprinkle the green jimmies and press them down gently.

4 To create the scene, place the farm animals in the green grass, and set up the tractor, barn, and trees in the chocolate dirt.

5 Pull a decorator comb through the frosting on the sides of the cake, following the cake's circumference.

6 Use the #32 tip to pipe chocolate buttercream shells around the base of the cake.

Circus Roar Cake

This cake makes quite a statement and is likely to get little ones roaring. I like to use this cake, which utilizes two sizes of round pans, to showcase two cake flavors. For example, a 1-year-old can enjoy a lighter flavored cake in the 6-inch round while the adults enjoy a more decadent cake flavor in the bigger cake.

For this particular recipe, a luscious cinnamon flavor permeates the cake, from the Cinnamon Buttercream Frosting to the (optional) cinnamon-chip eyes to the pennant-shaped cinnamon gum that circles the cake.

Tools: *14-inch round cake pan, 6-inch round cake pan, #5 icing tip, #22 icing tip, #48 icing tip, #100 icing tip*

Preparation time: *30 minutes*

Baking time: *50 minutes plus 2 hours for cooling*

Decoration time: *90 minutes plus 1 hour for refrigeration*

Yield: *32 servings*

For the cake:

3 batches Delicious Yellow Cake batter (see Chapter 6)

For the frosting (recipe follows):

7 cups sifted confectioners' sugar

1 teaspoon cinnamon

¾ cup all-vegetable shortening

⅓ cup whole milk

For the decorations:

2 batches Stiff Decorator Frosting (see Chapter 8)

Dark brown food coloring gel

Warm brown food coloring gel

Egg yellow food coloring gel

¼ cup cinnamon or chocolate chips

8 sticks cinnamon-flavored chewing gum, cut into pennant-shaped triangles

2⅛-ounce box animal crackers

2 black licorice whips, cut into three 4-inch strips

Making the cake

1 Preheat the oven to 350 degrees F. Grease the two round pans and line them with parchment paper.

2 Fill both pans with cake batter, about ⅔ full, and place them in the oven. Bake the 6-inch cake for 20 minutes, and then remove it from the oven. Continue baking the 14-inch cake for another 30 minutes.

3 Let the cakes cool in their pans for 10 minutes. Run a knife around the edges, and invert them onto cooling racks to cool completely.

4 Level the 14-inch cake, but **do not level** the 6-inch cake. Let the domed shape of it remain as is.

Making the Cinnamon Buttercream Frosting

1 In the bowl of an electric mixer, add the cinnamon to the confectioners' sugar and combine by hand with a balloon whisk.

2 Turn the mixer on low, and add the shortening to the sugar mixture. Gradually add the milk until the frosting starts to come together.

3 Increase the mixer speed until the frosting becomes creamy. If necessary, add a few more drops of milk to achieve the desired consistency.

Decorating the cake

1 Apply a crumb coat (thin layer) of frosting to both cakes, and then place the small cake at the center bottom of the big cake. Refrigerate the cake for 1 hour.

2 Apply a second layer of cinnamon buttercream to the entire cake.

3 Divide and tint the Stiff Decorator Frosting as follows: 2½ cups dark brown, 1½ cups warm brown, and 1 cup egg yellow.

4 Using tip #5 and the dark brown frosting, pipe the outline of two lion eyes. From the inner corner of each eye, draw a line directly down and then up and over onto the 6-inch cake. Make the lines meet to form the lion's nose and snout, and then pipe the lion's mouth (it should look like a rounded W) from that meeting point.

5 Place cinnamon (or chocolate) chips inside the eyes to form the irises. Place chips in the snout on the small cake, too.

6 For the lion's mane, prepare three pastry bags of frosting as follows: one bag outfitted with a #22 tip and dark brown frosting; one bag outfitted with a #48 tip and warm brown frosting; and one bag outfitted with a #100 tip and yellow frosting.

7 Pipe the lion's mane by making thick curls (a mixture of stars and wavy lines; see Chapter 11) with the dark brown and filling in with wavy lines of warm brown. Use the yellow to add blonde highlights.

8 Stick the gum pennants into the frosting on the side of the cake, spacing them evenly all the way around.

9 Dab a bit of cinnamon frosting on the back of the animal crackers and stick them to the side of the cake in between the gum pennants.

10 Stick the licorice whips into the lion's jowls on the small cake to form his whiskers.

Vary It!: Pipe frosting around the base of the cake and stick powdered candy sticks vertically into the frosting at even intervals.

Getting Kids Involved

Kids have great imaginations, and their refreshingly fanciful ideas and love for certain confections can bring a lot to the table when you're facing the task of designing and making cakes. Never underestimate the whimsy that a child can add to your decorating projects.

When you get kids involved in cake design, baking, and decoration, be practical about their participation. Pick recipes that are simple, don't require much time, and let the kids get involved with stirring, scooping, placing, and other tactile endeavors.

Following are a couple general guidelines to consider as far as children in the kitchen are concerned. Obviously, unless they're older, you don't want them near the oven or stove top or working the mixer.

- ✔ At the age of 5, they usually can grease a pan, stir batter, and measure certain ingredients. In addition, they can add some decorations to the cake, like sprinkles or candies.
- ✔ By the age of 8, they can crack eggs, chop butter, and grate certain ingredients.

For your first attempt at baking and decorating with kids, consider using a box of cake mix as a foundation. The mix lets you can see what they're capable of and interested in while minimizing the work and mess!

Think of ways that, after the cake has come out of the oven and cooled, the kids can add their own creative flourishes to make it stand out or be their own. And make sure the kids see the end result. No matter how you think it looks, they'll be impressed that they made something that everyone will enjoy eating.

Before you begin baking with the kids in the kitchen, they need to understand the importance of being clean when preparing food. Take the following steps:

- ✔ Make sure that they've washed their hands thoroughly.
- ✔ Tie back long hair.
- ✔ Give them aprons to wear.
- ✔ Have damp dish cloths or wet paper towels (or even wet wipes) handy for them to keep their hands clean so they're less inclined to lick their fingers or smear ingredients together.

Trying Kid-Friendly Recipes

The recipes in this section enlist kids' help and let them actually be participants rather than on-lookers in the cake baking and decorating process. Follow these basic steps to get started:

1. **Get kids acclimated to the cake process by reading the recipe aloud from start to finish so that they know what's involved. If possible, let them see a picture of the finished product so that they know where they're headed.**

2. **Assemble all the ingredients and acquaint kids with each one.**

3. **Show kids the various equipment, from bowls and pans to measuring cups and spoons to decorating tools, that you'll be using to make the cake.**

4. **As you progress through a recipe, keep the kids tuned in by letting them see how each step brings the cake together. When possible, let them perform steps so that they have an even greater sense of accomplishment when the cake is finished.**

These recipes are really kid-friendly, but you may also consider letting imaginations run wild by baking one of the basic Most Excellent White, Delicious Yellow, or Cocoa Chocolate cakes (refer to Chapter 6 for recipes), mixing up some frosting, and letting the kids loose with an assortment of candies and other confections.

No-Bake Cherry Cake and Icing

This cake doesn't even require you to use the oven! It calls for already-prepared ingredients, so you and the kids can vary the taste to your liking with a variety of cake mixes, pie fillings, and fruits. So, if you or the kids don't like cherry filling, you can easily substitute blueberry, apple, strawberry, apricot, pineapple, or whatever else you find on your grocer's shelves!

Tools: *Microwaveable 12-cup traditional-shaped silicone Bundt pan, wooden spoon, balloon whisk*

Preparation time: *10 minutes*

Baking time: *12 minutes plus 5 minutes for cooling*

Decoration time: *10 minutes*

Yield: *12 servings*

For the cake:

18.25-ounce box white cake mix   *1 egg*

21-ounce can cherry pie filling

For the icing and decorations:

1 cup confectioners' sugar

1 tablespoon milk

Pink food coloring liquid

12 maraschino cherries

Making the cake

1 Combine all the cake ingredients in a medium bowl, and mix them together with a large wooden spoon. The batter will be quite thick.

2 Pour the batter into a microwave-safe Bundt pan. Microwave on high for 12 minutes. If your microwave doesn't have a rotating tray, turn the pan halfway around after 6 minutes.

3 Remove the cake from the microwave, and let it sit in the pan for 10 minutes. (It continues to bake for 5 minutes after coming out of the microwave.) Then turn it out onto a plate.

Preparing the icing

1 In a medium bowl, stir the confectioners' sugar with a balloon whisk to break up any lumps.

2 Add the milk and whisk it until the icing reaches a drizzling consistency. Add additional milk, a drop at a time, if you need to thin out the icing.

3 Stir in a few drops of pink food coloring.

Decorating the cake

1 Drizzle the icing over the cake.

2 Place the cherries around the top of the cake, either evenly spaced or arranged in clusters of two or three.

S'mores Cupcakes

No one can resist these campfire-inspired treats . . . particularly because they're in the form of cupcakes — the perfect single serving!

Tools: *Two 12-well muffin pans, cupcake liners*

Preparation time: *20 minutes*

Baking time: *20 minutes plus 30 minutes for cooling*

Decoration time: *15 minutes*

Yield: *24 servings*

18.25-ounce box yellow cake mix

½ cup vegetable oil

1⅓ cup water

3 eggs

2 cups miniature marshmallows

3 cups semisweet chocolate chips, divided

24 miniature graham cracker bears

1 Preheat the oven to 350 degrees F. Line the muffin pans with cupcake liners.

2 In a medium bowl, combine the yellow cake mix with the oil, water, and eggs. Beat on low speed for 30 seconds, and then on medium speed for 2 minutes, scraping down the sides of bowl twice during the mixing process.

3 Divide the batter evenly among the 24 wells. Place two marshmallows and a few chocolate chips into each well of batter.

4 Bake the cupcakes for 20 minutes, or until the tops spring back when touched lightly. Let the cupcakes cool for 30 minutes before removing them from the pan.

5 Place 1½ cups of chocolate chips in a 2-cup glass measuring cup, and microwave for about 1 minute on high, or until the chips are melted and smooth when stirred with a spoon. Let the chocolate cool slightly so that it's just warm to the touch.

6 Pour chocolate onto each cupcake. Before the chocolate hardens, place a graham cracker bear flat on the top of each cupcake.

Berry Good Crumble Cake

Kids love to smush food together, and as long as their hands are clean, I find nothing wrong with that . . . especially where this recipe is concerned. For the dough of this cake, they can use their fingers to crumble the butter into the flour and sugar and to press the dough into the bottom of the pan and onto the filling. However, the filling itself requires the help of an attentive adult!

Tools: *8-x-8-x-2-inch square cake pan, squeeze bottle*

Preparation time: *15 minutes*

Baking time: *40 minutes*

Decoration time: *10 minutes*

Yield: *9 servings*

For the cake:

1 cup granulated white sugar

4 cups flour

1 teaspoon baking soda

1 tablespoon cornstarch

1 cup unsalted butter, cut into ½-inch pieces

1 egg

1 teaspoon pure vanilla extract

For the filling:

3 cups fresh blueberries, raspberries, or strawberries, or a combination

½ cup granulated white sugar

1 teaspoon fresh lemon juice

3 tablespoons cornstarch

2 tablespoons butter

For the topping:

½ cup seedless raspberry or boysenberry preserves

1 Preheat the oven to 375 degrees F. Grease the square cake pan and set it aside.

2 In a large bowl, combine the sugar, flour, baking soda, and cornstarch. Mix in the butter chunks. Let the kids use their fingertips to distribute the butter into the dry ingredients, or use a pastry cutter to achieve a crumbly consistency.

3 Add in the egg and vanilla, and mix the dough (hands are great tools for this) until it just comes together. Set aside.

4 In a medium saucepan over medium heat, combine the berries, sugar, lemon juice, cornstarch, and butter. Cook for 2 minutes, stirring frequently. The mixture should thicken slightly.

5 Press half of the dough into the bottom of the cake pan. Pour the fruit mixture over it. Let the mixture cool before pressing the remaining dough on top of the fruit mixture.

6 Bake for 40 to 45 minutes, or until the crumble is golden brown.

7 Heat the preserves in the microwave for 30 seconds until they liquefy and are easily stirred with a spoon. Spoon the liquid into a squeeze bottle.

8 After removing the cake from the oven, squeeze the preserves on the top of the crumble in a decorative pattern.

Chapter 14

Cakes for Grown-Ups

. . . .

In This Chapter

▶ Thinking about what adults enjoy in a cake

▶ Creating cakes just for women and just for men

▶ Decorating cakes that appeal to everyone

. . . .

Recipes in This Chapter

▶ Jewelry Cake

▶ Luscious Luau Cake

▶ Vegas, Baby! Cake

▶ Golf Game Cake

▶ Rock Star Cake

Why should kids have all the fun at parties? Grown-ups enjoy delicious and well-decorated theme cakes just as much as the younger set.

Cakes designed for grown-ups require a little more imagination and preparation than cakes for children or teens simply because adults are more likely to pay attention to the details and look a little longer before digging in. But the results can be more impressive, too. Just paying attention to a few key details can put you well on your way to crafting a wonderfully sweet and special party centerpiece. In this chapter, I explore some traditional possibilities and more unconventional designs . . . all in the spirit of a grown-up celebration that really takes the cake!

Gearing Up for Grown-Up Cakes

A cake can be the ultimate, satisfying conclusion to a grown-up's party . . . especially if you take into account the guest of honor's personality and the party's theme when planning your cake decoration.

Further, adults are particularly honored when someone bakes and decorates a cake just for them. Kids love cake and gooey frosting, but adults are truly appreciative of not only the cake's taste but also the time, effort, and creativity involved in making it.

Brainstorming a design

As you start thinking about decorating the perfect cake for a grown-up's party, I recommend that you consider the following questions as you conceive the design:

- ✔ What kind of birthday party or special event will the cake be served at?
- ✔ How many people will be enjoying your creation?
- ✔ Who's invited to the party? Is it strictly for adults, or will kids be there too?
- ✔ If it's a dinner party, what kind of cuisine will be served?

Your answers to these questions can help you determine the size, shape, and decorations for the cake. Further, if the party is mostly for adults, you can consider branching out with a cake that embraces more adult flavors, such as coffee, liqueur, exotic fruit, or interesting spices.

Taking personality into account

In addition to the party's theme and logistics, consider what specifically suits the celebrant and the celebration. For example, an outdoors-themed party can mean camping for one, surfing for someone else, and mountain climbing for another. You want your cake to be spot on, so you have to look at the party and the guest of honor from all angles.

To really personalize your cake, do some digging to find out the celebrant's favorite flavors. Don't just make a strawberry cake because you think it will look pretty when you cut into it. Get a sense of the kinds of cake the celebrant really loves, and also find out if any ingredients are off-limits.

Simple Letter and Number Designs

The recipes in this chapter tell you how to make some impressive cakes for men and women, but you also can depend on some popular standbys — involving letters and numbers — to dress up a cake design.

As you become more comfortable in your cake baking and decorating, I encourage you to strike out beyond the tried and true. If you opt for the letter or number route (which is particularly popular for birthdays), do try to infuse your celebrant's personality into the cake decorating somehow, either with favorite colors or flavors or tokens of interest.

Playing the alphabet game

Similar to kids' cakes, you can make a grown-up's cake special by shaping it into letters to form a monogram, first name, last name, or nickname. Another option is to cut a cake or cakes into the number of the person's age for a milestone birthday such as 30, 40, or 50.

Check out Chapter 13 for more on how to carve cakes into letters and numbers and personalize them even more with a variety of adornments.

Piping monograms and initials

Carving cakes into letters and numbers is fun, but you should never underestimate the class, simplicity, and ease of scripting letters on top of a birthday cake. In the same vein as spelling out a name in cake shapes, you can pipe a single initial or entire monogram in frosting on top of a cake.

You can go fancy or keep it crisp and clean. For ideas and inspiration, check out the fonts in your computer's word processing program or type "fonts" into your favorite Internet search engine and browse the results. With a little practice and patience, you should be able to mimic the styles you find.

To script a name, monogram, or message, follow these steps:

1. **Use a ruler to mark on parchment paper the dimensions of the cake pan you plan to use, or — better yet — trace around the pan to provide an accurately sized space.**

    Make a few copies of this template so that you have plenty of practice space.

2. **In the available space, write out what you want to put on the cake, taking care with the size and spacing of your letters.**

3. **If it's your very first time scripting, practice piping with actual frosting.**

    Outfit a pastry bag with a #5 or #7 tip, and put ½ cup of frosting in the bag. (You can also use shortening to save your frosting for the main event.) Trace over your writing with your pastry bag, taking care to make the lines smooth and consistent.

4. **When you're confident in your piping, use a toothpick to delicately trace your strokes on the cake itself, using your practice sheet as a guide.**

5. **With the pastry bag outfitted with a #5 or #7 tip and the frosting you want on your final cake, follow the toothpick strokes.**

Designing Cakes Ladies Swoon Over

For special occasions with a female guest of honor, you may find that you have so many — maybe too many — cake design choices to consider and pick from.

In devising an idea and designing the cake, be cognizant of the celebrant's favorite color. Most men don't pay much attention to a cake's color, but you'll be amazed at how many women will marvel when you remember and incorporate the wild hues or soft pastels they're crazy about. (Some tend to have passionate, averse reactions to colors they don't like as well, so that's another good reason to keep color in mind!)

The Jewelry Cake and Lucious Luau Cake that follow are design concepts that have been vastly appealing at many women's parties I've been hired to provide cakes for. I give you colors and other design ideas for these cakes, but you can easily personalize and tailor each of the cakes to your particular celebrant or celebration.

Jewelry Cake

This cake benefits from a sparkly look and a clever saying. Most women I know are very fond of jewelry, and this is a cake that's as fun to look at as it is to eat. And with the right decorations, which are fairly easy to find, the decoration process moves very swiftly. This cake is shown on the third page of the color section.

Tools: *9-inch round cake pan, 14-inch round cake pan, #7 icing tip*

Preparation time: *30 minutes*

Baking time: *45 minutes plus 2 hours for cooling*

Decoration time: *25 minutes plus 1 hour for refrigeration*

Yield: *32 servings*

For the cake (recipe follows):

3 batches modified White Velvet Cake batter (see Chapter 6)

Pink food coloring gel

For the frosting

3 batches Buttercream Frosting (see Chapter 8)

For the decorations:

4 large chunks pink rock candy (side by side, they should measure 14 inches)

4 large chunks green rock candy (side by side, they should measure 14 inches)

1 clear rock candy stick

Deep pink food coloring gel

Making the Pink Velvet Cake

1 Preheat the oven to 350 degrees. Grease and flour the round pans.

2 Prepare the cake batters as described in Chapter 15. Combine the batters into one bowl, and mix in pink food coloring gel (as much as is needed for your desired color).

3 Divide the batter into the pans, filling each one about ⅔ full, and bake for 45 minutes, or until a toothpick inserted in the center of each one comes out with moist crumbs attached.

Decorating the cake

1 After the cakes have cooled, level them (see Chapter 7). Apply a crumb coat (thin layer) of frosting to both cakes, and refrigerate them for 1 hour.

2 Frost the 14-inch layer completely. Place the 9-inch layer on top of the 14-inch layer, toward the back of the cake so that the smaller cake creates what looks like a neckline on the larger layer.

3 Frost the smaller layer.

4 Nestle the pink and green rock candy jewels end to end against the edge of the smaller layer, alternating them to form a two-color necklace. Leave a small space in the exact center of the candy necklace and at each end (on either side of the small layer).

5 In the space in the center of the necklace, gently press the stick of clear rock candy into the cake, letting the clear crystal portion dangle like a pendant.

6 Mix deep pink food coloring gel into 2 cups of frosting.

7 Using the #7 tip, pipe dots around the edge of the top layer of cake. Pipe dots extending from both ends of the rock candy necklace, and then pipe dots around the base of the bottom cake layer.

8 Write "Have a Gem of a Birthday," "You're a Gem!," or the guest of honor's name or initials on the top cake layer.

Luscious Luau Cake

The lady of the hour doesn't have to be Gidget, it doesn't have to be summertime, and you don't have to be in Maui to love this cake. It's a perfect complement to so many different kinds of theme parties, having been served at beach blanket bingo, luau, surf 'n' sand, tropical, and pool party themes with rousing success. The finished cake is shown in Figure 14-1.

Tools: *12-x-18-inch cake pan, #11 icing tip, bamboo skewer*

Preparation time: *30 minutes*

Baking time: *45 minutes plus 2 hours for cooling*

Decoration time: *1 hour plus 1 hour for refrigeration*

Yield: *32 servings*

For the cake (recipe follows):

3 batches modified Delicious Yellow Cake batter (see Chapter 6)

4½ cups coconut milk, divided into 1½-cup portions

3 cups drained, crushed pineapple, divided into 1-cup portions

For the frosting:

3 batches modified Buttercream Frosting (see Chapter 8)

3 teaspoons cherry extract

For the decorations:

1½ cups packed light brown sugar

Royal blue food coloring gel

2 plastic palm trees

3 plastic beachgoers

3 plastic surfboards (or 3 pieces of fruit stripe gum cut into a similar shape)

3 hula dancer cupcake toppers

3 toothpicks

3 sugar Tiki masks

Birthday candle

4 miniature pretzel sticks

2 gummi fish (preferably clownfish)

1 gummi shark

4 gummi rings (for inner tubes)

1 gummi lobster

Making the Piña Colada Cake

1 Preheat the oven to 350 degrees. Grease and flour the cake pan.

2 Prepare the cake batters as described in Chapter 6, but in each batch, substitute 1½ cups coconut milk for the whole milk, and fold the pineapple into the batter before pouring it into the pan.

3 Pour the batter into the pan, and bake for 45 minutes, or until a toothpick inserted in the center comes out with moist crumbs attached.

Making the Maraschino Cherry Frosting

1 Prepare the frosting as described in Chapter 8, but in each batch, substitute cherry extract for pure vanilla extract.

Decorating the cake

1 After the cake has cooled, level it (see Chapter 7). Apply a crumb coat (thin layer) of frosting to the cake, and refrigerate it for 1 hour.

2 Frost the cake completely. Drag the bamboo skewer horizontally across the top of the cake, approximately one-third of the way down, to make a shoreline.

3 To create the sandy coastline, cover the upper third of the cake (including the sides) with brown sugar, pressing it lightly into the cake.

4 Mix blue food coloring gel into 3 cups of frosting until you achieve a color that looks like water. Using a large icing spatula, cover the bottom two-thirds of the cake with the frosting. Make ridges and swirls to resemble ocean waves.

5 Arrange the palm trees, beachgoers, surfboards, and hula dancers on the brown sugar beach. Stick toothpicks into the Tiki masks, and position them around the hula dancers.

6 Place a birthday candle in the brown sugar, and arrange the pretzel sticks around the candle so that they lean in toward each other like a camp fire. Be sure to leave enough space above the candle so that the pretzels don't catch fire when you light the birthday candle!

7 Place the gummi fish, shark, and rings in the ocean, and put a lobster on the shoreline.

8 Outfit a pastry bag with the #11 tip and ½ cup white frosting. Pipe a series of wave caps and foam on the blue ocean.

9 Use the skewer to write a message, such as "LUAU!" in the brown sugar sand.

Tip: *You can find many of the inedible plastic decorations for this cake at cake decorating Web sites (such as those listed in Chapter 21), and on the cake decorating aisle at national craft chains. For the gummi candies, check candy shops in your local shopping mall and also online candy retailers.*

Other ideas for women's cakes

When it comes to cakes designed for women, you have a host of ideas at your disposal. For instance, flowers are always a great choice for a woman. If you can find out the guest of honor's favorite varieties, you can incorporate fresh, unsprayed flowers on the top of the cake or create them out of frosting (check out possibilities in Chapter 11) or gum paste (which I discuss in Chapter 13). Dresses, shoes, hats, garden items, birds, polka dots, teacups, and ribbons are other design ideas that you can use to delicious, beautiful, and feminine effect.

Figure 14-1:
Break out the Don Ho records when you serve the Luscious Luau Cake.

Winning Over Men

You may feel a bit challenged where men and cake are concerned because, whereas themes for women's cakes may seem abundant, men's tastes may strike you as limited (but you really just need to brainstorm a bit). And, granted, far less attention has been given to cakes for men: You may see bakery display cases chock-full of cakes that would be perfect for a woman's party, but those for men are lacking or missing completely! But rest assured, the recipes in this chapter will satisfy even the hardest-to-please or impress . . . and foster your creativity in coming up with your own concept, too.

Consider the celebrant's particular interests, personality, and favorite flavors — as well as dislikes that you should avoid — to create a memorable decorated cake.

Other ideas for men's cakes

For cakes for men, consider cutting and shaping layer cakes into a yacht, cabin cruiser, sailboat, or airplane. Also, you can use decorations to create the theme, such as:

✔ Cigars and bars: Incorporate chocolate cigars and pipe frosting in the shape of martini glasses

✔ Barbecues: Use licorice strips for the grill and frosted cupcake tops for burgers

Vegas, Baby! Cake

When each of the kids in my family turned 21, my parents treated us to a trip to Las Vegas, where we came face to face with the almost kaleidoscopic sight of chips, tokens, coins, tumbling sets of dice, decks of cards, and spinning wheels. That perspective inspired this cake, which is (not surprisingly) a consistent favorite of men and ideal for poker-themed parties and casino nights. The rum-flavored cake batter adds another grown-up element to the cake. You can see a version of this cake in Figure 14-2.

Tools: *14-inch round cake pan, #3 icing tip, #5 icing tip, #7 icing tip, #11 icing tip*

Preparation time: *30 minutes*

Baking time: *45 minutes plus 2 hours for cooling*

Decoration time: *1¼ hours plus 1 hour for refrigeration*

Yield: *24 servings*

For the cake (recipe follows):

3 batches modified Delicious Yellow Cake batter (see Chapter 6)

½ cup dark rum

For the frosting:

3 batches Buttercream Frosting (see Chapter 8)

For the decorations:

Red red food coloring gel

Black food coloring gel

Lemon yellow food coloring gel

Sky blue food coloring gel

14 foil-wrapped dark chocolate poker chips (3 inches in diameter)

8 mint truffle chocolate playing cards (measuring 1⅜ x 2 inches)

14 gold foil-wrapped chocolate coins (3 inches in diameter)

12 dice lollipops, various colors

45 3-inch lengths black licorice

45 3-inch lengths red licorice

Making the Rum Cake

1 Preheat the oven to 350 degrees. Grease and flour the round pan.

2 Prepare the cake batters as described in Chapter 6, but in each batch, combine the milk with ½ cup dark rum before adding that mixture to the batter alternately with the flour mixture.

3 Pour the batter into the pan, and bake for 45 minutes, or until a toothpick inserted in the center comes out with moist crumbs attached.

Decorating the cake

1 After the cake has cooled, level it (see Chapter 7). Apply a crumb coat (thin layer) of frosting to the cake, and refrigerate it for 1 hour.

2 Frost the cake completely. Using a toothpick, create the iconic Vegas sign by making a horizontal diamond-shape that measures 5 inches across the middle. Create seven circles at the top of the sign in which to write "WELCOME." Underneath the circles, write "TO" in block letters and script "Fabulous" all on one line. Sketch the words "LAS VEGAS" in the exact center of the sign, and then center "Nevada" underneath that.

3 Above the sign and a bit to the left, sketch an eight-point star by forming one large cross and then skewering it with a second cross set at a 45-degree angle. Sketch a straight line radiating from each point of the diamond-shaped sign to the edge of the cake, dividing the cake into four quadrants.

4 Divide and tint the frosting as follows: 2 cups red, 2 cups black, ½ cup lemon yellow, and ½ cup sky blue.

5 Outfit a pastry bag with a #3 tip and black frosting; outline the seven circles at the top of the sign. Outfit another bag with a #5 tip and red frosting; pipe the "WELCOME" letters inside the black circles.

6 Remove the #5 tip from the red frosting bag, clean it, and place it in a pastry bag with the sky blue frosting; pipe "to Fabulous" and "Nevada," following your sketch.

7 Refit the red frosting bag with a #7 tip, and write "LAS VEGAS." Also pipe over your sketch of the star above the sign.

8 Outfit a pastry bag with a #11 tip and yellow frosting; outline the sign.

9 Remove the #11 tip from the yellow frosting bag, clean it, and place it in the black frosting bag (replacing the #3 tip that was in the black bag). Pipe over the lines radiating out from the sign, and outline the top edge of the cake.

10 Place the multicolored poker chips in the upper right quadrant, the chocolate playing cards in the lower right quadrant, the gold foil coins in the upper left quadrant, and the lollipop dice in the left lower quadrant. Press these decorations gently into the frosting.

11 To create the feel of a roulette wheel on the outside edge of the cake, arrange alternating vertical columns of three black and three red licorice segments. Press the licorice gently into the frosting.

12 Using the #11 tip, pipe a band of black frosting around the bottom edge of the cake.

Tip: You can find many Vegas-style candies and other edible decorations (such as gummi versions of cards, casino chips, and dice) online at www.candywarehouse.com *and* www.vegasimage.com. *In addition check out candy shops in your local shopping mall or online counterpart such as* www.sweetfactory.com.

Figure 14-2:
Your guests
will be
"all in"
when they
see the
Vegas,
Baby! Cake.

Golf Game Cake

You'll be on course to make a golfing guy feel above par with this cake, which draws on some delicious edible treats for the sand trap, water, greens, and even the golf ball! This cake is shown on the third page of the color section.

Tools: *12-x-18-inch cake pan, #7 icing tip, Mason jar or 16-ounce plastic container with a tight lid, 6-inch round cookie cutter or biscuit cutter*

Preparation time: *30 minutes*

Baking time: *45 minutes plus 2 hours for cooling*

Decoration time: *45 minutes plus 1 hour for refrigeration*

Yield: *32 servings*

For the cake (recipe follows):

3 batches modified Delicious Yellow Cake
batter (see Chapter 6)

6 cups firmly packed light brown sugar

2¼ cups smooth peanut butter

1½ cups unsalted butter, at room temperature
and cut into ½-inch pieces

For the frosting:

3 batches Buttercream Frosting (see
Chapter 8)

For the decorations:

Leaf green food coloring gel

1 cup raw sugar

1.5-ounce tube royal blue gel icing

3 cups flaked sweetened coconut

¼ cup green jimmies

24 leaf-shaped spearmint gumdrops

25 3-inch pretzel sticks

3-inch strip red sour fruit tape

Coconut-flavored jelly bean

Plastic golfer figurine

Making the Peanut Butter Cake

1 Preheat the oven to 350 degrees. Grease and flour the cake pan, and set aside.

2 Prepare the cake batters as described in Chapter 6, but in each recipe, substitute light
brown sugar for white granulated sugar and substitute ¾ cup smooth peanut butter
plus ½ cup unsalted butter for the unsalted butter called for in the original recipe.

3 Pour the batter into the pan, and bake for 45 minutes, or until a toothpick inserted in
the center comes out with moist crumbs attached.

Decorating the cake

1 After the cake has cooled, level it (see Chapter 7). Apply a crumb coat (thin layer) of
frosting to the cake, and refrigerate it for 1 hour.

2 Mix green food coloring gel into 2 cups of frosting until you achieve a color that looks
like grass. Frost the cake completely.

3 Use a toothpick to sketch a loose figure eight shape for the green of the course.

4 In the upper right corner of the cake (outside the curve of the figure eight), use a small
serving spoon to dig out a kidney-shaped patch. Repeat in the lower right corner of the
cake.

5 Fill in one patch with raw sugar to create a sand trap. Fill the other patch with blue icing
gel to create a water feature.

6 Put the flaked coconut into the glass jar or plastic container with a few drops of green
food coloring gel. Put the lid on tightly and shake to color the coconut. Press the colored coconut around the figure eight–shaped green and around the sand trap and water
feature. Press coconut onto the sides of the cake, too.

7 Place the cookie (or biscuit) cutter in the center of the green, and shake green jimmies into the center of the cutter. Lightly press them into place before carefully lifting the cutter.

8 To make the golf course trees, make a small hole in the bottom of the spearmint leaves with a bamboo skewer. Fit each leaf onto a pretzel stick, and insert the pretzels into the cake all around the course.

9 To make the flagstick, wrap the red fruit tape around one end of the remaining pretzel stick. Clip slanted ends from both the top and bottom of the fruit tape to form a sideways V-shape for a pennant.

10 Press the coconut jelly bean into the green jimmies, and position the golfer figurine next to it.

Pleasing Both Men and Women

Sometimes you need a party cake concept that's appropriate for either a man or a woman. In this section, I share ideas for cakes that are fun and festive for any birthday or party honoree.

Rock Star Cake

I've found that feeling like a rock star knows no gender bounds. It makes no difference whether the celebrant dreams of fronting a band or even knows how to play a guitar. Simply toasting and treating him or her like a rock star is what matters.

With regards to this cake's decorations, everyone always has fun trying to figure out what all the pieces of the electric guitar actually are. And don't skimp on the candy rocks — cake eaters love their double meaning. The cake itself — a confetti variation on the Most Excellent White Cake recipe — is appropriately celebratory as well.

Tools: *12-x-18-inch cake pan, #7 icing tip, #11 icing tip, toothpicks*

Preparation time: *30 minutes*

Baking time: *45 minutes plus 2 hours for cooling*

Decoration time: *1¼ hours plus 30 minutes for freezing and 1 hour for refrigeration*

Yield: *32 servings*

For the cake (recipe follows):

3 batches modified Most Excellent White
Cake batter (see Chapter 6)

1½ cups multicolor nonpareils

For the frosting:

3 batches Buttercream Frosting (see
Chapter 8)

For the decorations:

Red food coloring gel

Deep purple food coloring gel

Lemon yellow food coloring gel

2 sticks black chewing gum (such as Black
Black), cut in half lengthwise to create four
thin strips

16 red small, round hard candies

12 yellow small, round hard candies

9 purple gumdrops

6 purple small, round hard candies

6 18-inch lengths black shoestring licorice

4 cups candy rocks

Making the Confetti Cake

1 Preheat the oven to 350 degrees. Grease and flour the cake pan, and set aside.

2 Prepare the white cake batters as described in Chapter 6, but for each recipe, fold in ½ cup multicolored nonpareils as the last step.

3 Pour the batter into the pan, and bake for 45 minutes, or until a toothpick inserted in the center comes out with moist crumbs attached.

Decorating the cake

1 After the cake has cooled, level it (see Chapter 7). Then, cut it according to the directions in Figure 14-3 to create the pieces that will form the guitar. Freeze the pieces for 30 minutes.

2 Put the pieces together using frosting to connect the joints (the neck to the body). Apply a crumb coat (thin layer) of frosting to the entire guitar, and refrigerate it for 1 hour.

3 Use a toothpick to sketch flames licking across the body of the guitar.

4 Divide and tint the frosting as follows: 1 cup red, 2 cups purple, and ½ cup yellow.

5 Spread the red frosting inside the flames sketched in Step 3. Frost the rest of the body of the guitar, including the sides, with purple frosting.

6 Outfit a pastry bag with a #11 tip and yellow frosting. Outline the flames by piping yellow where the purple and red frostings meet, and add jagged accent strokes to the red flames. Also, pipe seven horizontal lines along the guitar neck to form the frets.

7 Starting at the base of the neck, place four black chewing gum strips on the guitar body about ¾ inch apart. These strips form three pickups and the bridge of the guitar.

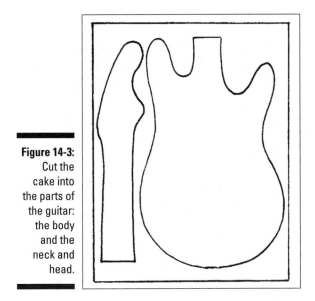

Figure 14-3:
Cut the cake into the parts of the guitar: the body and the neck and head.

8 Dab frosting on the back of 12 of the red hard candies and 12 of the yellow hard candies, and gently press six candies onto each piece of gum.

9 Place two purple gumdrops on the bottom right portion of the guitar body to look like tone controls. Place toothpicks into each of six gumdrops and stick them into the left-hand side of the head to be the tuning pegs. Place the last gumdrop on the bottom side of the guitar to be the strap holder.

10 Turn the six 18-inch lengths of shoelace licorice into guitar strings by placing them in between the hard candies (add a dab of frosting to the end of the licorice to make it stick to the chewing gum strip at the bottom of the body) and running them up the neck of the guitar.

11 Place the six purple hard candies at the top of the head to be the tuning knobs of the pegs. Dab frosting on each candy to stick it on top of a licorice string.

12 Place the remaining four red hard candies in between the two center strings to be the fret guides.

13 Press the candy rocks into the frosting on the sides of the cake, all the way around the guitar.

14 Outfit the yellow frosting bag with a #7 tip, and outline the body of the guitar by piping along the top edge. A version of this cake is shown in Figure 14-4.

Figure 14-4:
Rock on!

Following the invitation

Sometimes, the best ideas for a grown-up cake come from the party invitation itself. Several times, I've relied on the invitation to influence a cake's colors or design elements. After all, a party invitation is a great window into the theme, tenor, and scope of the celebration.

You can either mimic the actual design on the invitation or, if that seems daunting, just use it for inspiration. If you want to use the invitation itself for the design, enlarge it on a copy machine so that you can faithfully adapt it to the size of your cake. For a different look, consider re-creating only a portion of the invitation; for instance, if the invitation has a palm tree on it among other things, make a stencil out of the palm tree and focus your decorations on that.

Looking like the honoree

It may sound like a strange idea, but you can use a man's or woman's face as part of your cake design. It's not that difficult to pipe a pretty generic face on a cake, and then you just embellish it to suit your celebrant's visage or personality.

A colored copy you can eat?

I tend to favor frostings, icings, and embellishments when decorating a cake, but I have to admit that one newfangled invention is pretty handy. *Kopykake* sheets are basically edible color copies of your choice of artwork that you apply to cake surfaces for a quick and easy decoration solution. You can find them at most cake supply stores or online. You can either print an image yourself with a printer outfitted with edible color inks or have a cake supply shop do it. (The edible inks don't work with all printers, so you'll need to make sure yours is compatible or invest in one that is.) If you go with a sheet like this, I recommend that you enhance your cake with handcrafted adornments or it may come off as "manufactured" rather than decorated!

Visit www.kopykake.com to see firsthand if this decoration technique is a fit for your occasion and cake.

People usually have one or two very defining characteristics that you can exaggerate for a cake decoration: Long curly black hair can be strands of shoestring licorice, or bright blue eyes can be made with frosting, a rolled-out gumdrop, or crushed sour candies.

You can also use a face on a cake to show off an honoree's personality. For a birthday cake I was hired to make for a comedic actress, her husband requested that I let his wife's sense of humor somehow shine through in the decoration. I outlined her profile, and then — at the top of her head where her hair would be — I used Swiss candies shaped like fruits to give her a Carmen Miranda–style headdress.

Shaping up other cakes

Some adults love animals just as much as most kids do, so why not make a grown-up cake special by carving it into an animal shape? For example, think astrological signs: A lion-shaped cake like the one in Chapter 13 would work for a Leo birthday, and a fish-shaped cake would be ideal for a Pisces. It seems like butterflies are always in vogue for some ladies. And some people just have an affinity for certain animals: Let's face it, cakes in the shape of giraffes, penguins, or favorite dog breeds are fun for the guests of honor and conversation pieces for everyone else.

Like the other shapes of cakes covered in this chapter, you can embellish animal-shaped cakes with candies, coconut, gumdrops, and licorice strings.

Chapter 15

Showering Brides and Moms-to-Be

A s the excitement builds for couples who are getting married or expecting a child, showers usually feature cake in a starring role. For such a momentous occasion, not just any cake will do. That's why, in this chapter, I walk you through some cake decorating techniques for embellishing crowd-pleasing cakes that bring a "Wow!" factor to bridal and baby showers.

Along with sharing some helpful techniques, I show you how to make some common themes and treatments extra special and create a memorable confection that ideally anticipates the big event.

Analyzing the Occasion

When faced with designing, baking, and decorating a cake for a shower occasion, take some time to really assess what the event will be like. If you were ordering a cake from a bakery, you'd most likely have to fill out a questionnaire about what you wanted the cake to look like, so give your personally decorated cake the same consideration. Answer the following questions as you begin the process of designing, baking, and decorating a shower cake:

✔ How many people will be at the party?

✔ Is it for women only, or is it a coed event?

✔ What's the theme?

✔ Have specific colors been selected for the party?

✔ Will the cake be a centerpiece on a table? If so, what else will be on the table, and how much space will the cake have?

✔ What are the favorite cake flavors of the honoree(s)?

For both bridal and baby showers, the cake is often the centerpiece of a table setting at some point during the event. Further, cutting the cake is an event itself, either as a preamble to opening gifts, concurrently with unwrapping them, or as a sweet finale to the party. For these reasons, you want your creation to both look and taste amazing.

Whatever the event, I always suggest steering clear of the obvious, such as bootie shoe or building block–shaped cakes for a baby shower, and taking advantage of the opportunity to incorporate personality and inject warmth, spirit, and even a little humor into the event. When done with class and grace, your cake will stand out from run-of-the-mill alternatives and deeply impress the shower's guest of honor.

Bridal showers: Tying in to the main event

In many ways, I like to consider the wedding shower confection a fun, informal take on all the wedding goings-on. That's why I think it's important to gather information that's relevant to the actual wedding so that the cake becomes a colorful, memorable, integral part of that event and not just some cast-off notion.

Don't leave anyone out. If both the bride and groom-to-be will be guests of honor at the party, don't just concern yourself with the bride's favorite cake flavor. Check in with the groom, too. After all, you want both of them to enjoy the cake.

For a bridal shower, you may be asked to decorate the cake so that it ties in with design elements of the actual wedding (or you may decide to go this design route on your own, without being asked). For instance, if the couple is planning a wedding on the beach, the shower may have a tropical theme that should carry through to the cake (in both look and taste).

Although you want to make the most beautiful, most memorable cake possible, make sure that you don't upstage the confection that the bride and groom are planning for the big day itself.

When preparing a bridal shower cake, you may want to go a more nontraditional route. Lately, cupcakes have been in vogue for bridal showers. Not only do they offer a different take on cake in individual servings, but they also let you provide a number of different flavors. Petit fours are another popular alternative to traditional cake. Typically, they feature a host of different (but complementary) designs and icing colors that give off a chic yet playful vibe.

Baby showers: Making parents-to-be feel special

Partygoers definitely get excited about couples getting married, but celebrating the impending arrival of a little boy or girl sends relatives and friends into a gleeful frenzy. The baby shower cake should welcome a little one into the world and convey many good wishes.

To that end, definitely take the shower's theme into account. If the shower doesn't necessarily have a theme, consider a theme the new parents may be using for their nursery: Vintage cowboy, Dick and Jane, princess, alphabet, world traveler, surfer, mermaid, and seaside are all nursery themes that I've taken as inspiration to fashion shower cakes. Another option is to reflect the colors of the baby's new room into your design.

If the parents-to-be have opted not to know the sex of the child before it's born, you can rely on a host of gender-neutral, kid-cute options: A zoo or farm theme, the alphabet, or a playground scene are all appropriate possibilities.

Commanding Popular Shower Power Moves

Cutouts, edible flowers, and lace designs are always popular embellishments for shower cakes. Although the recipes in this chapter don't utilize all such techniques, mastering them will undoubtedly benefit your cake decorating repertoire, for showers and beyond.

Crafting cutouts

Fondant is a common choice for shower cakes because it's smooth, refined, and so versatile. I discuss how to make fondant in Chapter 9; in this section, I explain three methods for decorating a cake with fondant decorations. All three methods rely on using cookie or fondant cutters to cut fondant into the shapes of flowers, leaves, animals, or geometric designs, among other possibilities. You can use good-quality, sturdy cookie cutters you currently own to work with the fondant, or you can also purchase specialty fondant cutter sets to craft your fondant as well.

Although I talk about fondant cutouts as they apply to shower cakes, these instructions also apply to virtually any other occasion cake. For instance, you can cut holly leaves out of green-tinted fondant and arrange them on a Christmas-themed cake. Or you may want to cut out a fondant bird or chick to decorate an Easter or springtime treat.

Layered fondant

A layered fondant decoration is a fondant "stack" that features fondant cut in different sizes of the same shape. The three-dimensional effect adds depth to a cake design.

1. **Cut out the same or similar shapes in a gradation of sizes (see Figure 15-1).**

   To make the layers really pop, consider dividing and tinting fondant a number of colors and then cutting the different sizes of shapes out of different colors.

2. **Stack the shapes on top of each other.**

3. **Apply them to the cake.**

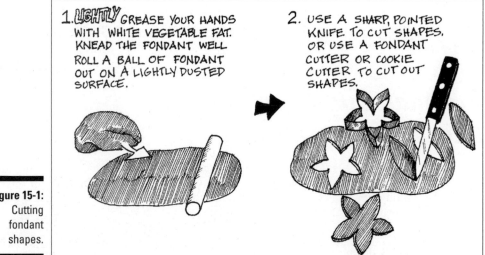

Figure 15-1: Cutting fondant shapes.

1. LIGHTLY GREASE YOUR HANDS WITH WHITE VEGETABLE FAT. KNEAD THE FONDANT WELL ROLL A BALL OF FONDANT OUT ON A LIGHTLY DUSTED SURFACE.

2. USE A SHARP, POINTED KNIFE TO CUT SHAPES, OR USE A FONDANT CUTTER OR COOKIE CUTTER TO CUT OUT SHAPES.

The fill-in

For this colorful fondant decoration, you fill in a larger fondant shape with a smaller size of the same shape that's tinted a different color.

1. **Cut your desired shape out of fondant.**

2. **Place a smaller cutter of the same shape inside the bigger fondant shape, and press.**

3. **With the smaller cutter, cut out a piece of fondant that's a different color from the fondant used in Steps 1 and 2.**

4. **Place the larger shape on your cake, and fill the empty space with the smaller shape in the different color (see Figure 15-2).**

Cake insets

For cake insets, you add interest to a cake covered in fondant by cutting out shapes in the fondant covering, and then inserting the shapes back in, but tinted a different color.

1. **Roll out a piece of fondant that you'll use to cover the entire surface of your cake. Carefully lay it on the cake.**

2. **Mark areas that you want to cut out and fill in with a colored shape. Transfer the fondant from the cake to a flat work surface.**

3. **Using a cutter of the desired shape, make cuts where you marked the fondant in Step 2.**

4. **Lay the fondant on the cake again, and smooth it so that it adheres to the cake's surface.**

5. **Use food coloring gel to tint a separate piece of rolled fondant to be used for the cutout insets.**

6. **Cut the inset shapes out of the colored fondant (as many as you need to fill in on the cake).**

7. **Press the colored insets into the spaces in the cake's fondant covering (see Figure 15-2).**

Figure 15-2:
Making
fondant
insets.

Adorning with flowers

Mostly in the arena of bridal showers, flowers in a variety of forms, textures, and colors are a preternaturally pretty and perky decoration choice. You can choose from the following options:

- ✔ **Frosting flowers:** With a little practice and the right icing tips, you can whip up roses, sunflowers, daisies, and chrysanthemums, to name just a few. For instructions on crafting frosting roses, check out Chapter 12.

- ✔ **Gum paste flowers:** Gum paste is a particularly good way to recreate fresh flowers that may be poisonous. Those shaped like roses and lilies of the valley are consistently popular; you can find a recipe for gum paste as well as instructions for creating roses and lilies of the valley in Chapter 12.

- ✔ **Fresh flowers:** Flowers and cake are a natural combination, and fresh flowers are even better! Incorporate some of the bride's favorites, use the same flowers planned for the big event, or play around with varieties and colors. For the ins and outs of decorating with fresh flowers, including which varieties are safe to use on cakes, flip to Chapter 12.

For a baby shower, a couple may be planning a garden or rose-themed nursery for a little girl on the way. In that case, a flower-adorned cake is a perfect choice.

Piping the lacy look

Piping frosting in a lace design (sometimes called *Corelli lace*) gives a more formal flair to shower cakes. You achieve the lacy look by creating a pattern of delicate squiggles across the cake's surface.

For best results, you need to use a fine, round icing tip, such as #1 or #2. (You can read about icing tips in Chapter 11.) Follow these steps to give your cake a lacy look:

1. **Outfit a pastry bag with an icing tip and frosting.**

   Check out Chapter 11 if you need a refresher on how to do this.

2. **With a toothpick, mark off the area of the cake that you want to fill with the lace design.**

   Ideally, the area should cover the cake's top surface and overlap onto the sides, which eliminates the need for a border and adds to the lace's realistic look.

3. **Working across the surface of the cake, pipe curving lines that are close together but not touching (see Figure 15-3).**

4. **As you pipe, maintain consistent, light pressure on the pastry bag. Cover as much of the area as possible without lifting the tip so that your lace looks continuous.**

5. **Define the lacy area by piping small beads (with a #3 tip, for example) around the edges of the design.**

When working on a lacy look, make sure that you start with an extra-smooth frosting surface so that the raised pattern truly stands out. The lacing pops even more if you pipe it in a color that contrasts with your cake's base frosting.

Figure 15-3:
Creating the lacy look.

Tossing Cheer into a Bridal Shower

The recipes in this section allow for both a coed approach and a cake with more feminine flair.

Tasteful Registry Cake

Gifts from wedding registries feature prominently at most bridal showers, and this cake takes its cue from that longstanding tradition. The cake's surface is adorned with the kind of "china" place setting — with the plates made from fondant — that so often appears on a couple's registry.

When I've made this cake in the past, I've incorporated colors and patterns unique or special to the groom and bride-to-be. This recipe calls for leaf green, pink, and burgundy frosting and fondant, but you should feel free to use whatever colors appeal to your honoree(s). However, do try to stick with one bright color, one muted color, and one accent color. This cake is shown on the fourth page of the color section.

Tools: 3 miniature loaf pans (5¾-x-3½-x-2 inches), 12-x-18-inch cake pan, #1 icing tip, #2 icing tip, #4 icing tip, #5 icing tip, #100 icing tip, 4 couplers, rotary pastry cutter, 2-inch round plastic lid (or cookie cutter), 4-inch round plastic lid (or cookie cutter), 6-inch round plastic lid (or cookie cutter), ruler

Preparation time: 30 minutes

Baking time: 45 minutes plus 2 hours for cooling

Decoration time: 50 minutes plus 1 hour for refrigeration

Yield: 32 servings

For the cake (recipe follows):

3 batches modified Delicious Yellow Cake batter (see Chapter 6)

3 cups toffee bits

For the frosting:

3 batches Buttercream Frosting (see Chapter 8)

For the decorations:

Leaf green food coloring gel

Deep pink food coloring gel

Burgundy food coloring gel

4.4-ounce sheet ready-to-use white fondant

4.4-ounce sheet ready-to-use pastel green fondant

Confectioners' sugar for dusting

Making the Toffee Cake

1 Preheat the oven to 350 degrees F. Grease and flour the miniature loaf pans, and prepare the 12-x-18-inch pan as follows: grease, line with parchment paper, grease, and flour.

2 Make the cake batters as described in Chapter 6, but in each batch, fold in 1 cup toffee bits as the last step. Divide the batter among the four cake pans, and put the pans in the oven.

3 Bake the miniature loaf cakes for 25 minutes. Remove them from oven, and let them cool in their pans for 10 minutes before turning them out onto cooling racks and letting them cool completely. Bake the larger cake for 25 minutes more than the miniature loaf cakes, or until a cake tester inserted in the center comes out with moist crumbs attached. Let the cake cool in the pan for 10 minutes. Then run a knife around the edges, turn it out onto a rack, and let it cool completely.

Decorating the cake

1 After the cakes have cooled, level them (see Chapter 7). Square off the sides of two miniloaf cakes so that each forms a 2-x-4-inch rectangle, and cut the third miniloaf into two 2-x-2-inch squares. Apply a crumb coat (thin layer) of frosting to all the cakes, and refrigerate them for 1 hour.

2 Divide and tint the frosting as follows: 2 cups leaf green, 2 cups deep pink, and 2 cups burgundy.

3 Frost the large cake with the leaf green frosting. Refrigerate that cake while you frost the others as follows: Frost one rectangular cake and one square cake with pink frosting, and frost the other two cakes with burgundy frosting. Refrigerate until set, about 1 hour.

4 Roll the sheet of white fondant to a thickness of ⅛ inch. Using the lids or cookie cutters, cut out three circles: one 6-inch (the dinner plate), one 4-inch (the salad plate), and one 2-inch (the bread and butter plate). These fondant rounds are the china in your place setting design.

5 Remove the large, rectangular cake from the refrigerator, and use a toothpick to lightly sketch the placement of the china. Place the fondant rounds on the cake, smoothing them evenly on the cake's surface.

6 Prepare four pastry bags with couplers (see Chapter 11). Fill one each with leaf green, pink, burgundy, and white frosting.

7 Outfit the burgundy bag with the #5 tip and the white bag with the #4 tip. Pipe the rim of a dinner plate with the burgundy frosting on the large fondant round. Inside the burgundy frosting, pipe a circle of white frosting. Repeat with another circle of burgundy frosting. Repeat this three-circle design on the salad and bread and butter plates.

8 Dust a clean work surface with confectioners' sugar. Roll the sheet of green fondant to a thickness of ⅛ inch. With a rotary pastry cutter (or a pizza wheel), cut six 1-x-6-inch strips, two 1-x-10-inch strips, and four 1½-x-6-inch strips. Place a 1-x-6-inch strip across the width of each rectangular miniloaf cake, and two of these strips across each square cake (so that they cross in the center) to look like ribbons on each package. Place each of the two 1-x-10-inch strips lengthwise across the rectangular packages, crossing the shorter ribbons in the center.

9 Loop each of the 1½-x-6-inch strips into a figure eight, and bend a square piece of fondant around the center of each one to form a bow. Place one bow on top of each package where the ribbons intersect.

10 Spread some white frosting on the bottom of each package to act as glue. Place the pink rectangular package at the upper right corner of the cake and the burgundy rectangular package at the upper left corner of the cake. Place the square packages in between them so that the colors alternate.

11 With a #2 tip and pink frosting, monogram the center of the fondant dinner plate with the initial of the couple's last name (after they're married). Monogram the salad plate with the initial of the bride's first name, and monogram the bread and butter plate with the initial of the groom's first name.

12 With the #100 tip and white frosting, pipe ruffles around the top and bottom edges of the large, rectangular base cake.

Tip: If the shower is a coed one, use a #1 tip to put the bride-to-be's monogram on one of the rectangular packages and the groom-to-be's monogram on the other. To make the monograms stand out, use contrasting frosting (burgundy on the pink package and pink on the burgundy package).

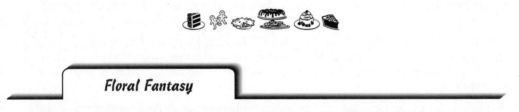

Floral Fantasy

I tend to reserve roses for wedding cakes, so for this cake design, I've picked two different flowers — hyacinths and chrysanthemums — that are unique, dramatic, and beautiful. You can certainly vary this design by incorporating any flower you like.

Although this is just a 9-inch double layer cake, the basket weave design and flowers make the decoration very time-consuming.

Tools: Two 9-inch round cake pans, #48 icing tip, #67 icing tip, #80 icing tip, #193 icing tip, 4 couplers, 3 bamboo skewers, wax paper, 6 plastic containers with 3¾-inch lids (or mason jars with comparable lids), double-stick tape, 10-x-10-inch polystyrene square (or florist foam or a wide-mouthed jar filled halfway with dry beans)

Preparation time: 30 minutes

Baking time: 45 minutes plus 2 hours for cooling

Decoration time: 2½ hours plus 1 hour for refrigeration

Yield: 16 servings

For the cake:

1 batch White Velvet Cake batter (see Chapter 6)

For the decorations:

Violet food coloring gel

Electric blue food coloring gel

Leaf green food coloring gel

For the frosting:

2 batches Stiff Decorator Frosting (see Chapter 8)

Electric green food coloring gel

4.4-ounce sheet ready-to-use pastel green fondant

21 regular marshmallows

Making the cakes

1 Preheat the oven to 350 degrees F. Grease and flour the pans, and set aside.

2 Prepare the cake batter according to the recipe in Chapter 6. Divide the batter into the two pans, and bake for 40 minutes, or until a toothpick inserted in the center comes out with moist crumbs attached. Allow the cakes to cool in the pans for 10 minutes before inverting them onto a cooling rack to cool completely.

Decorating the cakes

1 After the cakes have cooled, level them (see Chapter 7). Frost the top of one layer, stack the other layer on top, and apply a crumb coat (thin layer) of frosting to the entire cake. Refrigerate for 1 hour.

2 Divide and tint the frosting as follows: 1½ cups violet, 1½ cups electric blue, 1 cup leaf green, and 4 cups electric green.

3 Frost the cake electric green, and return it to the refrigerator while you work on the decorations.

4 Make the hyacinths: Thread 4½ marshmallows on a bamboo skewer, and frost them with untinted frosting. Outfit a pastry bag with a coupler, #193 icing tip, and violet frosting. Holding the skewer in your left hand if you're right-handed (swap this if you're left-handed), pipe hyacinth blossoms all over the stack of marshmallows. Start at the bottom edge of marshmallow and pipe out a blossom, pulling up and away gently from the marshmallow to form a point, and then moving to the next blossom, keeping them all very close together as you move up and down the stacked marshmallows. When you finish piping each hyacinth, insert the skewer into the polystyrene, and stick it in the freezer. Repeat the process with the other two skewers so that you have a total of three frosting hyacinths.

5 Make the chrysanthemums: Cut a 4-inch square of wax paper, and affix it to the top of a plastic container with double-stick tape. Outfit a pastry bag with a coupler, #80 icing tip, and blue frosting. Pipe a chrysanthemum petal from the center of the lid to the rim of it, lifting up at the finish so that the end stands up off the paper. Repeat this shape three times, forming a cross on the lid. Then, starting from the center point, press out more radiating petals until you've filled the spaces in between the first four petals. Add another layer of petals, placing these in between the petals of the first layer. Repeat with a third layer of petals, again alternating between the petals of the second layer. Continue with additional layers until the chrysanthemum is filled. Place the flower in the freezer to harden. Repeat the process until you have a total of six chrysanthemums (see Figure 15-4).

6 Outfit a pastry bag with a coupler, #48 icing tip, and electric green frosting. Remove your two-layer cake from the refrigerator, and, following the steps for the basket weave technique explained in Chapter 11, pipe a basket weave design around the sides of the cake.

7 Outfit a pastry bag with a coupler, #67 icing tip, and leaf green frosting. Pipe leaves all around the top edge of the cake. (If you need a refresher on piping leaves, flip back to Chapter 11.)

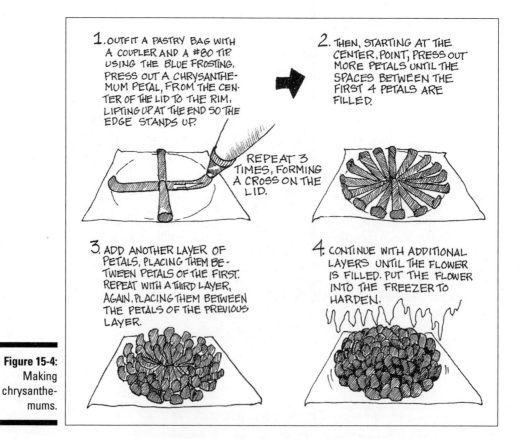

Figure 15-4:
Making chrysanthemums.

8 Remove the hyacinth skewers from the freezer, and stick them into the center of the cake. Remove the chrysanthemums from the freezer, and gently peel the wax paper off them. Set them on the cake surrounding around the hyacinths. If the chrysanthemums appear flat on the cake, dab a little frosting on the back of them, and rest them on the extra marshmallows.

9 Pipe leaf green leaves and tendrils in between the flowers to complete the floral arrangement.

10 Refrigerate the cake until you're ready to serve it. The cake is shown in Figure 15-5.

Vary It!: *If making the flowers proves too time consuming, consider using fresh ones (that aren't poisonous), or purchasing already-made gum paste flowers online or at a bakery supply store.*

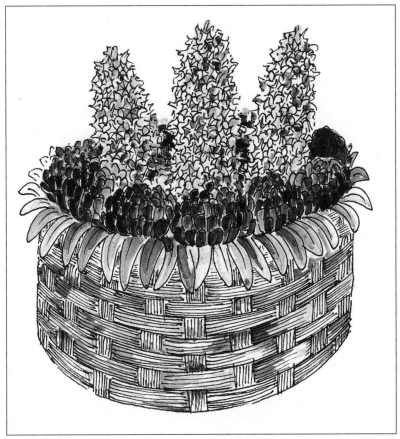

Figure 15-5:
The Floral
Fantasy
Cake isn't
easy, but it's
a show
stopper.

Bringing Up the Baby Shower

This section arms you with two recipes, both of which have been playfully, classily presented for a touch of whimsy at baby showers. The first one, a Cupcake Tower, doesn't require a tremendous time commitment and gives you room to play around with different decorations. The second recipe, the Baby Animal Zoo, takes more time to create but results in a charming cake that always draws "ooohs" and "aaaahs."

Cupcake Tower

This cupcake tower presents an appropriately grown-up version of cupcakes, which are often associated with kids but have become more popular in recent years as people experiment with cake flavors. One great thing about using cupcakes for a special occasion confection is that you don't have to worry about leveling or crumb-coating. Everyone enjoys a cupcake with a hearty round top!

I use blue-tinted frosting and blue confetti in this recipe, but you can easily substitute pink frosting and decorations if a baby girl is expected, or use yellow or green if the baby's gender is unknown. This cake is shown on the fourth page of the color section.

Tools: *Two 12-well cupcake pans, large star icing tip (such as #863), 2 couplers, cupcake stand or 3 pedestal cake plates*

Preparation time: *15 minutes*

Baking time: *20 minutes plus 30 minutes for cooling*

Decoration time: *40 minutes*

Yield: *24 servings*

For the cupcakes:

1 batch Key Lime Cupcake batter (recipe follows)

For the frosting:

1 batch Buttercream Frosting (see Chapter 8)

For the decorations:

Sky blue food coloring gel *White confetti*   *Light blue confetti*

1 Prepare the cupcakes as instructed in the following recipe. Carefully remove them from the pans, and line them up on a countertop or workspace with plenty of room for you to work.

2 Add sky blue coloring gel to 3 cups of frosting, tinting it to your desired shade of blue. Outfit a pastry bag with a coupler and the large star tip, and fill the bag with the blue frosting.

3 On 12 cupcakes, pipe the frosting in a clockwise swirling motion, starting around the outside edge of each cupcake and working in toward the center so that you create a circular cone shape that ends in a sharp point.

4 Outfit a pastry bag with a coupler and untinted frosting. Remove the star tip from the blue frosting bag, clean it, and refit it on the white frosting bag.

5 On the remaining 12 cupcakes, repeat the frosting procedure described in Step 3. You should end up with 12 blue-frosted cupcakes and 12 white-frosted cupcakes.

6 Sprinkle white confetti on the blue cupcakes and blue confetti on the white cupcakes.

7 Place the cupcakes — alternating blue and white — into the positions on the cupcake stand, or position them similarly on stacked cake pedestals.

Key Lime Cupcakes

2¼ cups granulated white sugar

3 cups sifted cake flour

¾ teaspoon salt

1½ teaspoons baking powder

¾ teaspoon baking soda

4.5-ounce package lime gelatin

7 eggs

1¾ cups vegetable oil

1⅛ cup fresh-squeezed orange juice

1½ teaspoons lemon extract

¾ teaspoon pure vanilla extract

3 tablespoons key lime juice

5 tablespoons sifted confectioners' sugar

1 Preheat the oven to 350 degrees F. Place 12 cupcake liners in the pans.

2 In a large bowl, combine the granulated sugar, cake flour, salt, baking powder, baking soda, and gelatin. Make a well in the center of these dry ingredients.

3 In a separate bowl, combine the eggs, oil, orange juice, and extracts. Mix lightly, and then pour the mixture into the well in the dry ingredients.

4 Beat on medium speed for 2 minutes, scraping down the bowl twice to make sure everything gets incorporated.

5 Pour the batter into the cupcake liners. Bake for 15 minutes, or until a cake tester inserted in the center comes out with moist crumbs attached.

6 While the cupcakes bake, whisk together the key lime juice and confectioners' sugar.

7 Remove the cupcakes from the oven. Let them cool in their pans for 15 minutes. Then prick holes in the tops and drizzle the lime mixture over them to be absorbed into the cupcakes.

Vary It!: *You can also arrange your decorated cupcakes on a succession of different-sized cardboard rounds. Cover each round with wrapping paper, and then cover that with heavy cellophane. Stack them using plastic miniature columns available at craft stores, and then arrange your cupcakes on each level.*

If you need to speed up the cookie decorating process in the following recipe, consider investing in a few #2 and #5 icing tips. They're inexpensive, and you make up for any money spent with the time you save in cleaning and reattaching the tips for the different colors of frosting you use.

Baby Animal Zoo

This cake, with its cavalcade of animals and humorous message, is always a hit at baby showers. It shows off the decorating technique of combining cookie cutters with cakes; for this cake, cookie cutters provide an easy but distinctive way of lining up the animals that entertain the cake eaters.

This cake also utilizes a technique called *flocking*, in which you basically use sanding sugar to give a decoration a glittery presence. Flocking a design directly on a cake is tough because the sanding sugar can stick to parts of your cake that you didn't want it on. That's why I recommend that you limit flocking to the cookies in this recipe; the sanding sugar is easier to control on the cookies and is less likely to muck up other parts of the cake design. The finished cake is shown in Figure 15-6.

Tools: *Three 10-x-10-inch cake pans, #2 icing tip, #5 icing tip, #7 icing tip, #16 icing tip, 4 couplers, 6 animal-shaped cookie cutters (such as a gorilla, lion, giraffe, elephant, camel, and kangaroo)*

Preparation time: *40 minutes*

Baking time: *45 minutes for the cake plus 2 hours for cooling; 10 minutes for the cookies plus 1 hour for cooling*

Decoration time: *1¾ hours plus 1 hour for refrigeration for the cake and overnight refrigeration for the iced cookies*

Yield: *32 servings*

For the cake:

2 batches Delicious Yellow Cake batter
(see Chapter 6)

For the decorations:

1 batch Royal Icing (see Chapter 9)

Neon pink food coloring gel

Neon blue food coloring gel

Neon green food coloring gel

6 cookies (recipe follows)

For the frosting:

2 batches Buttercream Frosting
(see Chapter 8)

White sanding sugar

Orange sanding sugar

Pink sanding sugar

Mint green food coloring gel

Decorating the cookies for the cake

1 Bake the cookies according to the recipe that follows. Divide and tint the Royal Icing as follows: ½ cup neon pink, ½ cup neon blue, and ½ cup neon green. (You should have ½ cup untinted icing left over for further embellishments to the cookies.)

2 Outfit a pastry bag with a coupler, #2 icing tip, and green icing. Outline the giraffe and gorilla cookies in green.

3 Attach a #5 tip to the green icing bag. Squeeze thick lines of icing within the outlines on the giraffe and gorilla cookies. Use an icing spatula to spread the icing out, giving the cookies a full, even coat of green icing. Transfer the cookies to a parchment paper-lined cookie sheet.

4 Outfit a pastry bag with a coupler, #2 icing tip, and pink icing. Outline the lion and kangaroo cookies in pink.

5 Attach a #5 tip to the pink icing bag. Squeeze thick lines of icing within the outlines on the lion and kangaroo cookies. Use an icing spatula to spread the icing out, giving the cookies a full, even coat of pink icing. Transfer the cookies to the parchment paper-lined cookie sheet.

6 Outfit a pastry bag with a coupler, #2 icing tip, and blue icing. Outline the elephant and camel cookies in blue.

7 Attach a #5 tip to the blue icing bag. Squeeze thick lines of icing within the outlines on the elephant and camel cookies. Use an icing spatula to spread the icing out, giving the cookies a full, even coat of blue icing. Transfer the cookies to the parchment paper-lined cookie sheet.

8 Place the cookie sheet in the refrigerator overnight to allow the icing to set up. When you're ready to finish decorating them, remove them from the refrigerator and arrange them on sheets of parchment or wax paper.

9 Outfit a pastry bag with a #5 tip and white royal icing. Outline the elephant's trunk, the lion's mane, the camel's hump, and the kangaroo's pocket. Also pipe eyes on all the cookies, and add spots and polka dots as you see fit. You're free to play around with the decorations.

10 While the icing is still wet, sprinkle sanding sugar on it, mixing and matching the sugar colors on the different-colored cookies. Let the cookies dry for 5 minutes, and then shake off the excess sugar.

Decorating the cake

1 Bake the cakes as instructed in the recipe in Chapter 6. After the cakes have cooled, level them (see Chapter 7). Apply a crumb coat (thin layer) of buttercream to the cakes, and refrigerate them for 1 hour.

2 Divide and tint the buttercream frosting as follows: 2 cups mint green, 2 cups a darker shade of green, and 1 cup neon green.

3 Arrange two of the square cakes side by side to form the bottom layer, and frost them with the mint green frosting. Place the third cake on top of the cake on the right.

4 Outfit a pastry bag with a coupler, #11 tip, and neon green frosting. Pipe neon green frosting in the shape of six ovals: three on the upper layer and three on the lower layer. These are the stands for the zoo animals.

5 In the center of the facing side of the double layer, use a toothpick to sketch an archway. Using an icing spatula, fill in the archway with dark green frosting. Outfit a pastry bag with a coupler, #11 tip, and dark green frosting, and outline the archway.

6 Refit the dark green frosting bag with a #7 tip, and pipe "It's Going To Be A . . ." in the center of the facing side of the double layer. Refit the dark green frosting bag with a #9 tip, and pipe "ZOO!" in an arc above the archway.

7 Using a bamboo skewer, sketch crisscrossing lines of latticework around the sides of the cake. Using the dark green frosting bag with the #9 tip, pipe the latticework on the sides of the cake, using your sketched lines as a guide and piping around the wording.

8 Refit the dark green frosting bag with a #16 tip, and pipe a zigzag border around the base of the top layer and around the base of the entire bottom layer of cake.

9 Stand one decorated cookie in the center of each frosting oval.

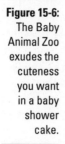

Figure 15-6:
The Baby Animal Zoo exudes the cuteness you want in a baby shower cake.

Decorative Cookies

1 cup all-purpose flour

⅛ teaspoon salt

¼ teaspoon baking powder

4 tablespoons unsalted butter, softened

½ cup sugar

1 egg

½ teaspoon pure vanilla extract

1 Preheat the oven to 375 degrees F. Line a cookie sheet with parchment paper.

2 In a medium bowl, sift together the flour, salt, and baking powder.

3 In a medium bowl, cream the butter and sugar until the mixture is light and fluffy. Add the egg and vanilla, and mix well. Add the dry ingredients, and mix just until blended.

4 Transfer the dough from the mixing bowl to a sheet of plastic wrap, wrap it up tightly, and refrigerate it for 20 minutes.

5 On a lightly floured surface, roll out the dough to a thickness of about ⅛ inch.

6 Cut out the desired shapes, rerolling dough if necessary to get more shapes. To decorate the cake, you only need one of each of six animal shapes, but I recommend that you make as many extras as you can in case some cookies break.

7 Place the cutouts on the cookie sheet, and bake them for 10 minutes, or just until they're golden. Leave them on the cookie sheet to cool completely.

Adapting recipes for other occasions

Although the cake recipes in this chapter have been typically used for showers, they're certainly appropriate for other festive occasions. Here are a few examples:

✔ The Floral Fantasy cake is ideal for ladies' birthdays and Mother's Day gatherings.

✔ The Cupcake Tower is so versatile that you can adapt it for practically any occasion with minimal tweaking, such as using different color combinations and adding cupcake picks, which come in a variety of designs.

✔ The Baby Animal Zoo cake is a hit at kids' birthday parties.

Chapter 16

Lifting a Fork to Weddings and Anniversaries

*W*ow! The wedding cake. For many, the wedding cake really does represent the pinnacle of skill, taste, look, style, and aptitude in cake decorating. Because of its importance, the thought and work associated with making and decorating a wedding cake tends to send some decorators screaming from their kitchens.

Because it's associated with that most revered of special events — the wedding — more is expected of the cake. It's on display at the reception, featured as the bride and groom take a first bite together, devoured by wedding guests, and even lasts until the couple's first anniversary, when they follow an age-old tradition and partake of the cake's top layer.

But fear not: You *can* master the techniques that produce a very impressive, very classy wedding or anniversary cake. Furthermore, with some surprisingly simple architecture, you can extend your skills to tiered cakes that are much taller than normal. This chapter covers all that and shares a few simple tricks to make a couple's anniversary cake an exceptional part of an affair to remember.

Considering the Event's Theme and Colors

You'd be surprised at how many cake decorators (both aspiring and professional) pass over an all-too-important aspect of planning a wedding (or anniversary) cake's design and flavors: They get stuck on what they envision for the cake . . . rather than what the couple wants. And believe me, the couple remembers the cake far longer than the person who made it does.

As you undertake the task of creating a wedding cake, make sure to gather some important details about the impending nuptials so that you get a true sense of the look and size of the cake that will fit the couple's tastes (regardless of whether it matches your taste).

I always think it's best to sit down with a couple and plan their personalized cake with them rather than have them pick a cake from a catalogue or a gallery of cakes you've made in the past. Of course, they may have collected pictures of cakes from magazines and such, but by planning the cake together, you take into account the wedding's particular dynamics. The details of the wedding should influence the style of the decorations, the size of the cake, and the overall look of your creation; tying together all these elements makes the cake truly special and unique for the couple celebrating.

Figuring out the logistics

Get answers to the following questions to inform the cake's direction:

- How many people will be at the wedding?
- Where is the couple getting married?
- What time of day is the wedding?
- Is the reception being held indoors or outside?
- Where will the wedding cake be set up?
- What's the feel of the wedding? Exceptionally formal, starkly modern, or rather casual and in a woodsy location?

Although the special couple should provide you with the overwhelming inspiration, you have plenty of choices and resources to draw from in designing and decorating a cake that suits them. For example, you may want to consider the following:

- Decorating the cake with the colors of the bridal bouquet
- Coordinating the cake with the design of the wedding gown, incorporating details such as lace, buttons, and swags
- Using the wedding locale as inspiration, such as using candy shells if it's a beachfront ceremony

In the case of an anniversary cake, consider the following:

✔ How many years of marriage are being celebrated? You may want to take into account certain gifts that are traditionally associated with specific years, such as tin (10th), crystal (15th), china (20th), silver (25th), and rubies (40th).

✔ Are certain colors particularly significant to the couple?

✔ Is there a symbol that's especially meaningful to the celebrants that could be incorporated or serve as a jumping off point for the design?

✔ Is there a particular place, city, or locale that's important to them and may guide you in your endeavor?

In addition to asking these questions, find out how many people are expected, the location and decorations, and the general tenor of the event (for instance, a formal dinner, a barbecue, or a humorous roast).

Daring to be different?

Wedding cakes used to be white inside and out, but times have changed! Now they can be any color and flavor, and decorations are limited only by the imagination. In fact, my wedding cake was chartreuse (thanks to my wife for letting me incorporate my favorite color), two tiers were fudge chocolate, the other two were caramel, and friends who were there still comment on it (in a good way, of course!).

As for shape, wedding cakes don't have to be circular. In fact, lately, trends have pointed to all kinds of shapes: hexagons, squares, octagons, diamonds, and ovals. They also don't have to be neatly tiered: Lopsided creations have become quite the rage, different-shaped cakes grouped together but standing on their own make for a chic presentation, and even cupcakes beckon a welcome, refreshing change in already perfectly portioned individual servings.

Similarly, don't feel regimented with an anniversary cake either. You have the leeway to adopt and adapt any number of shapes. And because anniversary parties often eschew the formality of a wedding, you have even more opportunity to create a unique flavor combination that boasts a fun, unconventional design.

Staying in style

I encourage you to embrace some nontraditional ventures in decorating a wedding or anniversary cake, but there are a few guidelines of good taste that all such occasion cakes benefit from.

✔ **Scripted decoration:** On a wedding cake, stay away from scripting words; a monogram may be suitable, but the wedding isn't the setting for a witty message or playful lettering. On the other hand, for an anniversary cake, you may want to script a cheery "Happy Anniversary," include the couple's name, or put their wedding date or number of years married on the cake.

✔ **Cake covering:** Wedding cakes are usually topped with buttercream, fondant, or a combination thereof. These coverings are the most popular because they create the smoothest finish. Some brides choose fondant because they want the cake to have a smooth, almost porcelain look. However, other brides find that fondant looks too manufactured or plastic, so they go with buttercream.

Personally, I'm in the buttercream camp. To my eye, it looks more natural, and to my palette, it always tastes better. I've found that some guests are confused by the taste and texture of fondant and aren't sure what to do with it, which means that it often ends up heaped up in the corner of each cake plate.

✔ **Filling:** Great fillings make wedding cakes even more extraordinary and special. If you usually use frosting as your filling, wedding and anniversary cakes are your opportunity to break out of the box. A tiered cake is a fantastic way to feature a filling (or fillings) that differs from your cake's covering but that both accents and highlights the flavors. Also, because wedding cakes are often prepared a couple of days in advance, flavored syrups are a popular way of ensuring that the cake doesn't dry out. The additional depth of flavor also amps up a wedding cake's exclusivity and originality. For some ideas about fillings syrups, peruse the recipes and techniques in Chapter 10.

Positioning to stand out

In the case of each and every wedding cake, keep in mind what the wedding cake will be actually sitting on. Because the cake won't be served directly off a table, you want to make sure that you decorate its placement — on a platter or pedestal — and its surroundings on a table. Of course, this strategy applies to anniversary cakes as well.

With the placement of a wedding or anniversary cake, you have a perfect opportunity to tie in to a theme. You may want to decorate the cake board with a coordinating fabric that has been integral in the party's design. Or if your cake includes floral arrangements, you may want to reserve some stems, buds, or petals to place around the base of the cake. Finally, if the cake will rest on a platter, you may choose to surround the cake with decorations that relate to the wedding's look or locale, such as shells for a beach wedding or chocolate pinecones for a mountain setting.

For wedding cakes and nostalgic anniversary cakes, take into account the possibility of a wedding topper. These figurines tend to fall in and out of vogue, but couples routinely request vintage ones from the 1950s and 1960s. You can even have a topper made in a couple's likeness (for a tidy sum and much advance notice, that is).

Creating a Simple Wedding Cake

With some organization and an understanding that yours doesn't have to be a towering, multitiered, 400-pound creation bursting with dozens of hard-to-find flowers, you'll be well on your way to making and decorating a wedding cake that will make any couple proud.

You can often dress up a white or chocolate cake with simple measures that lend elegance, such as:

- A bounty of fresh flowers
- Cherries (particularly uncommon varieties such as Rainier), strawberries, or raspberries that have been dipped in dark or white chocolate
- Fresh, unblemished fruits, particularly more exotic ones like kiwis and figs, which bring vibrancy, color, and variety when sliced and arranged on a cake
- Grosgrain or organza ribbon pinned around the circumference of the cake

Italian Chocolate Wedding Cake

With this recipe, I've deconstructed the traditional wedding cake. This cake has three separate tiers, but they remain unstacked for a presentation that's out of the ordinary. To tie the cakes together, try to find three platters of the same metal or material in sizes that fit the cakes.

Taste-wise, this cake has class, a little unexpected sass (it's chocolate!), and a sweet filling. Violet candies are a delicate touch that bring a dash of color to the cake and make it even more eye-catching. You can even sprinkle fresh violets in between the platters on your presentation table.

Additionally, you don't have to worry about *torting* these cakes (splitting the layers into halves). You can just focus on baking up nice cakes, whipping up two delicious frostings, and letting everyone enjoy your simple but impressive results. This cake is shown on the sixth page of the color section.

Tools: *14-inch round cake pan, two 9-inch round cake pans, 6-inch round cake pan, 14-inch cardboard round, 9-inch cardboard round, 6-inch cardboard round, bamboo skewer*

Preparation time: *40 minutes*

Baking time: *50 minutes*

Decoration time: *40 minutes plus 1 hour for refrigeration*

Yield: *50 servings*

For the cake:

5 batches Cocoa Chocolate Cake batter (see Chapter 6)

For the frosting:

2 batches Chocolate Buttercream Frosting (see Chapter 8)

1 batch Creamy Chocolate Syrup (recipe follows)

1 batch Pourable Chocolate Ganache (recipe follows)

For the decorations:

1 pound Italian violet candies

2 dozen fresh violets (optional)

Baking the cake

1 Preheat the oven to 350 degrees F. Grease the pans, and line them with parchment paper. Grease them again, and flour them.

2 Prepare the cake batters as described in Chapter 6, divide it among the four pans, and place all the pans in the oven together. Bake the 6-inch layer for 25 minutes; the 9-inch layers for 35 minutes; and the 14-inch layer for 50 minutes, or until a toothpick inserted in the center comes out with moist crumbs attached.

3 As you remove the cakes from the oven, let them cool in their pans for 10 minutes. Then invert them onto cooling racks, and invert them again onto racks so that they're right side up.

4 With a bamboo skewer, poke small holes all over the cakes' top surfaces. Drizzle the creamy chocolate syrup all over the cakes, letting it soak in through the holes. Cover the cakes with plastic wrap, and refrigerate them until you're ready to decorate them.

Decorating the cake

1 Place each layer on a cardboard round of corresponding size. Spread chocolate butter-cream on the top of one 9-inch layer, and set the second 9-inch layer on top of it. Frost each cake with chocolate buttercream, and refrigerate them for 1 hour.

2 Place each layer on a rack that's sitting on parchment paper or aluminum foil. Pour the chocolate ganache over each cake, proceeding slowly so that the chocolate completely covers the top and sides of each cake.

3 Transfer the cakes to their platters. While the ganache is still wet, place the Italian violet candies around the top rim of each cake. Place another row of violet candies around the base of each cake.

4 To display the cakes, stagger them on the presentation table so that guests can see each layer. Scatter fresh violets around the cakes.

Creamy Chocolate Syrup

18 ounces semisweet chocolate chips   1½ cups half-and-half

1 Combine the chocolate chips and half-and-half in a 2-quart glass measuring cup. Microwave on high for 1 minute.

2 Stir the mixture until it's smooth and the chocolate is completely melted.

Pourable Chocolate Ganache

24 ounces semisweet chocolate chips   3 cups heavy cream

1 Combine the chocolate chips and cream in a 2-quart glass measuring cup. Microwave on high for 1½ minutes.

2 Stir the mixture until it's smooth and the chocolate is completely melted.

Tiering Up for Success

Wedding cakes tend to be *stacked,* with each layer resting on the one below, or *separated,* with tiers supported by columns or pillars. In either case, a few supplies are necessary to provide support for your vertical creation.

- ✔ **Dowels:** To provide support for each tier, you snip these ¼-inch round wooden poles to the height of the cake layer and stick them into the center of the cake. Without them, the cake would collapse! Some cake decorators substitute straws for dowels, but I prefer the resolute sturdiness of wooden dowels.

- ✔ **Cardboard rounds:** You place your finished tiers on cardboard rounds. The cardboard gives the tier a solid surface to rest on the dowels below, and the rounds aid in removing the tiers for cutting and serving.

✔ **Presentation board:** This board, usually made of plywood or Masonite, holds your finished tiered cake. It's bigger than the cake both to make for a better presentation and to allow for proper transportation. The presentation board often is covered with cake foil lining or a similar grease-resistant but decorative wrapping. Another option for covering is spreading royal icing over the board so that, when dried overnight, the board has a smooth, pearly surface. For more on cake presentation boards, turn to Chapter 7.

✔ **Separator set:** If you intend to separate cake tiers rather than stack them, you need a separator set that contains separator plates, which the tiers rest on, and columns or pillars that snap into each plate from the tier below.

Inserting dowels into your cake tiers is much less daunting than it sounds. To begin, you need cake layers (duh!), dowels (which you can get at a hardware store or craft store), garden pruning shears, a rubber mallet, a pencil, a bamboo skewer, and the empty cake pans from the cake layers you baked.

I'm picky when it comes to clean utensils, so if you plan to do quite a bit of cake baking and decorating, I recommend that you keep a set of supplies devoted exclusively to cake-related tasks. For instance, label a brand-new pair of pruning shears with "Cake" in a permanent marker so that you don't use the same pair to snip dowels and cut roses.

To insert dowels in cake layers, follow these steps:

1. **Rest the pan from your second largest tier in the center of your largest tier, and press gently to make a very light impression in the cake.**

2. **In the center of the impression made in Step 1, use a bamboo skewer to mark evenly spaced holes in a circle around the center of the tier in which you'll insert dowels.**

   As a general rule, plan on resting an 8- or 9-inch round layer on five dowels and a 6-inch layer on four dowels. You have to strike a delicate balance: You don't want to pepper your layers with too many dowels, but you want each layer to have enough support.

3. **Insert a dowel in one of the holes, and press it all the way down until you hit the cardboard round. With a pencil, mark the height of the tier on the dowel.**

4. **Remove the dowel from the cake, and use the pruning shears to cut it to the appropriate height. Reinsert the dowel into the cake (see Figure 16-1).**

5. **Repeat Steps 3 and 4 with the other dowels for that tier.**

6. **Repeat Steps 1 through 5 for each additional tier except the top tier, which doesn't need multiple dowels because it doesn't bear any weight.**

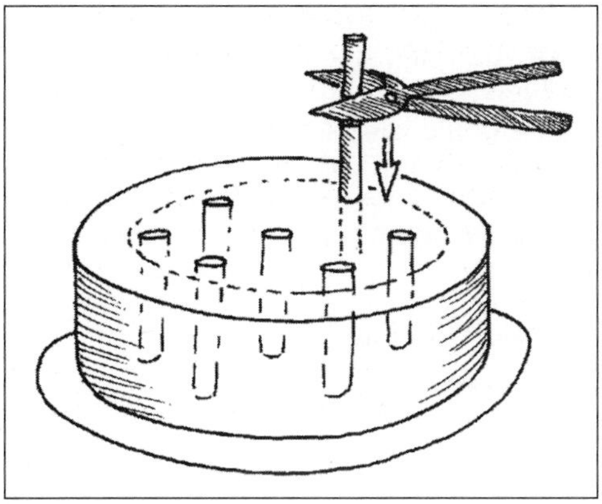

Figure 16-1:
Inserting
dowels to
give cake
tiers support.

7. **Measure one dowel to the height of your entire cake. Sharpen one end of the dowel to a point with a pencil sharpener. Insert the dowel in the center of the top tier, and stake it all the way through the center of the cake.**

When you encounter the cardboard round at the base of each tier, use a rubber mallet to pound gently on the dowel and pierce through the cardboard to the next layer.

Moving Up to a More Elaborate Wedding Cake

When taking on a cake that requires tiers and more elaborate decorations, it's smart to create a schedule for the baking and decorating required. As a general rule, I usually start two days out from the big event. For example, if the wedding is taking place late Saturday afternoon, this is my schedule:

✓ **On Thursday,** I bake the cake in the evening, and refrigerate it.

✓ **On Friday,** I frost the tiers, assemble the cake, and decorate it. Then it goes back into the refrigerator. If you don't have a refrigerator that accommodates the entire, assembled cake, skip the assembly stage and simply decorate and refrigerate the tiers individually. Plan extra time on-site to assemble the cake and touch up the decorations.

✓ **On Saturday,** I concern myself with futzing, checking to make sure that frosting covers any cardboard rounds and that all aspects of the cake are presentable; transporting; arranging the presentation; and incorporating fresh decorations, such as flowers.

Transporting your work of art safely is extremely important when you're dealing with a wedding cake. Although staking the entire cake with a dowel (refer to the preceding section) is essential, you also can assemble the cake on-site if transporting an assembled cake seems too risky. If you're transporting individual tiers, get your hands on appropriately sized skillets — one for each tier. Place a damp dish towel in the bottom of each skillet (to prevent sliding), and rest the tier on the towel.

Tahiti-in-SoHo Wedding Cake

In a nod to some of my favorite style icons — Kate Spade, Lulu Guinness, Dorothy Draper, and Elsie de Wolfe — this cake incorporates a color combination that never goes out of style . . . and is always in good taste. This cake is shown in Figure 16-2.

Don't skimp on the Tahitian vanilla in this recipe; it's distinct, rich, and ultrafragrant. Tahitian vanilla is available at specialty markets, gourmet stores, and on the Web.

Tools: *14-inch round cake pan, two 9-inch round cake pans, two 6-inch round cake pans, 14-inch cardboard round, 9-inch cardboard round, 6-inch cardboard round, #10 icing tip, silicone pastry brush*

Preparation time: *15 minutes*

Baking time: *50 minutes plus 2 hours for cooling*

Decoration time: *60 minutes plus 1 hour for refrigeration*

Yield: *24 servings*

For the cake (recipe follows):

6 batches modified Most Excellent White Cake batter (see Chapter 6)	*9 teaspoons Tahitian vanilla extract*

For the frosting (recipe follows):

3 batches modified Buttercream Frosting (see Chapter 8)	*3 teaspoons Tahitian vanilla*

For the filling:

1 batch Strawberry Syrup (recipe follows)	*50 medium-size fresh strawberries*

For the decorations:

Pale pink food coloring gel	*3 dozen unsprayed bright pink roses, such as the Sexy Rexy, Color Magic, Bewitched, or Disneyland varieties*
Warm brown food coloring gel	
Dark brown food coloring gel	*48 inches pink polka dotted chocolate brown grosgrain ribbon, optional*

Making the Tahitian Vanilla Cake and Buttercream Frosting

1 Preheat the oven to 350 degrees F. Grease the pans, and line them with parchment paper. Grease them again, and flour them.

2 Prepare the cake batters as described in Chapter 6, but in each batch, substitute 1½ teaspoons Tahitian vanilla for pure vanilla extract.

3 Divide the batter among the pans, and place them all in the oven together. Bake the 6-inch layers for 25 minutes, the 9-inch layers for 45 minutes, and the 14-inch layer for 50 minutes, or until a toothpick inserted in the center comes out with moist crumbs attached.

4 Remove the cakes from the oven, and let them cool in their pans for 10 minutes. Then invert them onto cooling racks, and invert them again onto racks so that they're right side up.

5 Prepare the buttercream as described in Chapter 8, but in each batch, substitute 1 teaspoon Tahitian vanilla for the pure vanilla extract.

Assembling and decorating the cake

1 After the cakes have cooled, level them (see Chapter 7), and torte them by slicing them in half horizontally.

2 Lightly wash and thoroughly dry the strawberries. Slice each one into eight even slices, and place them on paper towels to dry. Keep the slices as flat and even as possible.

3 Assemble the 14-inch tier: Place one 14-inch layer on the 14-inch cardboard round. Brush with strawberry syrup, and spread on a layer of frosting. Add a single layer of sliced strawberries before setting the corresponding 14-inch layer on top.

4 Repeat Step 3 with the four 9-inch layers and the four 6-inch layers.

5 Apply a crumb coat (thin layer) of frosting to each tier, and refrigerate them for 1 hour.

6 Divide and tint the frosting as follows: 8 cups pale pink, 2 cups light brown, and 2 cups dark brown.

7 Frost each tier with pink buttercream, taking each tier out of the refrigerator one at a time and returning it to the refrigerator after it's frosted.

8 Remove all the tiers from the refrigerator. Center and stack them, following the steps in the earlier section "Tiering Up for Success"; use five dowels in the 14-inch tier and four dowels in the 9-inch tier.

9 Outfit a pastry bag with a #10 tip and light brown frosting. Working clockwise, pipe light brown dots around the top and bottom edges of each tier, leaving space in between for alternating dark brown dots. (If you plan to use grosgrain ribbon on the cake, don't pipe around the base of the 14-inch tier.)

10 Outfit a pastry bag with a #10 tip and dark brown frosting. Pipe dark brown dots in between the light brown dots.

11 Arrange pink roses artfully between and around the cake layers, resting a few on the edges of both the 14-inch and 9-inch tiers.

12 Tie several roses with a 12-inch piece of grosgrain ribbon. Place the bouquet on top of the 6-inch tier to crown the cake.

13 Affix the remaining grosgrain ribbon to the base of the 14-inch tier using a beaded head pin to secure the ribbon ends. (Make sure that you remove the ribbon and pin before serving!)

Figure 16-2:
The elegant (and delicious) Tahiti-in-SoHo Wedding Cake.

Strawberry Syrup

2 cups sugar	2 cups water	½ cup strawberry flavoring syrup (used in coffee drinks)

1 In a medium saucepan, stir together the sugar and water over low heat for 2 minutes. Raise the heat to medium, and continue stirring until the mixture thickens and the sugar dissolves.

2 Remove the syrup from the heat, and let it cool to room temperature. Mix in the strawberry syrup.

Tip: *If you can't find enough unsprayed roses of a single shade, opt to blend a couple of varieties together for a nice effect.*

Celebrating Another Year with Anniversary Cakes

Although you may opt for a formal approach to an anniversary cake that celebrates 10, 25, or 50 years, I always enjoy taking a more relaxed route with anniversary cakes — particularly when kids are part of the celebration.

For instance, if the cake will be part of a black-tie affair celebrating the couple, consider making a tiered cake and covering the layers in white fondant. With royal icing, you can pipe simple dots all over the cake and pipe the number of years the couple has been married on the front side of the middle tier. If the gathering is more intimate, you can take a similar tack by covering a smaller, single-layer cake with fondant and dots.

For any anniversary occasion, consider taking a cue from the couple's wedding and wedding cake to settle on the colors, flavor, and style of the cake that they celebrate with. And consider adding a thoughtful memento or special touch to the cake, such as the couple's original cake topper or a small arrangement of flowers similar to the ones at their wedding.

Bubble Dot Anniversary Cake

If you've never worked with rolled fondant before, this cake is an easy introduction to the confection. Fondant adds formality to the cake without being stodgy.

I've opted for yellow, red, and orange as the cake's primary decorative colors, but you should use colors that you know are special for the couple. In addition, if blending colors into fondant doesn't appeal to you, check out the range of already-made colored fondant available in craft and baking stores as well as online. This cake is shown on the fifth page of the color section.

Tools: *9-x-13-inch cake pan, #1 icing tip, #2 icing tip, coupler, round fondant or cookie cutters in the following sizes: 3-inch, 2-inch, 1¼-inch, 1-inch, and ¾-inch*

Preparation time: *30 minutes*

Baking time: *45 minutes plus 2 hours for cooling*

Decoration time: *1½ hours plus 1 hour for refrigeration*

Yield: *24 servings*

For the cake:

1 batch Honey Cake batter (recipe follows)

For the frosting: *1 batch Buttercream Frosting (see Chapter 8)*

1 batch Royal Icing (see Chapter 9)

For the decorations: *Red food coloring gel*
3 4.4-ounce sheets ready-to-use white fondant   *Lemon yellow food coloring gel*
Orange food coloring gel   *Confectioners' sugar*

Assembling and decorating the cake

1 Level the cake (see Chapter 7). Apply a crumb coat (thin layer) of buttercream frosting to the cake, and refrigerate it for 1 hour.

2 Frost the cake with buttercream, and return it to the refrigerator to chill while you prepare the decorations.

3 Dab orange coloring gel into one sheet of fondant with a toothpick, and knead it to mix the color in evenly; add more gel to get the desired color. (You may want to wear plastic gloves to keep your hands dye-free!) When you've turned a sheet into a colored ball, place it in a sealed plastic bag to keep from drying out. Repeat the process with the red and yellow coloring gels and the other two sheets of fondant.

4 Sprinkle confectioners' sugar on your work surface, and roll out the orange fondant ball to a thickness of ⅛ inch. Cut one 3-inch circle, two 1¾-inch circles, two 1-inch circles, and two ¾-inch circles. Set them aside.

5 Roll out the red fondant to a thickness of ⅛ inch, and cut two 2-inch circles, one 1¾-inch circle, two 1-inch circles, and three ¾-inch circles. Repeat with the yellow fondant.

6 Remove the cake from the refrigerator, and place the large orange fondant circle in the center of it. Arrange the remaining circles (orange, red, and yellow) all over the cake. Bend them over the edges and stick them to the sides of the cake as well, if you like.

7 Outfit a pastry bag with a coupler, a #2 tip and royal icing. Pipe the anniversary date or years married in script on the large orange circle in the center of the cake. Refit the bag with the #1 tip. On the smaller circles, pipe family names, important dates, and meaningful locations.

Honey Cake

4¾ cups sifted cake flour

4½ teaspoons baking powder

1 teaspoon baking soda

¾ teaspoon salt

2 teaspoons ground cinnamon

1½ cups vegetable oil

1¼ cups honey

1¾ cups granulated white sugar

¾ cup firmly packed light brown sugar

5 eggs

1½ teaspoons pure vanilla extract

2 rounded teaspoons instant espresso powder

¾ cup fresh-squeezed orange juice

1 Preheat the oven to 350 degrees F. Grease and flour the cake pan.

2 Dissolve the espresso powder in 12 ounces of boiling water. Let it cool to room temperature.

3 In a large bowl, whisk together the cake flour, baking powder, baking soda, salt, and cinnamon. Make a well in the center of this mixture.

4 In a separate large bowl, combine the oil, honey, sugars, eggs, vanilla, espresso, and orange juice. Mix lightly, and then pour the mixture into the well in the dry ingredients.

5 In a mixer outfitted with the whisk attachment, mix the ingredients on low speed, just until blended (about 2 minutes). Pour the batter into the pan, and bake for 45 minutes, or until a cake tester inserted in the center comes out with moist crumbs attached.

6 Let the cake cool in its pan for 20 minutes before running a knife around the edges and inverting it onto a cooling rack to cool completely.

For anniversaries, I'm also fond of a double ring cake, in which you shape two 10-inch double-layer cakes into interlocking rings (see Figure 16-3). After outlining the rings, you can pipe on dates, years, names, or initials.

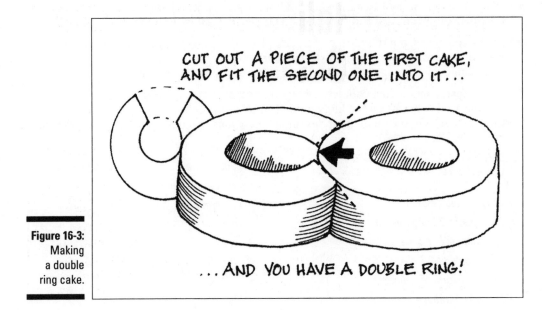

Figure 16-3:
Making
a double
ring cake.

Chapter 17

Savoring Holidays and Special Occasions

In This Chapter

▶ Taking advantage of seasonal confections
▶ Working with seasons and holiday themes
▶ Celebrating milestones with special cakes

*I*f you're looking for a reason to get your creative juices flowing and whip up a creative, delicious, and visually appealing cake, look no further than your calendar. With the seasons, holidays, and various other special occasions, each year abounds with opportunities for creative cakes.

This chapter mixes some decorating elements that I cover in other chapters with a few new techniques and ingredients to put you on track to creating some spectacular celebratory cakes.

Bringing Seasonal Treats to Your Decorating

Candy corn, conversation hearts, or shamrock mints, anyone? Almost every holiday has its own unique confections that you can incorporate into your cake decorating plan. Not only are such treats appropriate for your occasion, but they also make decorating a snap!

As each holiday or season rolls around, be on the lookout for treats and sweets that could be the perfect accompaniment — or even play a starring role — in your special cake.

Seasonal confections are just that — seasonal. For instance, cinnamon chips, which are particularly good for fall and harvest themes, may only be available in your grocery store for a few months in the fall, so stock up when you can. Similarly, brightly colored marshmallow confections in the shapes of chicks and bunnies are only available around Easter, and some chocolate candies come in seasonal colors that you can find only at certain times of the year. So if a product has a good shelf life and you've deemed it a favorite, stock up! You can always use it in the appropriate season, or it may be just what you need for another cake's design at another time of the year.

Saluting Spring and Summer

The spring and summer seasons bring great opportunities for decorating cake. For these spring and summer cakes, you get to work with a range of seasonal colors while trying out a variety of piping techniques and — in one cake — marzipan molding. A garden patch adorned with sweet crops, lemony cupcakes, and a razzmatazz red, white, and blue confection all promise to make your cake (and you!) a hit at warm weather gatherings and celebrations.

Garden Path Cake

After winter passes and spring fever hits, this cake is guaranteed to wow guests with its whimsical marzipan vegetables (which I cover in Chapter 12) set against a dirt background of finely ground chocolate wafers.

I've made this cake for many birthday celebrations, but the carrot cake flavor and overall design is versatile and works with a variety of occasions; it's an ideal theme for Easter or home-themed bridal showers. A version of this cake is shown in Figure 17-1.

Tools: *12-x-18-inch cake pan, bamboo skewer, 6 drinking straws, #6 icing tip, #7 icing tip, #67 icing tip*

Preparation time: *25 minutes*

Baking time: *50 minutes plus 30 minutes for cooling*

Decoration time: *3 hours plus 2 hours for refrigeration*

Yield: *32 servings*

For the cake:

*2 batches The Best Carrot Cake Ever batter
(see Chapter 6)*

For the frosting:

3 batches Cream Cheese Frosting (see Chapter 8)

For the decorations:

10 marzipan tomatoes	*4 marzipan watermelons*
10 marzipan pumpkins	*24 chocolate wafer cookies, finely ground*
6 marzipan carrots	*1 cup candy rocks*
8 marzipan eggplants	*Leaf green food coloring gel*
10 marzipan lettuce heads	

Preparing the cake

1 Preheat the oven to 350 degrees F. Grease the cake pan, and line it with parchment paper. Then grease and flour the parchment.

2 Prepare the cake batter as described in Chapter 6, and pour it in the pan.

3 Bake the cake for 50 minutes, or until a toothpick inserted in the center comes out with moist crumbs attached. Remove the cake from the oven, and let it cool in the pan for 10 minutes. Invert the cake onto a cooling rack.

Decorating the cake

1 Prepare the marzipan vegetables as instructed in Chapter 12.

2 After the cake has cooled completely, level it (see Chapter 7). Apply a crumb coat (thin layer) of cream cheese frosting to the cake, and refrigerate it for 1 hour. Frost the cake all over, and refrigerate again for 1 hour.

3 Using a bamboo skewer, etch a 4-inch wide pathway that winds the length of the cake.

4 Position drinking straws end-to-end along each side of the pathway to serve as a temporary barrier between the chocolate dirt and the path.

5 Use a large soup spoon to carefully pour the dirt into the garden area on either side of the pathway. Press the chocolate down lightly with the back of the spoon.

6 Lift off the straws, and place the candy rocks along each side of the pathway to mark it.

7 Lay out your garden of marzipan vegetables on each side of the path. (I like to group the crops together — a bunch of tomatoes in one spot, a bunch of eggplants in another spot, and so on.)

8 Mix 2 cups of cream cheese frosting with leaf green food coloring gel. Outfit a pastry bag with a coupler, a #7 tip, and the green frosting.

9 Pipe your desired message on the path.

10 Outfit the green frosting bag with a #67 tip, and make leaves around the border of the cake. Switch to a #6 tip, and finish off the leaves with tendrils. (Check out Chapter 11 for help piping leaves and tendrils.)

11 Place candy rocks along the base of the cake.

Figure 17-1:
The Garden
Path Cake.

Chick-Chick Cupcakes

Kids and adults are always thrilled to dive into these cupcakes, which feature a marshmallow and jelly bean scene atop lemony cake and frosting. Keep in mind, however, that the marshmallow chicks in this decoration are only available around Easter time.

Tools: *Two 12-well cupcake pans, jar with a screw-top lid (or large plastic container with a snap-on lid)*

Preparation time: *15 minutes*

Baking time: *20 minutes plus 30 minutes for cooling*

Decoration time: *1 hour plus 2 hours for refrigeration*

Yield: *24 servings*

For the cupcakes (recipe follows):

1 batch modified Delicious Yellow Cake Batter (see Chapter 6)

3 tablespoons grated lemon zest

¾ cup buttermilk

¾ cup fresh-squeezed lemon juice

For the frosting:

1 batch Lemon Buttercream Frosting (see Chapter 8)

For the decorations:

3 cups flaked sweetened coconut

Lemon yellow food coloring gel

Leaf green food coloring gel

2 cups jelly beans in pastel colors

24 marshmallow chicks

Preparing the Lemon Cupcakes

1 Preheat the oven to 350 degrees F. Line the pans with cupcake liners.

2 Prepare the cake batter as described in Chapter 6, except add 3 tablespoons grated lemon zest with the eggs, and substitute ¾ cup buttermilk mixed with ¾ cup fresh-squeezed lemon juice for the milk.

3 Bake for 20 minutes. Remove the pans from the oven, and lift the cupcakes out to cool on cooling racks.

Decorating the cupcakes

1 In the jar, combine 3 cups of coconut with several drops of lemon yellow food coloring. Screw on the top, and shake to tint the coconut yellow.

2 Set aside 1 cup of lemon buttercream frosting, and tint the remaining frosting leaf green. Use an icing spatula to spread green icing on each cupcake.

3 Press coconut onto the top of each cupcake to form a nest.

4 Pour the jelly beans into a medium bowl, and gently separate the marshmallow chicks.

5 Outfit a pastry bag with a #5 tip and white frosting.

6 Using the frosting as glue, pipe dots on the bottoms of six jelly beans and the marshmallow chick, and affix them to the top of one cupcake so that the chick is surrounded by jelly bean eggs.

7 Repeat with the remaining cupcakes. Check out what they look like in Figure 17-2.

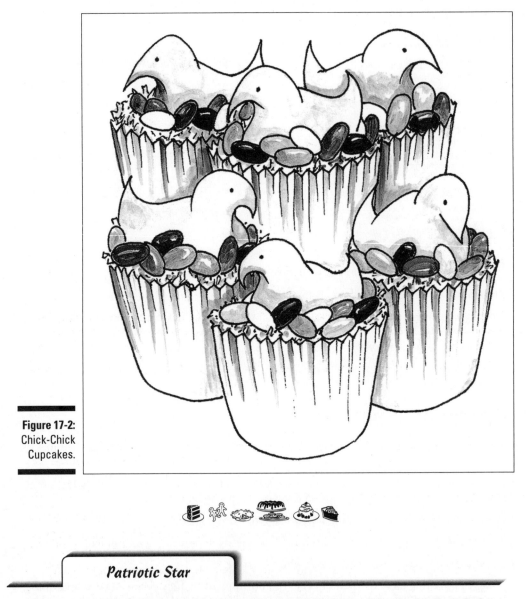

Figure 17-2:
Chick-Chick
Cupcakes.

Patriotic Star

Liven up a holiday cookout or picnic for Memorial Day or the Fourth of July with this festive and refreshing confection. The cake takes advantage of summer berries, and the inexpensive star-shaped cake pan is widely available each year as summer approaches. A version of this cake is shown in Figure 17-3.

Tools: *12¾-x-1⅛-inch star-shaped cake pan, #30 icing tip, bamboo skewer, silicone pastry brush, ruler*

Preparation time: *15 minutes*

Baking time: *30 minutes plus 30 minutes for cooling*

Decoration time: 45 minutes plus 1½ hours for refrigeration

Yield: 12 servings

For the cake:

1 batch Most Excellent White Cake batter
(see Chapter 6)

For the frosting:

2 batches Buttercream Frosting (see Chapter 8)

For the decorations:

½ cup seedless strawberry jam

1 batch Blueberry Compote (recipe follows)

1½ cups flaked sweetened coconut

3 cups fresh strawberries (washed, hulled, and dried)

1½ cups gummi stars in red, white, and blue

Star decoration

Preparing the cake

1 Preheat the oven to 350 degrees F. Grease and flour the pan.

2 Prepare the cake batter as described in Chapter 6.

3 Bake the cake for 30 minutes, or until a toothpick inserted in the center comes out with moist crumbs attached. Remove the cake from the oven, and let it cool in the pan for 10 minutes.

4 Run a knife around the edges of the cake, and then invert it onto a cooling rack to cool completely.

Decorating the cake

1 Apply a crumb coat (thin layer) of frosting to the cake, and refrigerate it for 1 hour. Then frost the cake all over with buttercream, and refrigerate it while you prepare the decorations.

2 In a small saucepan, heat the strawberry jam over low heat.

3 Following the cake's star shape, use a bamboo skewer to sketch a star about 1½ inches in from the outside edge of the cake. Sketch a second star about 3 inches in from your first sketch.

4 Carefully spoon blueberry compote into the smallest star in the center of the cake. Spread coconut around the blueberry star, staying within the lines of your star sketch. Place the strawberries, hulled side down, along the edge of the top of the cake, all the way around the star's perimeter.

5 Brush the strawberries with melted strawberry jam.

6 Outfit a pastry bag with a #30 tip and buttercream frosting. Pipe stars in an outline the blueberry compote star, the coconut star, and the strawberry star. Also pipe stars around the base of the cake.

7 Push the gummi stars on the sides of the cake, all the way around. If the stars don't stick well because the frosting's too cold, dab the undersides of them with more frosting before placing them.

8 Insert the star decoration into the center of the blueberry compote star.

Blueberry Compote

2½ cups frozen blueberries   ⅓ cup sugar   ⅓ cup water

1 In a small saucepan, combine 1½ cups berries with the sugar and water.

2 Simmer over medium heat until the berries burst, about 10 minutes, stirring frequently.

3 Add the remaining berries, and simmer for about 8 minutes, until the compote coats the back of a spoon. Chill the compote before using it on the cake.

Figure 17-3:
The
Patriotic
Star Cake.

Having Fun in the Fall

Before you leap headlong into the year-end holidays, savor the feeling of fall with a few festive cakes. Halloween and Thanksgiving are ripe with cake decorating possibilities, and each offers up an array of goodies to help bring on the fun.

Haunted Mansion

The recipe for this spooky showstopper calls for fudgy chocolate cake layers, but you can also make it out of honey cake (see Chapter 16 for a recipe), which imparts a sweet fall scent. And although you have to stack up a few cakes for this creation, you don't have to worry about using dowels because you have enough support from underneath.

The skeleton pops and cupcake picks in the decorations list are easy to find around Halloween time. And you also may find additional candies or novelties that you'd like to include in the windows and on the lawn of this haunted place. This cake is shown on the second-to-last page of the color section.

Tools: *Two 9⅛-x-5¼-inch loaf pans, two 10-inch square cake pans, #4 icing tip, #7 icing tip, #10 icing tip, #67 icing tip, food processor, meat tenderizer mallet*

Preparation time: *25 minutes*

Baking time: *30 minutes plus 30 minutes for cooling*

Decoration time: *1¼ hours plus 2 hours for refrigeration*

Yield: *12 servings*

For the cake (recipe follows):

2 batches modified Cocoa Chocolate Cake batter (see Chapter 6)

6 ounces semisweet chocolate, chopped

For the frosting:

1 batch Stiff Decorator Frosting (see Chapter 8)

2 batches modified Stiff Decorator Frosting (see Chapter 8 and instructions that follow)

2 tablespoons cocoa powder

For the decorations:

1 pound black licorice

4 2-x-4-inch squares of chocolate (from a 7.5-ounce chocolate bar)

Black food coloring gel

Red red food coloring gel

36 red and purple square-shaped sour hard candies, broken into jagged pieces with a meat tenderizer

14.4-ounce box chocolate graham crackers, finely ground in a food processor

4 skeleton pops

2 ghost cupcake picks

2 pumpkin cupcake picks

1 plastic glow-in-the-dark skull-and-crossbones ring

1 witch cupcake pick

Preparing the fudgy chocolate cake

1 Preheat the oven to 350 degrees F. Grease the cake pans, and line them with parchment paper. Then grease and flour the parchment.

2 Prepare the cake batter as described in Chapter 6, but for each batch, melt 3 ounces of chopped semisweet chocolate in ⅔ cup boiling water. Stir the mixture until smooth and slightly cool. Mix the chocolate into the cake batter after the eggs but before the flour.

3 Bake the cake loaves for 30 minutes and the squares for 40 minutes. Cool all the cakes in the pans for 10 minutes, and then run a knife around the edges of each cake. Invert the cakes onto cooling racks, and then invert them again so that they're right side up.

4 Prepare two batches of Stiff Decorator Frosting as described in Chapter 8, but in each batch, whisk 1 tablespoon cocoa powder into the confectioners' sugar.

5 After the cakes have completely cooled, cut one loaf cake in half vertically. Set one half aside, and cut the other half into quarters, keeping one quarter, and discarding the others. (The remaining quarter piece is one eighth-loaf.)

6 Level the cakes (two squares, one loaf, one half-loaf, and one eighth-loaf). Apply a crumb coat (thin layer) of chocolate decorator frosting to each cake, and refrigerate them for 1 hour. Frost the cakes again, and refrigerate them while you prepare the decorations.

Decorating the cake

1 Prepare a cake board that's approximately 18-x-24 inches in size. Use plywood or fiberboard that's wrapped with cake foil or Halloween wrapping paper covered with clear heavy cellophane wrap.

2 Stack the cakes toward the back of the board as follows: Set the two square cakes one on top of the other to form the bottom floor of the house. Center the loaf cake on top of the bottom floor; set the half-loaf on top of that floor; and set the one-eighth piece on top of the half-loaf to form a witch's perch.

3 Lay lengths of licorice around the top and base of each level, except for the witch's perch.

4 Using chocolate frosting as glue, affix chocolate bar squares to the center of the bottom layer to make the mansion's door.

5 Mix 2 cups of chocolate decorator frosting with black food coloring gel. Outfit a pastry bag with a coupler, a #7 tip, and black frosting.

6 With black frosting, pipe a square window on either side of the mansion door. Pipe four square windows on the second story of the house, three square windows on the third story, and an oval-shaped window on the witch's perch. Also pipe a doorknob and an awning on the door.

7 Mix 1 cup of white decorator frosting with red food coloring gel. Outfit a pastry bag with a coupler, a #4 tip, and red frosting. Along the top edge of the first three floors (not the witch's perch), pipe a string of pointed red drips to look like seeping blood.

8 With an icing spatula, spread 2 cups of untinted chocolate frosting in front of the house.

9 Outfit the black frosting bag with a #10 tip, and, over the chocolate frosting yard, outline a crooked walkway leading to the front door. Fill in the walkway with crushed hard candies.

10 Spread the chocolate graham cracker crumbs on either side of the walkway. With the black frosting bag, pipe frosting onto the candy tops of the skeleton pops. Scatter the skeleton pops to resemble trees in the mansion's yard, sticking them into the frosting in the front yard, and mound chocolate crumbs at the base of each pop. Refit the black frosting bag with a #67 tip, and pipe drooping black leaves on the skeletons' hands.

11 Stick the ghost picks and pumpkin picks on the second and third floors of the mansion, and push the skull-and-crossbones ring into the oval-shaped window on the witch's perch. Insert the witch pick into the very top of the house.

Jack-O'-Lantern

Here's a jack-o'-lantern that doesn't have to be scooped out! A fluted Bundt pan creates a realistic look, and the Brown Sugar Cake fits the tenor of October . . . but is delicious year-round. This cake is shown on the second-to-last page of the color section.

Tools: *Two 10-fluted Bundt pans, #11 icing tip*

Preparation time: *20 minutes*

Baking time: *50 minutes plus 30 minutes for cooling*

Decoration time: *35 minutes plus 1 hour for refrigeration*

Yield: *24 servings*

For the cake:

2 batches Brown Sugar Cake batter (recipe follows)

For the frosting:

2 batches Buttercream Frosting (see Chapter 8)

For the decorations:

Black food coloring gel

Leaf green food coloring gel

Sunset orange food coloring gel

Banana, unpeeled

Preparing the cake

1 Prepare the Brown Sugar Cake batter according to the recipe that follows. However, with two pans in the oven, rotate the pans midway through the baking time.

2 Let the cakes cool in the pans for at least 10 minutes, and then run a knife around the edges. Invert the cakes onto cooling racks, and then invert them again so that they're right side up.

3 After the cakes are completely cool, apply a crumb coat (thin layer) of buttercream frosting, and refrigerate them for 1 hour.

Decorating the cake

1 Divide and tint the buttercream frosting as follows: 1 cup black, ½ cup leaf green, and the remainder orange.

2 Turn one cake upside down, and frost it with orange buttercream. Put the other cake on top of it, right side up, and frost the entire cake orange. With the last coat of frosting, frost the cake with a downward motion to create the striations found on a real pumpkin.

3 Outfit a pastry bag with a coupler, a #10 tip, and black frosting. On the side of the pumpkin, pipe two triangles for the eyes, one triangle for the nose, and a series of smaller triangles for the mouth.

4 Cut the banana in half, and cover it with green frosting. Insert it stem side up into the hole at the top of the pumpkin.

Brown Sugar Cake

This is one of my most favorite and most requested cakes. Its caramel flavor also pairs well with milk chocolate frosting (see Chapter 8 for a recipe).

3¾ cups sifted cake flour

1½ teaspoons baking soda

2¼ cups vegetable oil

2¼ cups dark brown sugar

3 eggs

1½ teaspoons pure vanilla extract

1½ cups buttermilk

1 Preheat the oven to 350 degrees F. Spray a Bundt pan with baking spray that contains flour, and set it aside.

2 In a medium bowl, combine the cake flour and baking soda. Stir them together with a balloon whisk.

3 In a large mixing bowl, combine the oil and sugar, and beat the mixture until blended.

4 Add the eggs to the oil and sugar mixture, one at a time, beating well after each addition. Add the vanilla, and beat to blend.

5 Add the flour in four additions, alternating with the buttermilk. (Begin and end with the flour.) Mix each flour addition just until blended.

6 Pour the batter into the prepared pan, and bake for 50 minutes, or until a cake tester inserted in the center comes out with moist crumbs attached.

7 Let the cake cool in the pan for 10 minutes before inverting it onto a cooling rack to cool completely.

Cornucopia Cake

If you're eager to incorporate cake into your Thanksgiving buffet — or if you just want to lay off the pumpkin pie for a change — this not-too-sweet confection won't disappoint. Taking some time with the piped lace design makes it look as if the cornucopia is sitting on a tablecloth. This cake is shown in Figure 17-4.

Tools: *Two 9-inch round cake pans, #2 icing tip, #6 icing tip, #47 icing tip, 6-inch diameter plastic lid*

Preparation time: *20 minutes*

Baking time: *40 minutes plus 30 minutes for cooling*

Decoration time: *1 hour plus 1 hour for refrigeration*

Yield: *12 servings*

For the cake (recipe follows):

1 batch modified Delicious Yellow Cake batter (see Chapter 6)

3 teaspoons instant espresso powder

½ cup half-and-half

½ cup coffee liqueur

For the frosting:

1 batch Stiff Decorator Frosting (see Chapter 8)

1 batch Milk Chocolate Frosting (see Chapter 8)

For the decorations:

Egg yellow food coloring gel

Harvest brown food coloring gel

Waffle ice cream cone

2 cups Swiss fruits

Preparing the Coffee-Flavored Cake

1 Preheat the oven to 350 degrees F. Grease the cake pans, and line them with parchment paper. Then grease and flour the parchment.

2 Prepare the cake batter as described in Chapter 6, but stir 3 teaspoons instant espresso powder into the sifted flour, and substitute ½ cup half-and-half and ½ cup coffee liqueur for the milk.

3 Bake for 40 minutes, or until a toothpick inserted in the center comes out with moist crumbs attached. Let the cakes cool in the pans for 10 minutes, and then run a knife around the edges. Invert the cakes onto cooling racks.

4 After the cakes are completely cool, torte both cakes so that you have four layers. Frost one layer with milk chocolate frosting, and set the corresponding layer on top. Add a layer of frosting, followed by the third layer, another layer of frosting, and the final layer of cake. Apply a crumb coat (thin layer) of frosting to the entire cake, and refrigerate it for 1 hour.

Decorating the cake

1 Divide and tint the stiff decorator frosting as follows: 2 cups egg yellow and 2 cups harvest brown.

2 Frost the cake with yellow frosting.

3 In the center of the cake, use a toothpick to sketch an oval. Lay the ice cream cone on its side in the center of the oval.

4 Outfit a pastry bag with a coupler, a #47 tip, and brown frosting. Pipe a basket weave design on the ice cream cone cornucopia.

5 Arrange the Swiss fruits so that they appear to tumble out of the cornucopia.

6 Outfit the brown frosting bag with a #6 tip, and pipe an oval border around the cone, following your previous sketch.

7 Place the 6-inch plastic lid along the sides of the cake and press gently to create an impression of downward arcs. With the #6 tip and brown frosting, pipe little beads along the arcs. Also pipe a row of beads all around the base of the cake.

8 Outfit the brown frosting bag with a #1 tip, and in between the oval and the downward arcs, pipe a lacy design with a pattern of curves and lines.

Figure 17-4:
The
Cornucopia
Cake.

Greeting the Winter Holidays

In the throes of the holidays, occasion and opportunity abound for a themed cake that dishes up festive notions. In this section, you find recipes for two playful takes on holiday fare.

Take advantage of the myriad holiday-themed candies and sweets that are available to decorate cakes during the holiday season.

Christmas Tree Cake

This cake for a holiday crowd always draws raves . . . particularly after it's cut and partygoers get a peek at the color inside.

You can play around with your own color scheme for this cake. I like a multicolored approach because it reminds me of vintage Christmas trees decorated with glass ornaments of several different colors.

I like to keep the borders and edges free of any decoration so that the eye is drawn directly to the tree that appears to be standing amidst beautiful, fluffy snow. This cake is shown on the last page of the color section.

Tools: *12-x-18-inch cake pan, bamboo skewer, small rolling pin, #11 icing tip, #100 icing tip, paring knife*

Preparation time: *15 minutes*

Baking time: *50 minutes plus 2 hours for cooling*

Decoration time: *35 minutes plus 1 hour for refrigeration*

Yield: *24 servings*

For the cake (recipe follows):

2 batches Red Velvet Cake batter

For the frosting:

2 batches Cream Cheese Frosting (see Chapter 8)

For the decorations:

Leaf green food coloring gel	*36 large gumdrops in assorted colors*
Brown food coloring gel	*Large yellow gumdrop*

Preparing the cake

1 Preheat the oven to 350 degrees F. Grease a 12-x-18-inch cake pan, and line it with parchment paper. Then grease and flour the parchment.

2 Prepare the Red Velvet Cake batter according to the recipe that follows. Bake for 50 minutes, or until a toothpick inserted in the center comes out with moist crumbs attached.

3 Let the cake cool in the pan for 10 minutes before inverting it onto a cooling rack. After it is completely cool, apply a crumb coat (thin layer) of cream cheese frosting. Refrigerate for 1 hour.

Decorating the cake

1 Divide and tint the frosting as follows: 2 cups leaf green and ½ cup brown. Frost the cake with the remaining untinted cream cheese frosting.

2 With a bamboo skewer, sketch the shape of a Christmas tree on the surface of the cake. The tree trunk should be 3 inches tall.

3 Outfit a pastry bag with a coupler, #100 tip, and green frosting. Pipe boughs over the tree, overdrawing them for a full, lustrous look if you like. (Make sure to cover up your sketched lines!)

4 Outfit a pastry bag with a coupler, #11 tip, and brown frosting. Pipe the trunk in straight lines. If desired, smooth out the piping with an icing spatula.

5 Place the colored gumdrops on the tree, arranging them to look like ornaments.

6 To create the star, roll out a yellow gumdrop. Either carve out a star shape with a sharp knife, or cut the rolled gumdrop into five triangles and form them into a star. Place the star at the top of the tree.

Red Velvet Cake

3¾ cups sifted cake flour

1½ tablespoons cocoa powder

1½ teaspoons salt

1½ teaspoons baking soda

1½ tablespoons white vinegar

2¼ cups granulated white sugar

¾ cup vegetable oil

3 eggs

1½ cups buttermilk

1½ teaspoons pure vanilla extract

2 ounces red food coloring

1 Preheat the oven to 350 degrees F. Grease and flour a 9-x-13-inch cake pan, and set it aside.

2 In a large bowl, combine the cake flour, cocoa powder, and salt, and whisk them together with a balloon whisk.

3 In a small bowl, dissolve the baking soda in the vinegar. Stir well to make sure the baking soda is fully dissolved.

4 In a large bowl, beat the sugar and oil together until blended. Add the eggs one at a time, beating well after each addition.

5 Add the flour mixture to the sugar and oil mixture in four additions, alternating with the buttermilk. (Begin and end with the flour.) Mix each flour addition just until blended.

6 Beat in the vanilla and food coloring. Stir the baking soda mixture again, and fold it into the batter with a rubber spatula.

7 Bake the cake for 35 minutes, or until a toothpick inserted in the center comes out with moist crumbs attached.

Skating Rink Cake

Cake eaters will be amazed, surprised, and delighted by the visual impact of this design. Because the cake doesn't pay homage to a particular holiday, it's a great choice for any wintertime occasion. This cake is shown in Figure 17-5.

Tools: *Two 9-x-13-inch cake pans, #864 icing tip, 8-cup glass measuring cup, large glass bowl*

Preparation time: *15 minutes*

Baking time: *35 minutes plus 30 minutes for cooling*

Decoration time: *45 minutes plus 3 hours for refrigeration*

Yield: *12 servings*

For the cake (recipe follows):

2 batches modified Most Excellent White Cake batter (see Chapter 6)

1 cup flaked sweetened coconut

For the frosting:

2 batches Stiff Decorator Frosting (see Chapter 8)

1 batch Buttercream Frosting (see Chapter 8)

For the decorations:

6-ounce box berry blue gelatin

Leaf green food coloring gel

3 ice cream cones

Jumbo marshmallows

Gummi penguins and bears

Preparing the Coconut Cake

1 Preheat the oven to 350 degrees F, and grease and flour the pans.

2 Prepare the cake batter as described in Chapter 6, but in each batch, fold ½ cup flaked coconut into the batter before pouring it into the pan.

3 Bake for 35 minutes, or until a toothpick inserted in the center comes out with moist crumbs attached. Let the cakes cool in the pans for 10 minutes before you run a knife around the edges. Invert the cakes onto racks to finish cooling.

4 After the cakes are completely cool, level them (see Chapter 7). Apply a crumb coat (thin layer) of buttercream frosting to the cakes, place one atop the other, and refrigerate them for 1 hour.

Decorating the cake

1 Frost the stacked cake with buttercream. Use a bamboo skewer to sketch a free-form lake in the center of this cake. With a fork, carefully hollow out the lake, digging out the cake to a depth of 1 inch (only dig out the top layer of cake).

2 Prepare the gelatin as follows (don't use the directions on the box!): With a large bowl of ice water standing by, pour the gelatin into a large glass measuring cup, and stir in 2 cups of boiling water. Set the measuring cup in the bowl of ice water, and continue stirring the gelatin for about 8 minutes, just until it thickens very slightly. Pour the gelatin into the lake on the surface of the cake. Refrigerate at least 2 hours for the gelatin to set.

3 Tint 2 cups of stiff decorator frosting leaf green. Outfit a pastry bag with a #864 tip and green frosting.

4 Rest the ice cream cones upside down on a piece of wax paper. Moving vertically up and down the cones, pipe boughs on all the cone trees with the green frosting. Start at the base of each cone, and draw the frosting away from the cone to a point before moving onto the next bough. Place the trees on the cake around the lake.

5 Position marshmallows around the scene to resemble snowy drifts. Skewer the bottoms of the penguins and gummi bears with toothpicks, and insert them into the cake.

Figure 17-5:
The Skating
Rink Cake.

Celebrating Other Occasions

Not that you need a reason to bake and decorate a cake, but if you're looking for a reason, truth be told, you can celebrate any day of the year with cake.

Groundhog Day, Arbor Day, Secretary's Day, next Tuesday . . . the possibilities are endless, and you're only limited by your imagination.

For this section, I've picked a traditional holiday and a pair of life events to make even sweeter with beautiful cakes.

Heart-O'-Mine Cake

This heart-shaped cake was initially designed for a celebrity's Valentine's Day celebration-for-two. However, where hearts are concerned, any day's the right one to express love.

Candy hearts are part of the decoration for this cake, but you also can make all the decorations with frosting if you have the time. This cake is shown on the last page of the color section.

Tools: *Two 8-inch heart-shaped cake pans, three #7 icing tips*

Preparation time: *20 minutes*

Baking time: *35 minutes plus 1 hour for cooling*

Decoration time: *1¼ hours plus 1 hour for refrigeration*

Yield: *12 servings*

For the cake (recipe follows):

1 batch modified Most Excellent White Cake batter (see Chapter 6)

4 ounces white chocolate, chopped

For the frosting:

3 batches Buttercream Frosting (see Chapter 8)

For the decorations:

Fuchsia food coloring gel

Bright red food coloring gel

Purple food coloring gel

Fuchsia, red, and purple candy hearts

Preparing the White Chocolate Cake

1 Preheat the oven to 350 degrees F, and grease and flour the pans.

2 Prepare the cake batter as described in Chapter 6, but melt 4 ounces of white chocolate into ½ cup of boiling water, cool the mixture, and beat it into the batter after the egg whites and before the flour.

3 Bake the cakes for 35 minutes, or until a toothpick inserted in the center comes out with moist crumbs attached. Let the cakes cool in the pans for 10 minutes before running a knife around the edges. Invert the cakes onto cooling racks.

4 After the cakes are completely cool, level them (see Chapter 7). Frost the top of one cake, stack the other cake on top, and apply a crumb coat (thin layer) of buttercream frosting to the entire cake. Refrigerate it for 1 hour.

Decorating the cake

1 Frost the cake with buttercream, and return it to the refrigerator to chill while you prepare the tinted frosting.

2 Divide and tint the remaining frosting as follows: 1½ cups fuchsia, 1½ cups red, and 1½ cups purple. Outfit three pastry bags — one for each color — with a #7 tip and frosting.

3 Outline the outer edge of the top of the cake with red frosting. Position fuchsia, red, and purple candy hearts all along the top of the cake, sitting just inside the red outline.

4 Pipe stripes along the sides of the cake by alternating the frosting colors.

5 Put a conversation heart in the very center of the cake. Outline the heart in red frosting, then in purple frosting, and finally in fuchsia frosting.

Vary It!: Instead of placing heart-shaped candies around the cake's top border, you can pipe hearts in different colors. To do that, use a #10 icing tip and pipe two facing upside-down teardrops. In lieu of the conversation heart in the center of the cake, you can pipe a message to a special someone. Just keep the script on the small and subtle side.

Housewarming Cake

This cake evokes a homey scene and scent, and you can adjust the colors to match the palette of the home being celebrated. Edible glitter and pearls make for a very realistic sparkly chandelier. A version of the finished cake is shown in Figure 17-6.

Tools: 12-x-18-inch cake pan, bamboo skewer, ruler, #2 icing tip, #4 icing tip, #5 icing tip, #11 icing tip

Preparation time: 30 minutes

Baking time: 50 minutes plus 2 hours for cooling

Decoration time: 1 hour plus 1 hour for refrigeration

Yield: 32 servings

For the cake (recipe follows):

3 batches modified Delicious Yellow Cake batter (see Chapter 6)

1½ teaspoons ground cinnamon

1½ teaspoons cinnamon extract

For the frosting:

3 batches Cream Cheese Frosting (see Chapter 8)

For the decorations:

1 batch Royal Icing (see Chapter 9)

Gold shimmer dust

Ivory food coloring gel

Nut brown food coloring gel

Black food coloring gel

3 2-x-2-inch gourmet marshmallow cubes

12-inch yellow marshmallow stick

12-inch pink marshmallow stick

1-ounce bag edible yellow pearls

1-ounce bag edible pink pearls

Preparing the Cinnamon Cake

1 Preheat the oven to 350 degrees F. Grease the pan, line it with parchment paper, and then grease and flour the paper.

2 Prepare the cake batter as described in Chapter 6, but in each batch, add ½ teaspoon ground cinnamon to the cake flour, and substitute ½ teaspoon cinnamon extract for the vanilla.

3 Bake for 50 minutes, or until a toothpick inserted in the center comes out with moist crumbs attached. Let the cake cool in the pan for 10 minutes before running a knife around the edge and inverting it onto a cooling rack.

4 After the cake is completely cool, level it (see Chapter 7). Apply a crumb coat (thin layer) of cream cheese frosting, and refrigerate it for 1 hour.

Decorating the cake

1 Outfit a pastry bag with a coupler, #2 tip, and royal icing. On a sheet of wax paper, pipe eight teardrops at least 1 inch apart. While the icing is still wet, shake gold shimmer dust over the teardrops to cover them completely. Place the wax paper on a plate or tray, and set it in the freezer.

2 Divide and tint the cream cheese frosting as follows: 2 cups ivory, 2 cups nut brown, and ¾ cup black.

3 Frost the cake with ivory frosting.

4 Use a ruler to measure 2 inches in from the sides of the cake, and sketch a frame with a bamboo skewer. Sketch a 4½-x-1½-inch rectangle in the center of the frame; this is the sofa back. Underneath the sofa back, sketch the sofa's seat: a trapezoid that's 1½ inches tall on each side, 6½ inches across the top, and 8 inches across the bottom.

5 Above the sofa back, sketch a 5-inch tall chandelier with swag lights that branch out 3 inches at the top, 4½ inches in the middle, and 6 inches at the base.

6 Outfit a pastry bag with a coupler, #11 tip, and brown frosting. Pipe along the inside edge of the frame, but leave a 1½-x-4-inch rectangle in the center of the bottom of the frame.

7 Outfit a pastry bag with a coupler, #11 tip, and black frosting. Outline the frame, giving it mitered corners. Refit the frosting bag with a #4 tip, and outline the center rectangle on the bottom of the frame. In the rectangle, script the homeowner's last name, such as "The Waltons."

8 Cut three 1½-x-1½-inch squares out of the gourmet marshmallow cubes, and place them side-by-side to form the sofa's rectangular back cushion. Snip the marshmallow sticks to form the sofa's trapezoid seat: one ¾-x-6½ inches and the other ¾-x-8-inches. Stick them all in place.

9 Outfit the black frosting bag with a #5 tip, and pipe an outline around the sofa. Add pointed legs to the bottom.

10 Pipe the chandelier structure, making sure to include eight light holders. Place strands of edible pearls on the frosting to give a beaded appearance.

11 Remove the royal icing teardrops from the freezer. Using an icing spatula, gently lift them one at a time from the wax paper and slide them onto the chandelier's light holders.

Figure 17-6:
The House-
warming
Cake.

Cap 'n' Tassel Graduation Cake

This cake is perfect for graduates of any age. With just one commonly found ingredient — fruit streamers — you can easily personalize the colors of the mortarboard's tassel. This cake is shown in Figure 17-7.

Tools: *Two 9-inch round cake pans, silicon cupcake holder, #6 icing tip, #10 icing tip, #18 icing tip, paring knife, cutting board*

Preparation time: *20 minutes*

Baking time: *30 minutes plus 2 hours for cooling*

Decoration time: *40 minutes plus 1 hour for refrigeration*

Yield: *12 servings*

For the cake:

1 batch Cocoa Chocolate Cake batter (see Chapter 6)

For the frosting:

1 batch Chocolate Buttercream Frosting (see Chapter 8)

1 batch Buttercream Frosting (see Chapter 8)

For the decorations:

1 cupcake

Royal blue food coloring gel

Lemon yellow food coloring gel

Dark brown food coloring gel

1 pouch fruit streamers in the appropriate school colors

4-x-4-inch chocolate bar square

Preparing the cake

1 Preheat the oven to 350 degrees F. Grease and flour the pans.

2 Prepare the cake batter as described in Chapter 6, and pour it into the prepared pans and the cupcake holder.

3 Bake the cupcake for 20 minutes and the two cakes for 30 minutes, or until a toothpick inserted in the center comes out with moist crumbs attached. Let the cakes cool in the pans for 10 minutes before running a knife around the edges. Invert all three cakes onto a cooling rack.

4 After the cakes are completely cool, level them (see Chapter 7). Frost the top of one layer, and stack the other layer on top of it. Apply a crumb coat (thin layer) of chocolate buttercream to both the layered cake and the cupcake, and refrigerate them for 1 hour.

Decorating the cake

1 Frost the cake with chocolate buttercream, and set it back in the refrigerator.

2 Divide and tint the plain buttercream as follows: 1½ cups royal blue, 1½ cups lemon yellow, and 2 cups dark brown.

3 Outfit a pastry bag with a coupler, #18 tip, and yellow frosting. Pipe a shell border around the top edge of the cake.

4 Outfit a pastry bag with a coupler, #18 tip, and blue frosting. Pipe a shell border in blue around the base of the cake. Return the cake to the refrigerator.

5 Frost the cupcake with dark brown frosting, and set it upside down in the top center of the layered cake.

6 Outfit a pastry bag with a coupler, #10 tip, and brown frosting. Separate the fruit streamers into individual, spaghetti-like strands. Measure and cut six 6-inch blue ones and six 6-inch yellow ones. Place the fruit strands on top of the chocolate square (which is the mortarboard), adhering them with a dab of brown frosting. With the #10 tip, pipe a circle of frosting to be the button on the top of the chocolate mortarboard.

7 Dab some frosting on the underside of the chocolate mortarboard, and place it on top of the cupcake. Refit the dark brown frosting bag with a #6 tip, and pipe "Congratulations" on the cake by the cap.

Figure 17-7:
The Cap
'n' Tassel
Graduation
Cake.

Part V
Thinking Outside the Cake Box

The 5th Wave
By Rich Tennant

"I know it tastes a little odd. Let's just say you should store your bundt cake in a cool dry place, <u>other</u> than your husband's humidor."

In this part . . .

Take pride in a job well-done. This part guides you in wrapping up the cake process by preparing your cake for the big reveal and getting your cake to its destination in perfect shape. I also share ways to create and decorate cakes in a snap for last-minute functions. At this point, you also may be so excited about your cake decorating skills that you're thinking about starting a cake decorating business, but don't make a move until you've read the details dished out here.

Chapter 18

Prepping for Showtime

. . . .

In This Chapter

▶ Reviewing the finished product with a critical eye

▶ Remembering everything you need for an event

▶ Planning an inspired cake staging

▶ Getting the cake to its final destination

▶ Making the most of uneaten cake

. . . .

*W*ith an amazing cake completed and ready for its time in the spotlight of a special occasion, you may think that you've reached the finish line of the cake decorating process. However, a few more tasks remain to be done, starting with scrutinizing the final product in order to ensure that it's the best it can be. As part of your final preparations, put the cake through the paces (not literally of course) by checking and double-checking its appearance, stability, and structure, and collect everything you need to make any touch-ups and serve the cake in style.

This chapter covers those tasks as well as the concerns associated with transporting your creation — a proposition that may make you nervous. I provide recommendations on the best tools and procedures for getting your cake to where it needs to be — safely and completely intact. You also get some suggestions of what to do with leftover cake.

Giving Your Cake the Once-Over

I know you want your cake to make the best impression possible and fete an honoree or celebrate an occasion in the most polished, festive way. To that end, first congratulate yourself on your accomplishment, and then spend a few moments inspecting your freshly decorated cake from all sides.

Not only does scrutinizing your cake's look and decorations benefit the upcoming event, but it also helps you with future cake decorating endeavors. Viewing your cake with a critical eye and answering the questions that follow help you identify your cake design's strengths and weaknesses, which you can take into account when creating the same cake or a different one in the future.

1. **Examine the cake's silhouette.**

   • Does it seem lopsided or uneven?

   • Does the frosting completely cover the cake?

   • Are the borders and edges tight and clean, or could they use some perfecting?

2. **Examine the cake's decorations.**

   • Do the decorations fit on the cake well, and are they proportionate to the cake?

   • Is there too much crowding of decorations or too much design going on?

   • Is there too much or not enough blank space?

   • Does every part of the decoration look like it belongs on the cake?

   • Is any scripting legible? Are you certain that words and names are spelled correctly?

3. **Examine its positioning.**

   • How does the cake board look? Is it clean?

   • Does the cake board enhance or detract from the cake?

   • Is the cake board sturdy enough to transport the cake?

4. **Examine the overall design.**

   • Does the overall look fit in with the event?

   • How does this decorated cake match up with your initial concept?

   • How does it compare to the sketch you made in the planning stages?

   • What changes did you have to make? Why?

   • Did the colors come out like you expected?

If you have a digital camera, take and save pictures of each cake you complete. It's amazing what a camera can pick up that you don't see when you stare right at your cake. With the ease, speed, and advantages of a digital camera — including the ability to instantly enlarge shots on a computer screen — you can inspect your cake from all angles, spotting both glaring blotches and tiny imperfections. A digital photo also gives you a visual to refer back to if and when you decide to create a particular cake again.

A Cake Decorator's Checklist for the Big Day

It sounds so elementary, but a checklist that includes all the accoutrements and accessories you need to arrange, present, and serve the cake really can save the day. Experience has taught me that, without a list such as this, you'd be surprised at what you can forget, particularly if you have to take the cake to another location. (Believe it or not, I've heard a few humorous anecdotes from other cake decorators that involved forgetting the cake itself!)

Include the following items on your checklist:

- ✔ The cake
- ✔ The cake board
- ✔ Materials for fast fixes (see the list later in this section)
- ✔ Candles, if appropriate for the celebration
- ✔ Accessories for the presentation table or area (see the section "Playing around with props" later in this chapter)
- ✔ Serving implements, such as a cake knife and server or lifter
- ✔ A reference diagram for cutting (check out Chapter 22 for slicing ideas)
- ✔ A tall ceramic vessel in which to clean the serving knife between cuts (see Chapter 22 for details)
- ✔ Plates and forks
- ✔ Decorations or edible embellishments, such as whipped cream, that will be added at serving time

And, make sure you also know the answers to the following:

- ✔ Does the cake need to be refrigerated until the last possible minute before serving because of its filling or frosting?
- ✔ Do you know the cake's final location before it's served?
- ✔ Have you established and figured out how the cake will be cut?

Suppose you take your cake out of the refrigerator or arrive at another site with it and notice some imperfections: smushed frosting, crooked decorations, or a crushed border. If you set aside a few extras as you prepare for the occasion, you'll be in good stead to make quick repairs. Nothing holds up a celebration longer than someone having to make a trip to the store. The items in the following list are particularly necessary to secure beforehand if you're serving the cake at an event outside your home.

More than likely, many of these items are part of your handy cake decorating kit (refer to Chapter 2). (If you're serving the cake away from home, put together a portable version of your kit that contains these items.)

- ✔ **Small and large icing spatulas:** These are instrumental for smoothing out any ridges, crinkles, or similar imperfections in frosting.

- ✔ **Frosting left from your decorating (and softened if necessary):** Because you never know what may happen before the cake is actually served, it's always a good idea to set aside a small amount of each of the colored frostings you used on your cake. You may need to call on one or all to repipe decorations, fix lettering, or repair a border.

- ✔ **Pastry bags, couplers, and tips appropriate for your cake's decorations:** With these tools on-hand, you can quickly outfit a pastry bag with the correct frosting you need for a particular repair.

- ✔ **Parchment paper:** Usually, if your cake has been refrigerated, it holds up fine until serving time. But if there's a delay or transporting the cake takes longer than expected, the frosting may soften and become uneven. In these situations, you can press strips of parchment paper on the frosted surface to smooth it out.

- ✔ **Office supplies, such as scissors, a tape measure, and low-tack tape:** You may need scissors to snip the pointed end of your pastry bag, a tape measure to figure out a new placement for the cake and cake board at the last minute, and low-tack tape to hold your cake board in place on the table. And wouldn't you know it? It's when you've forgotten one of these that you'll undoubtedly need it, so plan on collecting them and having them with you ahead of time.

Livening Up the Cake Presentation

In Chapter 7, I talk about dressing up the cake board that your beautiful cake rests on. You may have opted to drape it in fondant or cover it with fabric or a theme-appropriate collage under cellophane. In any case, you undoubtedly have an eye-catching display that fits your cake and the celebration perfectly.

However, too often the thoughtful, attractive presentation only goes as far as the cake board: The cake's final setting, where people gather and the cake is portioned out, is often overlooked in terms of decoration. When you have an awesome confection that you've spent time designing, baking, and decorating, don't let all your hard work go unnoticed or be diminished by a setting that doesn't suit the cake. In the end, a poor setting doesn't just take away from the cake; it also detracts from the celebrant's experience and the celebration itself.

Mapping out the space

Before the event kicks off, find the best place to set up the cake. Remember that you don't have to just plop it down on the table where you usually eat supper if the event is at your house. You're likely to have several other viable options at your home and a host of other locales. Most obviously, you can consider a brightly festooned table outdoors if the time of year is right. But don't resist the urge to get creative as long as you have a sturdy platform for your cake. For instance, you can build a miniature staircase out of bricks or stones, or carve a miniature stage out of plywood that features your cake in the starring role. I've served cakes atop a sand castle and a large dollhouse, on a small replica of a football field, peeking out from rows of flower arrangements, and even from a clean, new wheelbarrow (at a garden party).

As you consider different locations, use the following questions to narrow down your choices:

- ✔ Does space accommodate the width and length of the cake board and the height of the cake?
- ✔ Do you have enough space for the cake cutting implements and to cut the cake?
- ✔ Is the setting such that you should plan on showing the cake and then taking it to another area to cut it into servings?
- ✔ Will there be a beverage station set up near the cake? If so, is there ample room for both the cake and the beverages?
- ✔ Will the look of your cake be hampered by cords hanging from a nearby electrical outlet?

Playing around with props

When you choose an exact setting in which to display your cake, consider ways to dress up that area. Start by covering the cake table with a theme- and color-appropriate tablecloth. Then consider adding props that fit in with the theme. You don't want to junk up the space, but some tasteful additions really can enhance the presentation. Consider using

- ✔ Fresh flowers in vases, pots, or even tin pails
- ✔ Tea lights or votive candles
- ✔ Uplighting, using light canisters masked by a plant or placed behind and below the table
- ✔ Candelabras
- ✔ Garland threaded with twinkle lights

- ✔ Wide, wire-rimmed grosgrain ribbon

- ✔ Tulle (even if it's not a wedding)

- ✔ Vintage toys (for a children's party or baby shower)

- ✔ Sports memorabilia

- ✔ Spooky candies and marshmallow ghosts and pumpkins (for a Halloween celebration)

- ✔ Foliage, such as harvest leaves or holly

- ✔ Seashells, coral, and starfish

As you brainstorm and then decide on exactly what and how many props fit in with your look and spark up your cake's presentation, draw up a simple diagram to determine their final look and placement. If you aren't available to stage the presentation yourself, you can give your diagram to someone else with instructions to follow for the desired look.

Transporting Your Creation

With the aid of some handy items, most cakes, such as a two-layer or quarter-sheet, are a snap to transport. Still, you need to position them properly in the right packaging so that they don't arrive collapsed or with all the frosting shifted to and oozing down one side.

Taking measurements for fit

One of the biggest (and silliest!) mistakes that cake decorators make is over- or underestimating the vehicle space needed for a cake. You don't want to find yourself standing outside an open car door ready to place your cake inside but stumped by the realization that the space is actually too small, the cake is too tall, or there's way too much room for the cake to shift and slide around. Make things easier on yourself by collecting the following information:

- ✔ The width and length of your cake board

- ✔ The height of your cake

- ✔ The measurements of the available space in your car

Compare the measurements of the board and cake with the car space measurements to ensure that everything will fit. If necessary, arrange for a larger or smaller vehicle in which to transport your creation.

Before you have your cake in hand, clear the appropriate space for the cake inside the car, and gather up the right transportation materials, which I cover in the next two sections.

Using standard gear and procedure

Usually, unless you're dealing with a tiered wedding cake (see the next section) or similar cakes that involve separate tiers, I find that it's easiest to transport a cake that's already on its board, such as a layer or sheet cake. For those, follow these steps:

1. **Procure a sturdy cardboard box that's slightly larger than the cake board and slightly taller than the cake.**

   If you can't find a heavy cardboard box and your cake is small, it may fit in a large baking pan lined with dish towels.

2. **Place clean dish towels in the bottom of the box, and rest the cake board on top of the towels.**

3. **Position the box in the allocated space in your car, making sure that it sits level, with no room to slide along a seat, on the floor, or in the trunk.**

   To keep the cake box from moving, you may need to brace it with other boxes or large items.

As an additional measure of safekeeping, get a plastic cover like the ones that come on cakes from the grocery store bakery and place it over the cake before you set it in the box. If necessary, tape the cover to the underside of your cake board so that the cover doesn't accidentally slide into one side of the cake. You can get plastic covers at cake decorating stores, but in a pinch, friendly employees at grocery store bakery counters may also let you purchase them.

 If you're assembling a tiered cake on-site, you can carry the cake board separately and store the layers (which should be on their cardboard bases) in cake boxes, covered plastic carrying totes, or cast iron skillets lined with clean dish towels.

Stabilizing more complicated cakes

When you have a multitiered or extra-large cake that you've created for a special occasion, you need to take extra precautions, procedures, and packaging into account to get it to its final location.

Following are the safest procedures for transporting certain kinds of towering or tiered cakes:

- ✔ **For assembled, tiered cakes,** tap a long, slender dowel down through the center of the cake to hold the tiers in place (refer to Chapter 16 for instructions).

  Traveling with any tiered cake that's already assembled is a risky proposition because it could topple over during the drive if it's not properly secured. If you go this route, definitely have another person on board to be the cake monitor while you drive, or vice versa. Trying to drive while keeping your eye on a cake is even riskier than getting a cake to a site in good shape.

  Whether or not this dowel method is the best for your cake depends on the size of the cake and the length of the journey to the site. For instance, if you have three tiers that are 12-inches and smaller and your drive is ten minutes, getting your cake safely to its site is a better bet than transporting five 14-inch tiers on a 45-minute drive. Use common sense, and if you're into attempting this method, start small. Don't put yourself under undue pressure. Particularly with larger cakes that have to be tiered, you're better off assembling the tiers on-site.

- ✔ **For tiered cakes with pillars between the layers,** transport the layers separately (refer to the preceding section) and assemble the cake on-site. In this case, each layer should be on a separator plate that you situate on the pillars as you build the cake at the location.

- ✔ **For large sheet cakes with extra-fancy decorations or lots of embellishments,** invest in a large, hard plastic box with a cover. Get one that's just the right size to snugly fit a large cake board and has a nonskid bottom.

In all cases, if you have a large embellishment for the top of the cake, don't put it on until you're at the site. Otherwise, it may fall off or over, messing up your frosting or — worse — taking a tier or layer with it.

For special transporting items such as large boxes, plastic covers, and long dowels, cake decorating supply companies sell a bounty of goods (many of which are devoted to tiered cakes) that ease cake transportation. In addition, check out craft stores and catering stores, which I turn to time and time again. Caterers constantly deal with traveling to other sites to serve their fare, so any store that appeals to them is bound to have these types of products that can help you, too. And if you can find a wholesaler that specializes in restaurant supplies but is open to the public, you'll be amazed at some of the products that are suitable for cake transportation. (Chapter 21 contains the ten best places to find and buy cake supplies.)

What to Do with Leftover Cake

There's a good chance your cake will be so fabulous and so delicious that not a crumb will be left, but on that rare occasion that you have a few pieces left over, don't just toss them in the trash can. Share the remaining cake with others right away, or preserve it for future enjoyment.

Give parting gifts

If you can bear to part with pieces of your beautiful cake, plan ahead and purchase disposable plastic containers or precut squares of aluminum foil in which to package and send pieces away with departing guests.

If the event is upscale or glamorous, experiment with other (perhaps more creative) packaging. For example, to the thrill of delighted departing guests, I've doled out leftover squares of cake in vellum take-out boxes bedecked with organza and laminated tags; cupcakes in cellophane bags tied with striped grosgrain ribbon; and slices of cake in striped miniature hatboxes.

Refrigerate for good taste

Depending on the kind of cake you serve, you can probably keep it in the refrigerator for two to three days after the event. Most cake-frosting combinations, like white cake and buttercream frosting and chocolate cake iced with ganache, handle refrigeration well. But if your cake's frosting or filling is made with whipped cream, the cake isn't likely to last beyond the big night because the cream breaks down and leaves you with a soggy mess.

For optimal results, refrigerated cake needs to be stored properly. Don't just relegate it to the refrigerator resting on paper party plates. Either place pieces in plastic or glass containers with sealed tops or wrap them well in cellophane.

In my opinion, you should always refrigerate leftover cake. Even if it's in a tightly covered container, never leave it simply sitting on the counter after the event. Although it's considered safe to keep some cakes at room temperature in a sealed container, I prefer refrigeration to absolutely ensure safety. (And, truth be told taste-wise, I'd rather have cold cake than what's been left out at room temperature.)

With one exception, I don't recommend freezing leftover decorated cake pieces unless you're really intent on having someone who wasn't at the event try your cake. A frozen cake just doesn't have the same taste or appeal of a freshly prepared one. If it's going to sit in your freezer for a couple of days after the event before it gets eaten, I say toss it.

The exception: I realize that the tradition of keeping the top tier of your wedding cake and enjoying it on your first anniversary is cherished and time-honored. To freeze that tier, wrap it in two layers of cellophane and then in aluminum foil. If possible, tuck it away in a freezer that isn't opened on a regular basis.

Rework it for another occasion

In some situations, you may intentionally make more cake than you need for one event because you have a second event soon after. If you're intentionally planning to serve what's left of one designed cake at an occasion the next day, don't just present it in an unattractive pan or on a plate with plastic wrap laid over it.

Instead, figure out a way to rechristen it to be appropriate for the new event. Showcase the cake in a completely new light, such as being precut: Display the pieces individually by laying them out in a festive pattern or design on a freshly prepared cake board or by presenting them on dessert plates.

How you serve the cake the second time around may be the least of your problems. Your cake may have some wild design that looks messy in individual pieces served at an event with no relation to the one the cake was baked and decorated for. In that case, consider embellishing the cake slices or pieces or the plates you present them on in order to tailor them more for this event.

Whatever you do, don't overwork the pieces. In other words, don't refrost them or keep adding embellishments just to hide the initial decoration. If refashioning one cake for two occasions seems impossible, don't force it; take advantage of a great reason to bake another cake!

Chapter 19

Quick Cakes and Last-Minute Decorating Techniques

It's 10 p.m. and your son comes clean that he promised you'd provide a homemade cake for his teacher's birthday tomorrow. Or perhaps it's midday and you just found out that your spouse is desperately trying to impress a client who's dropping by after dinner tonight.

Let's face it: You don't always have the luxury of time in turning out a beautiful, delicious cake. If the thought of assembling a lot of ingredients and rolling up your sleeves drains your energy at the end of a long day, know that turning out an elegant or impressive cake doesn't have to be a demanding, exact endeavor.

For a quick assist, you can rely on several conveniences, starting with cake mixes, to help you make an ordinary cake special in a jiffy. Further, a vast collection of swift decorative techniques and handy embellishments can transform plain cake layers into a centerpiece dessert. In this chapter, you discover several possibilities and some unexpected tips for baking and decorating a cake in the throes of a time crunch.

Keeping a Well-Stocked Pantry

With the demands of your daily life, whipping up a pretty cake in a pinch may seem overwhelming. But just a handful of easily found products make the process a snap . . . and fun. To make any cake decorating endeavor easier — and especially last-minute ones — keep some items on hand in your pantry at all times.

The essentials

At a minimum, your pantry should include:

- Cake mixes in different flavors, such as white, yellow, and chocolate
- Instant pudding mixes in different flavors, such as vanilla, chocolate, lemon, and pistachio
- Chocolate chips
- White and dark chocolate bars
- Candied citrus fruits
- Nuts, such as walnuts and pecans
- Extracts, such as vanilla, lemon, and rum
- Confectioners' sugar
- Cocoa powder

Decorating odds and ends

Your imagination may surprise you when it comes to turning simple candies or on-hand pantry items into fun or classy decorations. Even when your time is limited, keep design in mind. Simple items may fill in a word that you've sketched out on a cake; some may form blossoms of a flower; others easily could be part of a geometric pattern, swirl, or polka dots; some would look lovely pressed into the sides of a cake.

Although you may feel like you're pressed for time, it's always wise to sketch out an idea on paper before you commit your design to cake. A little planning saves you frustration (and more time) in the long run.

The following items can really transform a cake in very little time. Notice that many of these decorations are impressive and impactive without being complicated or expensive. Take stock of other items available in your grocery store (or in your cupboard right now) to tailor the list for your own tastes and needs.

- Candy canes
- Cinnamon sticks
- Chocolate sprinkles
- Chopped chocolate
- Crushed peppermint candy

- ✔ Edible glitter
- ✔ Edible pearls
- ✔ Grated lemon peel
- ✔ Grated orange peel
- ✔ Gumdrops
- ✔ Halved or chopped pecans
- ✔ Maraschino cherries in different colors, such as red, blue, and yellow
- ✔ Metallic candy balls (also known as *dragees*)
- ✔ Multicolored sprinkles
- ✔ Nonpareils
- ✔ Pastel mints
- ✔ Peppermint patties
- ✔ Pillow mints
- ✔ Sanding sugars
- ✔ Slivered almonds
- ✔ Toasted or tinted flaked coconut

None of these pantry items are meant to be dumped on a cake to add color, texture, or interest. You never want a decoration — no matter how simple or quick — to look like it was just an afterthought to frosting a cake.

Quick Fixes with Mixes

Although almost everyone prefers the taste of a cake made from scratch, cake mixes are an alluring convenience. Usually you just have to add eggs, oil or butter, and water, and — presto! — you have cake batter. Plus, they come in a variety of flavors, so you can offer many different kinds of cake fairly easily for events like dessert buffets or bake sales.

I like to reserve baking with cake mixes for occasions that pop up unexpectedly. I don't ever like to serve store-bought baked goods, so when I'm in a jam at home, I turn to a cake mix for help.

Although cake mixes offer a shortcut, baking rules still apply. Read recipes from start to finish before beginning. Use eggs that are at room temperature. Follow mixing and cooking times, and check for doneness. Using a cake mix isn't a license for laxity . . . but it undeniably shaves minutes off mixing and clean-up.

Lori's Chocolatey-Chippity Cake

Although not made from scratch, this cake is one of my most requested creations. It made its premiere in 1999 when I had to come up with several small cakes for a film festival's dessert buffet following an evening's worth of screenings. (My wife's film was featured, thus the name of the cake!)

Tools: *10-inch Bundt pan*

Preparation time: *10 minutes*

Baking time: *50 minutes plus 30 minutes for cooling*

Yield: *12 servings*

For the cake:

18.25-ounce box chocolate cake mix	*4 eggs*
3.4-ounce box chocolate instant pudding mix	*8-ounce container sour cream*
¾ cup vegetable oil	*2½ cups semisweet chocolate chips*
½ cup water	

For the decorations:

1 cup semisweet chocolate chips	*½ cup miniature chocolate chips*
1 cup heavy whipping cream	

1 Preheat the oven to 350 degrees F. Spray the Bundt pan with a cooking spray with flour, and set it aside.

2 In a large bowl, combine the cake and pudding mixes, oil, water, eggs, and sour cream. Beat on low speed for 1 minute, or just until the ingredients come together. Then, beat on medium speed for 4 minutes, or until the batter is thick and silky.

3 Mix in the chocolate chips with a wooden spoon or rubber spatula.

4 Pour the batter into the prepared pan, and smooth out the top.

5 Bake for 50 minutes, or until a toothpick inserted in the center comes out with moist crumbs attached. Be careful not to over-bake!

6 Let the cake cool in the pan for 10 minutes, and then invert it onto a cooling rack to cool completely.

7 For the decoration, combine the regular chocolate chips and heavy whipping cream in a glass measuring cup. Microwave on high for 1 minute, remove from the microwave, and stir the mixture until smooth.

8 Drizzle the chocolate cream mixture over the cake. Sprinkle the miniature chocolate chips all over the top of the cake. Serve immediately.

Vary It!: Double or triple this recipe for a large sheet cake.

Cinco Leches Cake

This sponge cake is a tribute to my Cuban heritage and the more traditional tres leches cake you may be familiar with. Baking this cake in an attractive pan is important because you serve it out of the pan.

Tools: *9-x-13-inch cake pan, #22 icing tip*

Preparation time: *10 minutes plus overnight refrigeration*

Baking time: *35 minutes*

Yield: *16 servings*

18.25-ounce box yellow or white cake mix	*2 cups heavy whipping cream, divided*
1 cup water	*12-ounce can evaporated milk*
½ cup vegetable oil	*14-ounce can sweetened condensed milk*
3 eggs	*1 pint Dulce de Leche ice cream*

1 Preheat the oven to 350 degrees F. Grease the pan with butter, and set it aside.

2 In a large bowl, combine the cake mix, water, oil, and eggs. Beat on low speed for 30 seconds, and then beat on medium speed for 2 minutes. Pour the batter into the prepared pan.

3 Bake for 35 minutes, or until a toothpick inserted in the center comes out with moist crumbs attached.

4 In a large measuring cup or a bowl with a pouring spout, whisk together 1 cup heavy whipping cream, the evaporated milk, and the sweetened condensed milk.

5 Pierce the top of the hot cake all over with a fork. Whisk the whipping cream mixture briefly, and then pour it evenly over the top of the cake.

6 Cover the cake with plastic wrap, and refrigerate it for at least 3 hours. If possible, refrigerate the cake overnight for best results.

7 Just prior to serving, beat the remaining 1 cup of whipping cream until stiff peaks form. Outfit a pastry bag with a coupler, #22 tip, and the whipped cream. Cut the cake into 16 squares, and pipe a whipped cream star on top of each square.

8 Serve each piece of cake with a scoop of Dulce de Leche ice cream.

Summer Lovin' Lemon Cake

This vibrant and refreshing cake is a true quick fix because you don't need to remove it from the pan and you can serve it warm. Plus, it's a delicious finish to a variety of meals.

Tools: *9-x-13-inch cake pan*

Preparation time: *10 minutes*

Baking time: *35 minutes*

Yield: *12 servings*

18.25-ounce box lemon cake mix	¾ cup water
3.4-ounce box lemon instant pudding mix	1 batch Lemon Butter Glaze (recipe follows)
4 eggs	Candied lemon slices
¾ cup vegetable oil	

1 Preheat the oven to 350 degrees F. Grease and flour the cake pan, and set it aside.

2 In a large bowl, combine the cake and pudding mixes, eggs, oil, and water. Beat on low speed for 30 seconds and then on medium speed for 3 minutes. Pour the batter into the prepared pan.

3 Bake for 35 minutes, or until a toothpick inserted in the center comes out with moist crumbs attached. Let the cake cool in the pan for 10 minutes before running a knife around the edge. Invert it onto a serving tray.

4 While the cake is still warm, drizzle the lemon glaze over it.

5 Garnish the cake with candied lemon slices.

Lemon Butter Glaze

1½ tablespoons milk	1¼ cup sifted confectioners' sugar
1 tablespoon butter	1 tablespoon lemon juice

1 In a small saucepan, heat the milk and butter over low heat until the butter melts. Stir in the sugar, and mix well to combine.

2 Transfer the mixture to a heatproof bowl. Add the lemon juice, and beat the mixture until smooth.

Moussetachio Cupcakes

These moist, tender, and unusually flavored cupcakes invariably become conversation pieces. If you're setting them out for company, use decorative cupcake liners. They're also great as a take-along dessert to a picnic.

Tools: *Two 12-well cupcake pans*

Preparation time: *10 minutes*

Baking time: *20 minutes*

Yield: *18 servings*

18.25-ounce box white cake mix	*1 cup vegetable oil*
3.4-ounce box pistachio instant pudding mix	*1 batch Pistachio Mousse Frosting (recipe follows)*
3 eggs	*Chocolate-covered pistachios or chopped pistachios*
1 cup ginger ale	

1 Preheat the oven to 350 degrees F. Place 18 cupcake liners in the wells of two cupcakes pans.

2 In a large bowl, combine the cake and pudding mixes, eggs, ginger ale, and oil. Beat on low speed for 30 seconds until just combined, and then beat on medium speed for 2 minutes, scraping the bowl twice to make sure that all ingredients are fully incorporated.

3 Fill each cupcake liner about two-thirds full. Bake for 20 minutes, or until a toothpick inserted in the center comes out with moist crumbs attached. Let the cupcakes cool in the pans for 10 minutes before setting them on a cooling rack.

4 While the cupcakes are still warm, spoon the pistachio frosting over them and smooth it out with an icing spatula. Work quickly before the frosting sets.

5 Place a chocolate-covered pistachio on each cupcake, or sprinkle chopped pistachios over the top as decoration.

Pistachio Mousse Frosting

3.4-ounce box pistachio instant pudding mix	*½ cup cold milk*
1¼ cups sweetened condensed milk	

1 In a medium bowl, combine the pudding mix and sweetened condensed milk. Beat on low speed until the frosting begins coming together.

2 Gradually add the milk, and continue beating. Scrape the bowl twice to make sure that all the pudding mix is incorporated into the frosting. Use immediately.

Barbara and Vera's Rum Cake

Sometimes a single ingredient instantly makes a dessert seem more adult. As such, this rum cake should be reserved for grown-up functions. The mother and daughter who shared this recipe with me face a constant dilemma: Whenever they bring another dessert to a party, people always complain that they were looking forward to this rum cake!

Tools: *10-inch Bundt pan, #22 icing tip, bamboo skewer*

Preparation time: *10 minutes*

Baking time: *1 hour*

Yield: *12 servings*

1 cup chopped pecans	*½ cup vegetable oil*
18.25-ounce box yellow cake mix	*½ cup dark rum*
3.4-ounce box vanilla instant pudding mix	*1 batch Rum Glaze (recipe follows)*
4 eggs	*1 cup whipping cream*
½ cup water	*12 pecan halves*

1 Preheat the oven to 325 degrees F. Spray the Bundt pan with cooking spray that contains flour. Sprinkle the chopped pecans in the bottom of the pan, and set the pan aside.

2 In a large bowl, combine the cake and pudding mixes, eggs, water, oil, and rum. Beat on low speed just until blended, and then beat on medium speed for 2 minutes, scraping the bowl twice during mixing to incorporate everything.

3 Bake for 1 hour, or until a toothpick inserted in the center comes out clean. Let the cake cool in the pan for 10 minutes before inverting it onto a serving platter.

4 Pierce the top of the cake all over with a bamboo skewer, and drizzle rum glaze over the top and sides of the cake.

5 Just prior to serving, in a medium bowl, whip the cream until stiff peaks form. Outfit a pastry bag with a #22 tip and whipped cream. Pipe 12 stars around the top of the cake, and press a pecan half into the center of each star.

Rum Glaze

¼ cup unsalted butter	*1 cup granulated white sugar*
¼ cup water	*½ cup dark rum*

1 In a small saucepan, melt the butter. Stir in the water and sugar, and bring the mixture to a boil. Boil for 5 minutes, stirring constantly.

2 Remove the pan from the heat, and stir in the rum.

When You Have Only Minutes

Don't think that an absence of time equals a cake that looks like it was hastily assembled. It's possible to make a cake look festive and ultra-appealing in just a matter of minutes.

Making it special, quickly

With your endeavors geared toward a speedy — but beautiful — finish, put your own spin on an array of both delectable and stunning decorations that can add depth and style to your cake.

Getting fresh

In your time-saving take on cake decorating, don't forget the fresh approach that lends class, sophistication, and good taste to cakes. Part of the beauty using fresh items is that they're easy to find and don't require a lot of arranging or dressing up. Fresh decoration options include:

- **Fresh flowers:** Unsprayed varieties such as roses and daisies are great, colorful choices.

- **Fresh fruits:** Whole strawberries, raspberries, blueberries, and blackberries dress up a cake and add flavor. If you have time to make frosting, you can tint it green and pipe leaves and vines in between the fruits.

- **Fresh herbs:** Consider this original, earthy option for lending beauty and fragrance to your cake. Some unusual varieties that enhance a cake's aroma and presence include chocolate basil, lavender, lemon verbena, and mint.

Saucy encounters

Sometimes decorating a cake means decorating the plate the cake will be served on. Sauces and purees in a variety of colors, flavors, and textures — many that can be purchased from the grocery store or gourmet shop —can enliven your presentation, particularly when they're used in tandem with each other.

For instance, if you're serving white cake, place raspberry puree and mango puree in squeeze bottles. Make a pool of raspberry puree on the plate, and then decorate it with dots of mango puree. Or you can decorate the plates with puree hearts. To do that, just squeeze out a generous dot of raspberry puree, and draw a line through it with a toothpick to pull the puree into a heart shape.

You also can make stars out of sauce or puree by drawing lines out of a dot at several points. Another option is to create scrumptious swirls: Using squeeze bottles, draw a whirling circle with one sauce, and then draw another circle inside that one with a different sauce.

Decorating a cake plate with sauce or puree works well if you aren't satisfied with how your final cake turned out. Just slice it up and serve it on decorated plates.

Chocolaty endeavors

Chocolate provides a tasty, quickly mastered embellishment for cakes. The following sections walk you through a few variations.

Chocolate curls

All you need to make these chocolate curls is a block of chocolate, a vegetable peeler, and a microwave. Follow these simple steps:

1. **Microwave the chocolate for just a few seconds to soften it slightly.**

2. **Drag the peeler down the side of the chocolate.**

   The longer the piece of chocolate, the longer the curls will be.

3. **Place the curls on the cake using tongs or a bamboo skewer (so that the heat of your fingertips doesn't melt or smudge the chocolate), and refrigerate the cake until you're ready to serve it.**

Chocolate shavings

Nothing could be easier than chocolate shavings. Simply run a chocolate block against a fine grater, and let the chocolate shavings fall onto the surface of your cake.

Chocolate shapes

With a simply crafted pastry bag, you can pipe fun chocolate shapes that harden quickly. Follow these steps:

1. **Place a sheet of wax paper on a cookie sheet.**

2. **Place ½ cup semisweet chocolate chips in a resealable plastic food storage bag. Microwave the bag on high for 30 seconds.**

3. **Knead the bag to mix the chocolate, and then microwave it on high for 10 or 20 seconds, until the chocolate is completely smooth.**

4. **Snip off a corner of the bag, and pipe the chocolate out through the hole. Pipe hearts, stars, initials, numbers, or any desired shape onto the wax paper.**

5. **Let the shapes sit on the wax paper until the chocolate sets (but don't refrigerate them). After the chocolate has hardened, gently lift the shapes from the wax paper, and place them on your cake.**

Chocolate leaves

Not only are these chocolate leaves quick and easy to make, but they're also a strikingly realistic addition to any cake. To make them, follow these steps:

1. **Gather up clean, nontoxic, unsprayed leaves. Make sure that they're completely dry.**

2. **In a small bowl, combine ½ cup semisweet chocolate chips with 1 teaspoon vegetable shortening. Microwave on high for about 45 seconds, until the chocolate melts and the mixture is smooth when stirred.**

3. **Use a soft pastry brush to brush melted chocolate onto the back of a leaf. Leave a bit of the bottom of the leaf free of chocolate.**

4. **Repeat with the other leaves, setting them on a wax paper-lined cookie sheet as you finish them. Refrigerate until the chocolate is firm, about 10 minutes.**

5. **Remove the leaves from the refrigerator, and gently peel the chocolate away from the leaves. Arrange the chocolate leaves on your cake as desired.**

Salvaging a broken cake

If it so happens that your cake falls, collapses, or crumbles when you turn it out of the pan, don't panic. With a fondue pot and a few other ingredients, you can serve up your not-so-pretty cake in a very tasty and fun way.

Cake Fondue

One of my favorite cake celebrations revolves around this recipe, in which you cube a cake, melt a chocolate mixture in a fondue pot, and put out accompaniments for guests to decorate their own dipped cubes.

Tools: *Fondue pot*

Preparation time: *10 minutes*

Yield: *12 servings*

¼ cup milk

1 cup butterscotch chips

1 cup semisweet chocolate chips

14-ounce can sweetened condensed milk

1 teaspoon pure vanilla extract

1 prepared cake (9-inch round or 9-x-13-inch rectangle) cut into 1½-inch cubes

Flaked coconut, crushed candies, sanding sugars, sprinkles, chopped nuts, and other accompaniments

1 Combine the milk, butterscotch chips, and chocolate chips in the fondue pot. Warm over low heat, stirring until melted.

2 Add the sweetened condensed milk and vanilla, and stir until thoroughly combined.

3 Set out the cake cubes, and place the various accompaniments in individual bowls. Instruct guests to dip the cake cubes individually into the fondue pot and immediately press them into a chosen accompaniment.

Fast designs

Although picking up a pastry bag and piping flowers, words, and other embellishments is the most common form of cake decorating, it's not always the swiftest time-wise. Therefore, I've come up with a wide range of sweet designs that you can create in a flash.

Flying high balloons

Press round candies, such as pastel mint wafers, onto a frosted cake, and then attach balloon strings made of cherry or strawberry licorice.

Patchwork cake

Use a toothpick to section off the top of the cake into squares or diamonds. Then fill in the shapes with crushed candies (see Figure 19-1). This design looks best on square or rectangular cakes.

Swiss dot cake

Cover the entire cake (top and sides) with white chocolate, dark chocolate, milk chocolate, or butterscotch chips, or a mixture of these.

Carnival cake

With a bamboo skewer, divide a round cake into eight sections. On every other section, press multicolored nonpareils into the frosting (see Figure 19-2).

A toast to Mondrian cake

One of my kids has recently become fascinated with the 1970s sitcom *The Partridge Family* and the multicolored, Mondrian-inspired painting that covered the group's tour bus. To recreate this look on a cake, divide a round, rectangular, or square cake with thick licorice strips or thin licorice shoelaces. Fill the resulting geometric shapes with different colored crushed candies, cookies, or colored sugar (see Figure 19-3).

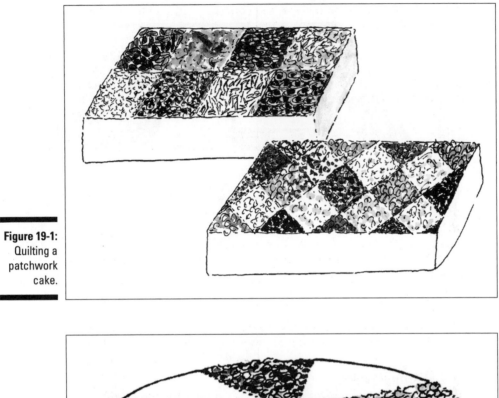

Figure 19-1:
Quilting a
patchwork
cake.

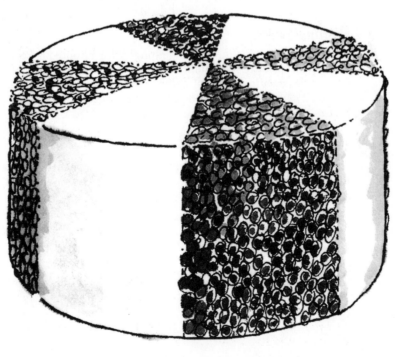

Figure 19-2:
Sectioning
a cake for
a carnival
appearance.

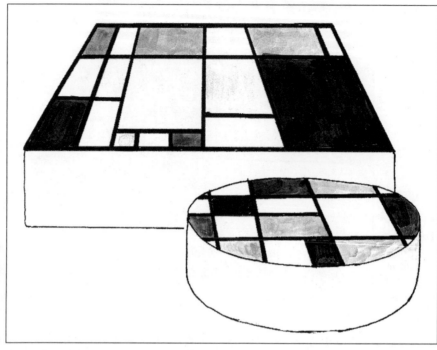

Figure 19-3:
Making a
Mondrian-
inspired
design.

Frosting flowers

If you decide to take the frosting plunge with a limited time frame, your creations can be more representative than life-like. For instance, five dots that form a circle with a different color in the center easily looks like a flower, even if it's not a multipetaled gum paste rose. Play around with frosting colors to make different flower varieties.

Candy creations

Carefully sprinkled colored candies turn into festive swirls in a flash. You can also use candies to form the petals of a flower or spell out a name.

Chapter 20

Starting a Cake Decorating Business

. . . .

In This Chapter

▶ Understanding the (sweet) mechanics involved

▶ Figuring out where to set up shop

▶ Keeping it legal with food service rules and regulations

▶ Drawing customers in by marketing your specialties

. . . .

*I*nterested in taking your cakes to the next level? This chapter gives you the lowdown and steps involved in turning the art of cake decorating into a moneymaking enterprise.

Everyone has a reason to celebrate, which means that, in the world of cakes, you have untold opportunities for entrepreneurial adventures that are rewarding both creatively and financially. That's the side of planning, organizing, and executing a cake decorating business that's a snap. However, just because it's creatively stimulating and results in delicious, eye-appealing confections doesn't mean that it's not a business. You have to carefully consider and review all the necessities involved with getting a business up and running and keeping it successful. For example, you have to balance your books, make sure you meet your city's or county's health department rules and regulations, keep your equipment in working condition and your staples stocked, source out new ideas, keep existing customers happy, and attract new customers. Whew! And that's just for starters.

But if you embark on this entrepreneurial adventure, you can rest assured that, with the right combination of know-how and chutzpah, all your efforts can truly pay off, making all those necessities niceties. With a successful cake decorating business, you reap profits, are in charge of your own time, and continually broaden your creative spectrum, bringing lip-smacking smiles to hundreds (and maybe even thousands!).

Setting Up Your Own Business

You love cake decorating, and you can't believe how much it stimulates you creatively. And you know that there's money to be made . . . I mean, what's with all the bakeries around, right? Plus, people have been talking about your cakes; they've complimented you at events featuring your cakes and even asked if you've thought about providing cakes for other occasions. Heck, someone even thought you were a professional cake decorator and asked for a price list!

If you're giving some serious thought to the idea of a cake decorating business (or if you're already booked to make a cake for an upcoming affair), take a step back to take stock of your particular situation. Although baking and decorating cakes provides an amazing amount of fun, enjoyment, and satisfaction, setting up a business to make money doing it requires commitment, the right equipment, a modicum of financial savvy, and time.

Deciding if you have what it takes

In order to make it as a professional cake decorator, you have to have know-how, skills, drive, specialties, and even equipment. I discuss all these elements in this chapter. But the first step in creating a cake decorating business is reflection and assessment . . . of yourself. Think about the aspects of cake decorating you truly enjoy, and spend some time answering the following questions. You may even want to share your answers and discuss these topics with trusted friends, family, or colleagues.

- ✔ Do you particularly enjoy the baking, the art involved in designing, the joy on a cake celebrant's face, or all of these aspects of cake decorating?

- ✔ What has prompted you to consider cake decorating as a commercial venture rather than simply an artistic one or a hobby?

- ✔ Do you have the time to build and maintain the business (including handling contracts and billing as well as marketing and possibly a Web site) as well as undertake the cake decorating?

- ✔ Do you already have the skill set necessary to turn out a succession of different, special cakes? If not, do you have a single specialty you can concentrate on?

- ✔ If you plan to rely on a specialty, will it be enough to carry your business?

- ✔ Do you know the best way to go about expanding your repertoire and skills?

- ✔ Do you have the resources to purchase (or rent) necessary equipment?

- ✔ Do you have resources you can call on to guide you in accounting, insurance, legalities, and marketing?

Doing your research

Don't just dive into a cake decorating start-up business because someone at a party where your cake was served placed an order for another cake of yours. Rather, do your homework by conducting research on several fronts.

- ✔ **Figure out your *market*, the people who will regularly buy your cakes and enthusiastically refer you to others for their celebration cake needs.**

  The people who may be willing to pay for your particular cakes may be the parents of children in your child's class who you know will probably be hosting at least one birthday party this year. Fellow members of a civic club, bowling league, or church group could be ambassadors for your business, giving you leads on people who have upcoming events that call for a cake. Outside of social circles, consider restaurants and hotels in your area; local eateries may be interested in featuring a unique cake as a specialty dessert menu item.

- ✔ **Analyze the specialties and the unique selling proposition you can offer your customers.**

  Make a list of all the bakeries and stores you can think of who sell specialty cakes, and for each retailer, list the characteristics that make your cake superior (think appearance, ingredients, and taste) to their offerings. (See the section "Determining your specialties" later in this chapter for more on figuring out what sets your cakes apart.)

- ✔ **Get a rough estimate of how much you can charge by researching costs of cakes in your area and costs involved in making and decorating your cakes.**

  It's perfectly fine to charge more than a grocery or warehouse store because your cake will almost certainly cater to your celebrant's style, be more tailor-made for the event and the celebrant's tastes, and not be a mass-produced creation. In the beginning, you should also pay close attention to how much it costs for you to make and decorate your cakes. Figure out

  - The cost of the ingredients and materials you need

  - An estimate of all the time involved, including working with the customer, making and decorating the cake, collecting necessary ingredients, and transporting it to the event site

  - The cost of rentals you may need for equipment, ovens, and kitchen space

The price of a cake shouldn't be simply a total of the cost of ingredients. When you know what confections you'll make and what specialties you'll focus on for the bulk of your business, decide how much those things cost so that you can make a profit on each and every cake you make and decorate.

Determining your specialties

Even if your town has a bakery on every corner, there still may be room for your cake creations because you can offer a product that's superior on many fronts. You just have to determine what categories your product will be a leader in.

To figure out what specialties your cakes will focus on, think about what has pulled you into considering a cake decorating business and what you think makes your cakes special. Use your answers to these ten questions to identify ways to distinguish your cakes from the local competition:

- Do you have a cake flavor that everyone loves but few have heard of?

- Do you use imported ingredients?

- Are your cakes made completely from scratch?

- Are your designs singularly unique? For instance, are your cakes particularly stunning or humorous or colorful in their design?

- Do you have signature frosting colors that no one can mimic?

- Do you use decorations that are particularly hard to find?

- Do you use only fresh flowers in your decorations?

- Do all your cakes include amazing marzipan creations or beautiful gum paste flowers?

- Do greetings on the cakes feature clever and memorable wordplay?

- Do your cakes come in interesting sizes or shapes (such as ovals and hexagons) or only one size (such as cupcakes)?

In organizing your business from the start, you must examine and define your cakes' incomparable qualities to come up with what marketing experts call a *unique selling proposition,* or USP. Your USP is what you know makes your cakes so different, so special, and so alluring that customers will flock to your business over others.

For instance, the combination of delicious, unusual cake flavors with whimsical designs was my USP. My red velvet cake was often the talk of a party — so much so that people often came up to me to ask if they could order one. When I started making red velvet cakes in Southern California, they were (and, often, still are) quite a novelty even though they're a staple of my Southern heritage. My other unusual cakes included the Bubblin' Brown Sugar Cake (with a subtle caramel flavor) and the Best Carrot Cake Ever (refer to Chapter 6 for the recipe). The cakes were out of the ordinary and delicious, and people always knew that the designs would take the cake to the next level, either with artwork and words that were very specific to the celebrant, vivid colors, or a humorous rendering for the event.

Regarding the upsides

When you're considering starting a cake decorating business, you can't ignore the risks; being cautious isn't cowardly, it's smart. But the world of cake decorating isn't totally treacherous — there are many upsides to encourage you. For example, there's no limit to the profits you can reap, and you'll be absolutely amazed at how flexible your schedule becomes. In fact, if you have access to the right equipment and workspace, you literally can bake and decorate any time of the day or night. Some of my best work has been done at 3 a.m.!

As I mention throughout this book, cake decorating allows you to be creative, experiment, and flex your artistic muscles. Your cakes are your canvases, your frostings are your paints, and embellishments are your assorted, colorful accoutrements. And being responsible for the sheer delight of partygoers as they dive into a cake they absolutely love is tantalizingly priceless (and the fact that you get paid in addition to the warm fuzzy feeling is even better!).

My many cautious words in this chapter aren't intended to scare you away from a cake decorating business but rather to make sure that you take necessary steps to avert costly mistakes and time-consuming surprises if you continue on toward your goal of starting a cake decorating business.

Finding a Location for Your Business

One of the greatest difficulties for an aspiring cake decorator who wants to turn a passion into a business is finding a kitchen suitable for cake decorating endeavors.

Working out of your home

When some people decide to launch a cake decorating business, they automatically think to just start it at home. That's not a bad idea, but it's not quite as easy as it sounds; you have to consider some legalities and the equipment involved.

Tackling pesky legal issues

Many people operate cake decorating businesses out of their homes, but you must make sure that doing so is permissible in your city. If it is, you may have to outfit your kitchen specially, expand it, or build another one to ensure safe food handling and proper sanitation that meets government regulations. For example, you may need to have three-compartment sinks, a private trash collection service, a separate entrance just for your kitchen, and an arsenal of required equipment such as National Sanitation Foundation (NSF)–approved food storage containers and cutting boards.

Research the regulations in your area pertaining to working in a kitchen that meets county health standards for food preparation and distribution. Check with your county's health department to get started on what you need to do and have to pass inspection in your area.

Gathering equipment

Some Web sites claim that you can start a cake decorating business with little more than an oven and a microwave. Those two appliances are essential, but they really aren't all you need. To work out of your home kitchen, you're likely to need the following equipment (depending on how big your business gets):

- ✔ A mixer that can accommodate large batters and extra mixing bowls for the mixer
- ✔ A convection oven
- ✔ Ample refrigeration for tall cakes or multiple cakes
- ✔ A supply source for boxes, carrying cases, and the like
- ✔ A supply source for unusual tips, standard decorating fare, and pans in different shapes
- ✔ A dependable and accommodating vehicle for safely transporting your works of art

For more info on kitchen equipment and layout, see Chapter 3.

Scouting for commercial kitchen space

Perhaps the rules and regulations involved in working out of your home are daunting; your existing kitchen is far too small to host a business; your kitchen isn't up to code and making the necessary changes and additions is cost-prohibitive; or your kitchen is the hub for a busy family and subjecting your cakes to the constant activity of daily life is a scary proposition.

Whatever your situation, you may have to find a kitchen outside your home in which to work. An increasingly popular option is the commercial kitchen. Commercial kitchens are facilities where food professionals can rent space by the day, hour, or week. Many are open 24 hours a day, seven days a week. Because the kitchens are licensed by health departments, you don't have to worry about bringing anything up to code.

Commercial kitchens generally feature restaurant-quality equipment (convection ovens, stand mixers, and the like) as well as ample refrigeration and counter space and sometimes even storage space. Depending on the size of the facility and the number of separate kitchens available, the commercial facility may be organized such that different spaces are devoted to different kinds of culinary pursuits; in other words, a pastry chef wouldn't work in the same area and with the same equipment as a chef who specializes in garlic-infused Italian cuisine.

For a commercial kitchen to approve your use of the facility, you probably need to have a business license and liability insurance. In addition, the facility may require you to be certified in safe food handling, which entails attending a class and paying a minimal fee. Be sure to inquire about any requirements the facility may have.

Find a commercial kitchen to rent in your area by checking listings in your local phone books, and also ask around at bakeries, catering supply houses, and cooking stores in your area. In addition, visit www.chefskitchens.com, a site for a commercial kitchen located in Los Angeles. Even if you don't plan to work in the L.A. area, the description, application process, rental costs, rules, and other information available on the site may be invaluable to you in trying to find a commercial kitchen suitable for your needs.

In addition to commercial kitchens, a social caterer, bakery, or restaurant in your area may be willing to rent space to you for baking and decorating cakes, particularly if you're willing to do your work during the location's off-hours. Some cake decorators rent out a kitchen in a church or school because of their restaurant-quality equipment.

Not-for-profit facilities may not be viable options for you to operate out of because you're running a for-profit business and therefore could end up with a problematic business and health-department licensing situation. And despite its impressive equipment, a not-for-profit facility may not be health department–licensed. Just because a space has restaurant-quality equipment doesn't necessarily mean that it's a licensed kitchen.

Getting Down to Basics

Just because cake decorating is extremely creative doesn't give you an exemption from using business savvy in setting up shop and attracting and keeping happy customers. Baking cakes, mixing frosting, and coming up with fanciful designs is fun, but you still have to take care of an array of practical demands required to make money on any business venture. Having a kitchen for an office doesn't mean you don't have to handle a variety of traditional office duties.

Running a cake-centric office

Review the following list of business necessities. Granted, at the outset, you may not need every last one (such as a fax line or Web site), but most aren't very expensive, and some — from a legal standpoint — are absolutely required.

- Office stationery, such as business cards, letterhead for invoicing, order forms, and contracts

- A dedicated phone line and e-mail address to communicate with customers, and a fax line to receive order forms

- A Web site to showcase your work and communicate with potential and existing clients (jump to the section "Designing a Web site for your designs" later in this chapter for more)

- A city or state business license, which is different than a food preparation license (see the next section)

- A federal ID number for tax purposes and to obtain a *resale number,* which allows you access to restaurant supply stores, wholesale florists, and the like for wholesale prices on equipment, tools, and embellishments

- Business insurance, because sometimes bad things happen and it's nice to be covered when they do

- Access to professionals such as a lawyer and accountant, preferably with experience in the culinary industry

For more information on starting, running, and managing a business, check out *Business Plans Kit For Dummies,* 2nd Edition (Wiley).

Finding out about licensing

I mention legal issues earlier in this chapter, but this recommendation bears repeating: Find out the rules in your area regarding food preparation and retail sales for your decorated cakes as well as zoning restrictions for where you can do your work. Start by contacting your county's health department.

Cake decorating isn't as common as, say, catering, so your first contacts may not know how to categorize your business or answer your questions immediately. But be patient and persistent. If you get transferred around, let each person know what you're asking for — the county's rules and regulations for operating a cake decorating business — and take down the name and phone extension of each person you speak with. You'll undoubtedly think of questions after you hang up, so try to get a single contact that you can return to for follow-up information.

Armed with the necessary information, you can do what's required to operate as a fully functional and law-abiding cake decorating business.

Drawing up contracts

Don't be content just to take orders over the phone and assume that verbal agreements suffice when you and a customer come to terms on the cake for an event. The colors involved, the wording on the cake, the kind of filling, the number of layers, the price . . . it's just too much to leave to chance, so create a contract in which all the details are recorded for both parties to review and sign off on.

Contracts for decorated cakes usually don't have to be fancy affairs. For instance, the contract may be a dated document with the following information:

- ✔ A description of the cake, including its dimensions, flavors, and design details
- ✔ The date of the event for cake delivery
- ✔ The charges associated with the cake
- ✔ A place for both you and the customer to sign indicating your understanding of the cake and services to be provided

An exception to using this simple contract is in the case of a wedding cake. Because of the cake's bigger size, more intricate designs, and typically higher costs, the contract should contain more detail about the cake you're providing. For instance, if someone other than yourself will serve the cake on-site, you can't guarantee the actual number of servings (the cake cutter may divvy up the cake in fat wedges far larger than what you would have done or anticipated); therefore, the contract should only have an estimate of the number of servings. However, in the contract, you can guarantee the size of the layers and provide a suggested diagram for how the cake should be cut.

Contact a reputable lawyer to review your contract and let you know if it includes all the right information or needs to be tweaked.

Attracting a Clientele and Marketing Your Cakes

As you launch and grow your business, you constantly must be thinking about ways to attract new customers while you keep your name fresh with your existing ones.

Spreading the word

People are passionate about good cakes that they've enjoyed. So when you're looking to launch your cake decorating business, begin your marketing efforts by contacting your cake fans. Let them know that you're launching a cake decorating business and would love to have them — and their friends, colleagues, family, and business associates — as customers.

Before you contact the first person, finalize a price list and put together a portfolio of your creations. That may mean making several cakes just for the purpose of taking pictures of them, but people want to see your work . . . even if you've been highly referred.

Outside of your social circle, think about professional ties you already have to companies with a vested interest in cakes. For instance, do you know any professionals involved with events, such as wedding or party planners, corporate event organizers, special event planners, restaurant managers whose venues frequently host parties, and even florists and photographers? Aligning yourself with individuals in these fields can bring you loads of referrals and lasting connections with many people who have the potential to come back to you repeatedly to order cakes.

Do you plan to specialize in children's birthday cakes? Wedding cakes? Cakes for dinner party dessert buffets? Your target audience dictates the media you should focus on with your advertising. For example, if you specialize in kids' cakes, your initial advertising should be low-cost but high-visibility placements, such as in community parenting magazines, local weekly newspapers, and even church bulletins.

Brainstorming cool marketing methods

Before you start your business — and certainly as it expands — identify and monitor your target audience and niche demographics. They dictate where you should plunk down your marketing dollars to reach those most likely to buy your beautifully decorated cakes.

Marketing encompasses a variety of tools, including advertising and publicity, but it also refers to nontraditional methods. To spread the word outside typical marketing streams, keep in mind that virtually any occasion you provide a cake for is an opportunity to market your work beyond the event at hand. For instance, consider placing your cakes in a specially designed cake box that's distinctly yours and displays your contact information. And provide your client at an event with business cards to be passed out to anyone at the party who inquires about ordering a cake from you.

An interesting way of marketing your product to increase your exposure is to donate cakes to community events, fundraisers, end-of-season parties for sports teams, PTA committee meetings, church functions, and so forth.

Don't go broke giving away free cakes. Ascertain which events will have the highest exposure to your target audience, and plan your donations accordingly for maximum benefit.

If you've been hired to make a truly unique cake for a high-profile event, take advantage of the occasion's attention by issuing a press release in your city's newspaper about your cake with a picture of it. Or if the cake is particularly eye-catching, send the release to local news stations, especially if you know that they're covering the event. With a little advance notice, TV crews may make sure to get footage of your cake at the event.

Designing a Web site for your designs

In recent years, creating and maintaining a Web site for a business has become more of a necessity than an option.

It's true that Web sites can require substantial financial investments to create, launch, and maintain. However, you also can set up a fairly simple but nice-looking site for a modest sum. Your site can be a *billboard,* meaning that it just contains your company name, logo, and contact information. Or you can make it highly interactive, complete with online order forms, a gallery of cake photos, price lists, frequently asked questions, and even a shopping cart component for visitors to purchase cake decorating supplies. Also consider a feature that allows visitors to enter their e-mail addresses to receive communication via e-mail newsletters.

Suppose you've just started a cake decorating business called The Coolest Cakes Ever, and you specialize in cakes that highlight extreme sports (such as skateboarding, surfing, and mountain climbing) for boys, girls, and sports aficionados. You procure a domain name for your business: www.thecoolest cakesever.com. On your Web site, you have a brief description of your cake decorating business, your phone number and e-mail address, and a selection of photos that spotlight some of your best work. Existing and potential customers can visit your site to get a feel for your specialty cakes and how your business operates.

For creating marketing materials that best suit your business and tackling a host of marketing initiatives such as designing a Web Site and launching publicity and advertising campaigns, check out my book *Streetwise Business Communication: Deliver Your Message with Clarity and Efficiency* (Adams Media, 2007).

The cakes on your site are your calling card. Invest in sharp photography for images that appear on your Web site. Depending on your expertise in the photography arena and your own photography equipment, you may need to hire a professional photographer with a high-resolution digital camera to give your cakes the detailed attention they deserve.

People often think that, with a fully functioning and interactive Web site, they never have to talk to a customer again. What a mistake that is! Your Web site should welcome customers, not shut a door on them. Letting them take some information down from the Web site and communicate with you by e-mail to confirm some details is acceptable, but remember that, in phone and face-to-face conversations with your customers, you learn about any upcoming events for which they may need more cakes, find out about referrals, and get ideas and feedback for growing your business and keeping customers satisfied.

Part VI
The Part of Tens

The 5th Wave   By Rich Tennant

"Don't blame us! The recipe clearly states, 'Add 4 tablespoons of sugar.'"

In this part . . .

Not sure where to get cake decorating supplies? Curious about how to cut and serve a cake to its maximum potential? Interested in saving time when decorating? Worried about what to do if your hopes for a beautiful cake are suddenly on the verge of being dashed? Never fear. In the grand tradition of *For Dummies* books, this part contains lists of handy tips and pointers — and some flat-out, little-known secrets — on all these topics.

Chapter 21

Ten Great Sources for Cake Supplies and Ideas

In This Chapter

▶ Procuring the right supplies

▶ Looking outside the box for products and inspiration

*Y*our local grocery store may carry some basic cake decorating supplies, like pastry bags, plastic icing tips, and parchment paper. However, plan on venturing out to other retailers — both bricks and mortar and online — for specialty products, including coloring gels and pastes, tips, novelty candies, fondant, marzipan, gum paste, cake pans, and more.

The stores and sites covered in this chapter put you well on your way to following any recipe and cake decorating instruction or bringing any imaginative cake design of your own to sweet, delectable life. Some of these resources carry ingredients and supplies, whereas others can provide you with tantalizing inspiration and ideas.

Wilton

800-794-5866; www.wilton.com

Many Web sites boast an extensive array of cake decorating essentials, but Wilton is often regarded as the flagship company for cake decorating supplies. It offers a bevy of products — from petal-shaped pans to ready-made fondant, from gum paste cutters to bottles of glycerin — in numerous product lines. You can peruse the company's Web site to shop for products, find out more about certain items before purchasing them at a retailer, or gather ideas for future cake designs.

Jo-Ann and Michael's

www.joann.com; www.michaels.com

Both of these national retail chains sell a variety of cake decorating products, which usually are located on one or two aisles in each store. They carry many of the basics, such as pans, icing tips, coloring gels, cardboard rounds, and cutters. In addition, in other parts of the stores, you may find inedible embellishments perfect for your particular cake or for decorating your cake board.

Both Jo-Ann and Michael's have Web sites where you can find project instructions as well as purchase products. Further, the sites provide information about cake decorating classes — each one concentrating on a different skill — at store locations if you're interested in getting hands-on experience with an instructor in a classroom setting.

Williams-Sonoma

877-812-6235; www.williamssonoma.com

This kitchen and housewares store has locations nationwide, with many stores found in malls. Williams-Sonoma products, gadgets, and appliances cover a wide range of culinary skills and areas; many stores feature a nice selection of cake decorating tips and accoutrements that usually tie in with the current or upcoming season (such as Easter or Christmas). In addition, Williams-Sonoma carries a famed selection of utensils, such as icing and rubber spatulas, and a complete line of popular stand mixers (including colors exclusive to the store). You can visit the store's Web site and click the Bakeware link on the home page for items related to cake decorating.

Surfas

8777 Washington Blvd., Culver City, CA 90232; 866-799-4770; www.surfas restaurantsupply.com

Being a Los Angeleno, I'm very fond of this store, which bills itself as a "Chef's Paradise." As such, it offers a wide and compelling assortment of tips, tools, and such hardware as decorating turntables, cake pans, and cake plates and boards. Surfas also carries a nice range of decorations — such as sanding sugars and sprinkles in a rainbow of colors — and such fun cake design accoutrements as retro-patterned cupcake liners, unique birthday candles, and a set of paper gorillas climbing up a stick! You can shop Surfas online or visit the store if you're in the area.

Orange Novelty Cake Supplies

3625 West MacArthur Blvd., Suite 305, Santa Ana, CA 92704; 714-556-4661

Stores devoted exclusively to cake decorating supplies seem increasingly rare; this store — the largest cake decorating supply store in California — offers exceptional service and an eye-popping assortment of supplies, food-stuffs, pans, and cake toppers. If you ever have the chance to visit it, you'll be absolutely amazed.

Orange Novelty Cake Supplies initially set up to sell supplies to bakeries in the area but decided to open to the public because of demand. The store is well organized and well stocked; essentially, it's a one-stop shop, with licensed character sets (such as decorations inspired by kids' TV shows and animated films), rolled fondant supplies, every color of food coloring gel you could imagine, and a plethora of products from well-known cake suppliers. If you can't find what you need for your design, give the store a call, and they'll take your order over the phone and ship it out.

Sweet Factory

877-817-9338; www.sweetfactory.com

This national self-serve candy store may have just the chocolate, sour, gummy, or jelly treat you need for your cake design. Retail stores in 23 states offer more than 450 varieties of traditional, hard-to-find, and nostalgic candies. And if you can't find it there, just ask and a store manager may be able to order it for you for prompt delivery. At the chain's Web site, you can order candy as well as find a store location near you.

GroovyCandies

www.groovycandies.com

This expansive Web-based retailer offers dozens of categories of candy, from holiday to retro and wrapped to bulk. If you're looking for any particular kind or brand of confection, or if you just need some inspiration, turn to GroovyCandies for an extensive selection, easy searching, and great customer service.

HometownFavorites

888-694-2656; www.hometownfavorites.com

This retailer's "old-town favorites" and "regionally exclusive foods" coupled with divisions called "The Hard-to-Find Grocer" and "The Candy Store" make it a tremendous asset for a cake decorator, particularly if you're searching for a whimsical touch or a surprise for a celebrant. Peruse this site's candy aisles for amazing treats, including those you thought disappeared long ago but actually are still in production and seasonal items that are available year-round.

Toys "R" Us

800-ToysRUs (800-869-7787); www.toysrus.com

On many occasions, I've been stumped trying to find the perfect cake topper or embellishment for a cake's theme, such as the Sea Creature Birthday, the Murder Mystery Affair, and the Pirate Cruise Barbecue. I searched Web sites and stores in vain. In each instance, I ended up finding just what I needed at Toys "R" Us. With its large and varied assortment of toys, amusements, and entertainment products for nearly all interests and ages, I found a bucket of small but realistic plastic ocean animals, a detective crime scene set, and a small treasure chest full of sea-faring paraphernalia.

Often a cake decorating supply resource has the embellishments you need, but when it doesn't, try this trusty — and convenient — retailer. You can shop online or visit the Web site to find a store near you.

Kate Spade and Paul Smith

www.katespade.com; www.paulsmith.co.uk

Inspiration for your cake designs can come from any source. These two top designers concentrate on apparel and accessories, but I find their use of colors, textures, fabrics, and lines constantly inspiring. Both infuse their cheery, classic styling with a sense of humor, and, in so doing, they've unwittingly provided me with cake decorating inspiration.

For even more inspirational fodder, Kate Spade has even ventured into elegant china (perfect for serving cake slices) and stationery with cake illustrations. You can browse both designers' work at their respective Web sites.

Chapter 22

Ten Ways to Cut a Cake

In This Chapter

▶ Formulating a plan of attack

▶ Divvying up cakes of all shapes and sizes

*N*eedless to say, there's more than one way to cut a cake. Even if the best way to slice and dice seems absolutely obvious, you may find that the servings don't come out all the same. Or in the case of a double- or triple-tiered cake or a three-dimensional cake, you may find yourself totally stumped when trying to figure out the best way to yield the most even, nicest-looking pieces.

In this chapter, I explain that, no matter if the cake is round, square, rectangular, hexagonal, or petal-shaped, a cake doesn't have to be parceled out in uneven pieces that leave the cake remains a mishmash of crumbs. Trust me: If you can bake it, you can cut it!

Coming Up with a Game Plan before You Cut

A well-cut cake starts with a game plan. Don't just come at your cake with a sharp knife and hope for the best. Instead, draw a diagram of the cake and map out how you'll divide up the whole cake (or refer to this chapter).

Use a ruler to divide your cake diagram into sections that flow into subsequent pieces. If you feel like getting really technical, draw your diagram to scale and use a calculator to size up pretty and even pieces of cake that aren't squished, marred, or irregular.

When you're ready to start cutting, arm yourself with a sharp knife and a cake server. The pair doesn't have to be the sterling silver set Aunt Betty gave you when you got married. A simple set will get the job done just as well. The knife should be slightly serrated with a blade that's between 7 and 8 inches long. The cake server allows you to lift each piece of cut cake and neatly transfer it to the dessert dish.

In addition, have a clean dishtowel and a tall round vessel of hot water close by as you cut. To keep the slices tidy, you'll occasionally need to dip the knife into the hot water and then wipe it off between cuts, particularly if the cake you're cutting is sticky or very moist. The water vessel can be a tall, wide glass, but I prefer to use a colored, earthenware vase that's food-safe and used only for food prep such as this (that is, it never holds flowers). If you use a clear glass, you end up with an unattractive glass of murky water standing by your beautifully presented cake.

Round Cakes

With a cake up to 9 inches in diameter, you slice the cake in half and then into quarters. Cut each quarter into equal wedges, depending on how big you want the pieces to be (see Figure 22-1). For cakes that are 12 or 14 inches in diameter, see the section "Round Wedding Tiers" later in this chapter.

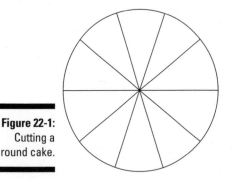

Figure 22-1:
Cutting a
round cake.

Square Cakes

For a 10-inch square cake, slice it in half vertically and then in half horizontally. Divide each of the four resulting quadrants into even pieces according to the number of pieces you need or the desired serving size (see Figure 22-2). If the square is 12 or 14 inches, use a ruler to divide the cake into three even vertical columns and then three columns horizontally. Divide up each quadrant depending on how big you want the pieces to be.

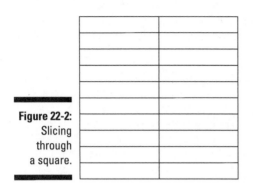

Figure 22-2:
Slicing
through
a square.

Sheet Cakes, Straight Cut

Cut the cake in half vertically and then in half horizontally. From there, depending on the size of the cake and the size of the pieces you'd like to serve, gently mark off each quadrant first vertically, and then horizontally, with hash marks to guide your slices (see Figure 22-3).

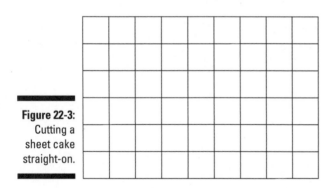

Figure 22-3:
Cutting a
sheet cake
straight-on.

Sheet Cakes, Diagonal Cut

To mix things up a bit, cut the entire length of the sheet cake diagonally through the center, creating two triangles. On each side of the center diagonal line, mark off a succession of evenly spaced diagonal lines. Then make one horizontal cut through the center of the cake, bisecting the diagonal, and follow that with evenly spaced straight horizontal cuts on each side (see Figure 22-4).

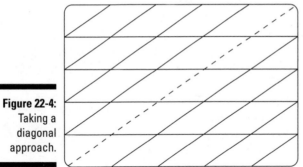

Figure 22-4:
Taking a
diagonal
approach.

Oval Cakes

With an oval cake, your best bet is to get *slices* out of your mind and instead concentrate on squares. Divide the cake into four quadrants (each with a rounded arc on the outside). Slice each quadrant with evenly spaced vertical cuts, and then divide those cuts into squares (see Figure 22-5).

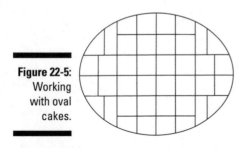

Figure 22-5:
Working
with oval
cakes.

Hexagonal Cakes

For a 9-inch or larger hexagonal tier, begin by etching out a smaller hexagon in the center of the cake. From there, you can carve out pieces in different shapes, as shown in Figure 22-6.

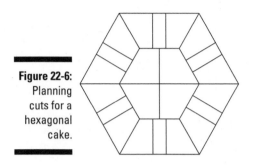

Figure 22-6:
Planning
cuts for a
hexagonal
cake.

Petal-Shaped Cakes

Although the shape is different, you can follow the same guidelines for cutting a petal-shaped cake as you would for a round cake (see the section "Round Cakes" earlier in the chapter and check out Figure 22-7).

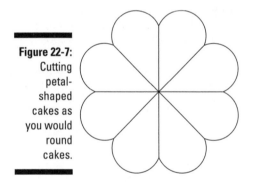

Figure 22-7:
Cutting
petal-
shaped
cakes as
you would
round
cakes.

Heart-Shaped Cakes

I find the heart-shaped cake the hardest to slice up because it's basically impossible to produce a majority of same-sized pieces unless the cake is 12 inches or larger at its widest point. With a heart of any size, divide the large central area into quasiquadrants that you can cut evenly into squares (see Figure 22-8). You'll still have odd-shaped pieces around the edges, but fortunately, the heart reminds everyone that love conquers all . . . even when it comes to cake cutting.

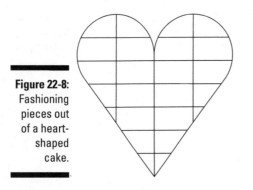

Figure 22-8:
Fashioning pieces out of a heart-shaped cake.

Round Wedding Tiers

Round wedding tiers tend to throw people for a loop. They look at the cake and know they don't want to just hand out extra-big slices, but how do you make sense of such a large round? It's easy. Separate the layers first, removing any dowels or separators in the process. Then use your knife to cut a large circle inside one layer's circumference; cut more evenly spaced circles, working your way toward the center of the cake so that it essentially looks like a bull's-eye. Cut individual pieces from the outer ring, working your way around the circumference of the cake. The pieces should look like wedges with squared-off ends (see Figure 22-9). After you've served up the outer ring of cake, move on to the next ring, and so on.

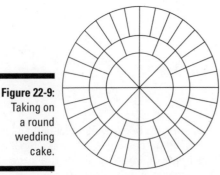

Figure 22-9:
Taking on a round wedding cake.

Square Wedding Tiers

After making sure that you've removed any set pieces necessary to the architecture of your cake, cut square-shaped wedding cake tiers by following the same process as you use for round wedding tiers, except that you use a square as your guide. Start by slicing an inner square, and then another square inside of that, and another, if necessary. Then cut the first rim into even squares, working your way around the outside edge of the cake. Repeat the process on the inside squares (see Figure 22-10).

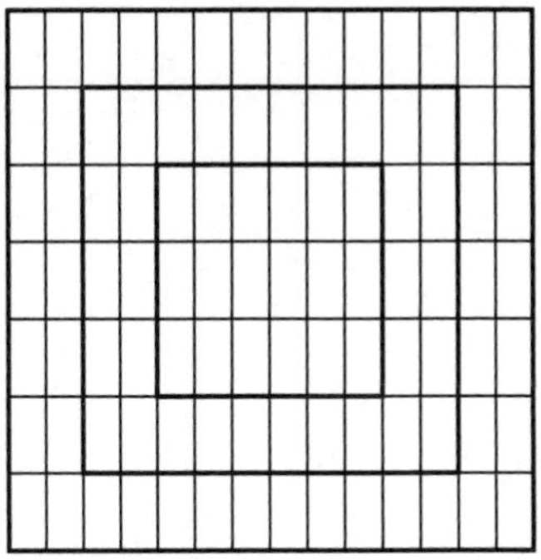

Figure 22-10:
Slicing up
a square
wedding
cake.

Chapter 23

Ten Easy Baking and Frosting Alternatives

In This Chapter

▶ Piping simple patterns with frosting

▶ Adding tasty toppings

▶ Playing with shapes and accessories

*I*f you've committed to decorating a cake and find yourself suddenly short on time or completely overwhelmed by the prospects, don't just head out to your grocery store's bakery department. Take a more personal but just as easy approach with the baking and frosting alternatives covered in this chapter. You may even be surprised by some of these quick methods that professionals routinely call on.

The resources and techniques covered in this chapter work for both formal and informal presentations, for shaving time off your preparation, and for fashioning decorations. I even include a couple of solutions if you don't want to whip up frosting.

Finding Elegance in Simplicity

Never underestimate the sheer beauty of a cake itself. I'm not recommending that you smooth some frosting all over the cake and call it a day, but a few fast-and-furious decorating moves can make for an absolutely beautiful cake. For example:

✔ Pipe a simple bead border (with a #5 tip) all around the top edge and base of the cake.

✔ Pipe big puffs of swirled star frosting (with a #21 tip) all over the top of the cake.

✔ Frost the cake using a #789 tip. You can either leave the striations that the tip creates or smooth them out with an icing spatula. (This tip doesn't fit with a coupler; you simply drop it into a pastry bag.)

Playing with Cupcakes

Cupcakes have recently found favor with a whole new legion of fans, but they've always presented an endless stream of decorating opportunities. First off, because they're small, they bake faster than cake layers. And even though they're little, you can put them together to make something big and visually impressive. For instance, you can put them together to form a bigger design that's pulled apart as guests take their pieces. I've used cupcakes as roses in a big rose bush with greenery interspersed among the cakes, and I've also used them as balloons joined together by fanciful string against a painted sky backdrop on a table. Another design idea is to form a tortoise shell out of several cupcakes and make one cupcake the turtle's head.

You also don't necessarily need to painstakingly frost each cupcake. Dip and swirl them in thin icing for quick coverage. The roses in my cake bush were made using rose cakelet molds, and the thin icing actually helped delineate each rose's unfurling petals; a thick frosting would have hidden those details.

Rolling Out Allover Patterns

This method of design requires some skill but moves very quickly. First pick a repetitive pattern that you're partial to, such as swirls, gingham, dots, open paisleys, plaids, herringbone, lace, squiggly lines, or geometrics like circles, squares, or diamonds. Outfit your pastry bag with a small tip (such as a #2, but you can go up to a #7), and cover every square inch of your cake with the pattern. If you're new to this type of work, go for a pattern that's more forgiving and less rigid, like lace or swirls.

Melting Away Frosting Worries

Don't have the energy (or ingredients) to frost your cake? Serve a cake in its (attractive) baking pan and, immediately upon removing it from the oven, top it with miniature marshmallows and coconut. As an example, for a 9-x-13-inch cake, you need 4 cups of mini marshmallows and ½ cup coconut to cover.

Or you can cover a warm cake with any one of a variety of chips available in stores, such as chocolate, butterscotch, or mint. Use 2 cups for a 9-x-13-inch cake. Melt them in a microwave on high for one minute, and stir until smooth.

Smooth the mixture onto the cake with an offset spatula, create a pattern of swirls, or, once spread, use a decorating comb to make ridges. Just work quickly. Similarly, you could make a chocolate glaze (see Chapter 9 for the recipe) and pour it on the cake.

A s'mores-like topping is popular, too — especially for late-evening dessert buffets. Sprinkle equal parts chocolate chips, marshmallows, and chopped nuts on a warm cake, and place it under the broiler for 1 to 2 minutes, until the chocolate is slightly warm and the marshmallows are toasted.

Pinning on Ribbons

Although certainly a favorite for cakes at weddings and showers, ribbon adds chic elegance to cakes for all occasions. If you find a ribbon with colors or a pattern particularly appropriate for a gathering or an honoree, place it around the bottom of the frosted cake for a classic touch. Fasten it with a beaded pin (that you remove before cutting and serving the cake, of course!). Use ribbon that's thick and sturdy (such as grosgrain) and that has a strong color or design so that it isn't too sheer to be seen and doesn't absorb the frosting.

Freezing Layers for Future Use

This idea requires you to plan ahead, but trust me, you'll be glad you did. When baking a cake, bake extra layers and freeze them for up to 1 month. After they're cooled, wrap them tightly in cellophane and then again in aluminum foil. To thaw, let the wrapped layers sit at room temperature for a couple of hours. Then just frost, decorate, and enjoy!

Applying Sprays and Shimmer Dusts

One of the newer developments in cake decorating is sprayable, edible color that makes a white cake vibrant with just the push of a button. Sprays are available in many colors and can even be used with stencils.Generally, you'll just take the can of spray, point it, and press the nozzle to spray around your cake. However, cans have different widths of applications, so practice on a paper towel first to get an idea of the coat it makes and the area it covers. In addition, depending on the size of your cake (or how much you're covering), you'll probably want to cover the area underneath the cake with paper towels or newspaper to keep areas other than the cake color-free.

Another option for quick but striking decoration is shimmer dust. The dusts come in an array of colors (metallics, pastels, and rich hues) and can turn a bland base into a sparkling, lustrous affair. You can mix the dust with a few teaspoons of lemon extract, and apply the mixture with a small craft paintbrush to the cake's surface. Or, if your cake's frosting is particularly sticky (such as cream cheese frosting), you can simply sprinkle the colorful dust on the cake's surface.

Getting More Out of Cookie Cutters

Put all those cookie cutters in the back of your pantry to work. Use them as outlines for stenciling, or cut shapes in colored marzipan or fondant. Apply a bit of frosting to the underside of the marzipan or fondant shapes, and press them onto the cake.

Using Intricate Molds

Molded pans turn out cakes that attract oohs and aahs. With attention rightly diverted to the striking shape of the cake, there's less pressure on you to decorate every inch of it. Besides, the intricate designs of many molds would be obliterated by gobs of thick frosting. Often, a light dusting of confectioners' sugar or cocoa powder or a drizzle of powdered sugar icing is all you need for a finishing touch.

Gathering Bouquets

When someone says "bouquet," you may immediately conjure up an image of flowers. That works fine, but bouquets can take on other forms, too. Although one of my favorite ways to dress up a cake in a flash is to gather nonpoisonous blooms and arrange them on a cake, other bouquets look great on cakes as well. For example, with a handful of lollipop sticks (available at craft stores) and a little time, you can turn cookies, candies, chocolates, and even photos into a lovely grouping to top your cake. If you like baking cookies, insert sticks into your parceled-out cookie batter before you bake them. With candy molds, you can make quick work with melted chocolate chips to create 3-D chocolates mounted on a stick. For the photos, use double-stick tape on the backs of a pair of them. Press the lollipop stick onto the back of one, and then press the other photo's back on the other side.

Chapter 24

Ten (or So) Troubleshooting Techniques

In This Chapter

▶ Planning ahead to prevent problems

▶ Saving the (cake) day when disaster looms

When you take your cake out of the oven, you may be faced with an array of dilemmas. Or when you start to decorate, you may encounter a plethora of problems.

Even in the throes of a cake crisis, remember that you'll learn from the mistake. I realize that's not much consolation when your cake's supposed to be at a major event and you don't have time to make another one, but the real tragedy would be repeating the mistake with future cakes.

The suggestions in this chapter are intended to help you either avoid or work around cake-related problems. If you take heed of these handy guidelines, you'll be forearmed to prevent many mistakes from happening. Still, because the occasional snafu is bound to occur, you also get some hints and tips for after-the-fall to bring your decorated cake up-to-snuff.

Ruthlessly Organize

The best way to ward off any problems is to be organized. Before you begin mixing to bake or frost, read through all your recipes thoroughly. Then create a game plan for decorating. Often, cake decorators bake the cake the day before so that the layers firm up overnight in the refrigerator and so that they have the whole next day to focus on decorating. Consider taking that approach, and even think about making a to-do list that you check off as you proceed with baking, frosting, filling, and decorating. The list can include cues to keep track of time, such as turning the oven light on to periodically check on the cake as it bakes and checking for doneness 5 to 10 minutes before the timer goes off.

Beware Melting Cakes

If you're planning on serving your cake outdoors, be mindful that buttercream doesn't hold up well in warm temperatures (such as hotter than 78 degrees), so fondant is a better choice. If it's hot outdoors and you're bringing in a buttercream-covered cake, hold off on showing off the cake until it's time to slice and serve. If it's a hot month but the cake event is being held inside, make sure that the celebration place is cool (and that no one's waiting until everyone arrives to turn on the air conditioning) before you bring in the cake and set up its presentation.

Know Where the Cake Will "Land"

If you're planning to bake and decorate a large sheet cake or one that's tiered or constructed, make sure that you know where that cake will be refrigerated for its crumb coat and where it will be served. Don't leave your decorated cake's transport or final home to chance; that's just inviting disaster. If necessary, get out a ruler or measuring tape to make sure that the final product will fit on the cake board, cardboard circles, or whatever else you may be lining up for both decorating on and serving from.

Consider the Great Cover-Up

Some days your cake layers may just turn so lopsided that leveling them could turn a once-high cake into a too-short version of itself. Or you may try all the tips and tricks possible for a smooth frosting finish but still be left with a lumpy or streaked exterior. Your best bet in these circumstances is to divert the eye. For instance, if you're planning on sparse decorations that expose much of your base cake, enhance your design with more embellishments, such as frosting garlands, vines, and flowers or candies such as jelly beans or dragees that fit in with your overall scheme. If your cake's surface is a message, pipe a wide band of stars or rosettes around it.

I'm not suggesting that you go on a decorating binge or start piping willy-nilly. Instead, when you're looking at a cake that just isn't up to your standards, turn to your original drawing and explore ways to best fill in your design such that the lumps, bumps, and slants underneath aren't so noticeable.

Handle Sticky Cake Pans with Care

If you try to remove your cake from the pan and it just won't budge, don't knock the pan on the counter or try prying the cake out by hand. Instead, return the cake to the oven for a few minutes to let the pan heat up again. Run a clean dishtowel under cool water (or dip it into a bowl of icy water), and spread it out on the countertop. Remove the hot pan from the oven and place it (right side up) on top of the wet dishtowel. The coolness from the dishtowel may help loosen the cake's hold on the bottom of the pan.

Serve Off-Site

If your cake just doesn't turn out as you'd hoped, salvage what you can and redirect your decorating efforts so that cake eaters concentrate on their own individual pieces rather than the overall cake. To do so, decorate what you can, but keep in mind that no one but you will see the whole cake. Then, away from everyone, slice and serve the cake on individual plates instead of presenting it as an entire creation. You can garnish the plates with melted chocolate, raspberry coulis, cut fruit, or piped frosting.

Prevent a Fondant Faux Pas

Because fondant dries out quickly, make sure to keep what you're not working with well-wrapped or tightly covered. If the fondant tears when you place it on the cake, you have two options: Smooth more nice, pliable fondant on it to fill in the ripped holes, or put a little bit of shortening on your fingertips and roll your fingers over the tear.

Many people think that a little water can fix any fondant problem, but that's far from the truth. Fondant is made mostly of sugar, so it will dissolve if you use water to smooth over cracks or tears.

Don't Skip the Crumb Coat

For the most professional results, always crumb coat your cake after it's baked and cooled. Without a thin layer of frosting to start, you're sure to end up with flecks of crumbs in your frosting, resulting in an unattractive and unprofessional appearance. So don't skimp on this step! And remember, as long as you cover the cake completely, the crumb coat doesn't have to be pretty — that's what the second coat of frosting is for. With a crumb coat underneath, the final coat of frosting will be much easier to tame for smoothing and decorating . . . and much sweeter to look at.

Take Care to Prevent Cracks

Usually a cake starts to crack when it's being transported, like from a cardboard round to its presentation tray or board, and disaster can ensue when those cracks become deep fissures. When transporting a cake, take care to support its center, not its sides. Holding the edges of any shape of cake causes the center of the cake to dip down or bow up from cracks.

Shore Up Runny Frosting

If you mix up frosting that's far too runny to coat your cake properly, don't just keep mixing in more confectioners' sugar, hoping that it will start to thicken up. Instead, divide the frosting in half (or thirds or fourths, depending on how much frosting you have and how runny it is). When the volume is more manageable, you have a greater chance at correcting the consistency. Add confectioners' sugar gradually to one batch, taking note of how much you mix in at a time so that you can do the same with the other batches.

Offer Cake Sundaes

Everyone loves cake, so even if you have a disastrous-looking baking effort on your hands, you don't have to trash it. As long as the cake tastes good, you can serve up cake sundaes.

To make cake sundaes, chop up the cake as neatly and evenly as possible, and make it the starring foundation for an ice cream sundae bar complete with ice creams, toppings, and whipped cream. And, of course, make sure that frosting is one of the sundae bar offerings! In fact, if you were planning to decorate the cake with tinted frostings, set those out in individual pastry bags with decorative tips and let the guests have their way with them. The cake experience may not be what you had in mind, but it will be memorable!

Index

BUSINESS, CAREERS & PERSONAL FINANCE

0-7645-9847-3   0-7645-2431-3

Also available:
- Business Plans Kit For Dummies
  0-7645-9794-9
- Economics For Dummies
  0-7645-5726-2
- Grant Writing For Dummies
  0-7645-8416-2
- Home Buying For Dummies
  0-7645-5331-3
- Managing For Dummies
  0-7645-1771-6
- Marketing For Dummies
  0-7645-5600-2

- Personal Finance For Dummies
  0-7645-2590-5*
- Resumes For Dummies
  0-7645-5471-9
- Selling For Dummies
  0-7645-5363-1
- Six Sigma For Dummies
  0-7645-6798-5
- Small Business Kit For Dummies
  0-7645-5984-2
- Starting an eBay Business For Dummies
  0-7645-6924-4
- Your Dream Career For Dummies
  0-7645-9795-7

HOME & BUSINESS COMPUTER BASICS

0-470-05432-8   0-471-75421-8

Also available:
- Cleaning Windows Vista For Dummies
  0-471-78293-9
- Excel 2007 For Dummies
  0-470-03737-7
- Mac OS X Tiger For Dummies
  0-7645-7675-5
- MacBook For Dummies
  0-470-04859-X
- Macs For Dummies
  0-470-04849-2
- Office 2007 For Dummies
  0-470-00923-3

- Outlook 2007 For Dummies
  0-470-03830-6
- PCs For Dummies
  0-7645-8958-X
- Salesforce.com For Dummies
  0-470-04893-X
- Upgrading & Fixing Laptops For Dummies
  0-7645-8959-8
- Word 2007 For Dummies
  0-470-03658-3
- Quicken 2007 For Dummies
  0-470-04600-7

FOOD, HOME, GARDEN, HOBBIES, MUSIC & PETS

0-7645-8404-9   0-7645-9904-6

Also available:
- Candy Making For Dummies
  0-7645-9734-5
- Card Games For Dummies
  0-7645-9910-0
- Crocheting For Dummies
  0-7645-4151-X
- Dog Training For Dummies
  0-7645-8418-9
- Healthy Carb Cookbook For Dummies
  0-7645-8476-6
- Home Maintenance For Dummies
  0-7645-5215-5

- Horses For Dummies
  0-7645-9797-3
- Jewelry Making & Beading For Dummies
  0-7645-2571-9
- Orchids For Dummies
  0-7645-6759-4
- Puppies For Dummies
  0-7645-5255-4
- Rock Guitar For Dummies
  0-7645-5356-9
- Sewing For Dummies
  0-7645-6847-7
- Singing For Dummies
  0-7645-2475-5

INTERNET & DIGITAL MEDIA

0-470-04529-9   0-470-04894-8

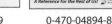

Also available:
- Blogging For Dummies
  0-471-77084-1
- Digital Photography For Dummies
  0-7645-9802-3
- Digital Photography All-in-One Desk Reference For Dummies
  0-470-03743-1
- Digital SLR Cameras and Photography For Dummies
  0-7645-9803-1
- eBay Business All-in-One Desk Reference For Dummies
  0-7645-8438-3
- HDTV For Dummies
  0-470-09673-X

- Home Entertainment PCs For Dummies
  0-470-05523-5
- MySpace For Dummies
  0-470-09529-6
- Search Engine Optimization For Dummies
  0-471-97998-8
- Skype For Dummies
  0-470-04891-3
- The Internet For Dummies
  0-7645-8996-2
- Wiring Your Digital Home For Dummies
  0-471-91830-X

* Separate Canadian edition also available
† Separate U.K. edition also available

WILEY

SPORTS, FITNESS, PARENTING, RELIGION & SPIRITUALITY

0-471-76871-5

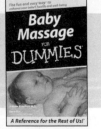

0-7645-7841-3

Also available:
- Catholicism For Dummies
  0-7645-5391-7
- Exercise Balls For Dummies
  0-7645-5623-1
- Fitness For Dummies
  0-7645-7851-0
- Football For Dummies
  0-7645-3936-1
- Judaism For Dummies
  0-7645-5299-6
- Potty Training For Dummies
  0-7645-5417-4
- Buddhism For Dummies
  0-7645-5359-3

- Pregnancy For Dummies
  0-7645-4483-7 †
- Ten Minute Tone-Ups For Dummies
  0-7645-7207-5
- NASCAR For Dummies
  0-7645-7681-X
- Religion For Dummies
  0-7645-5264-3
- Soccer For Dummies
  0-7645-5229-5
- Women in the Bible For Dummies
  0-7645-8475-8

TRAVEL

0-7645-7749-2   0-7645-6945-7

Also available:
- Alaska For Dummies
  0-7645-7746-8
- Cruise Vacations For Dummies
  0-7645-6941-4
- England For Dummies
  0-7645-4276-1
- Europe For Dummies
  0-7645-7529-5
- Germany For Dummies
  0-7645-7823-5
- Hawaii For Dummies
  0-7645-7402-7

- Italy For Dummies
  0-7645-7386-1
- Las Vegas For Dummies
  0-7645-7382-9
- London For Dummies
  0-7645-4277-X
- Paris For Dummies
  0-7645-7630-5
- RV Vacations For Dummies
  0-7645-4442-X
- Walt Disney World & Orlando
  For Dummies
  0-7645-9660-8

GRAPHICS, DESIGN & WEB DEVELOPMENT

0-7645-8815-X   0-7645-9571-7

Also available:
- 3D Game Animation For Dummies
  0-7645-8789-7
- AutoCAD 2006 For Dummies
  0-7645-8925-3
- Building a Web Site For Dummies
  0-7645-7144-3
- Creating Web Pages For Dummies
  0-470-08030-2
- Creating Web Pages All-in-One Desk
  Reference For Dummies
  0-7645-4345-8
- Dreamweaver 8 For Dummies
  0-7645-9649-7

- InDesign CS2 For Dummies
  0-7645-9572-5
- Macromedia Flash 8 For Dummies
  0-7645-9691-8
- Photoshop CS2 and Digital
  Photography For Dummies
  0-7645-9580-6
- Photoshop Elements 4 For Dummies
  0-471-77483-9
- Syndicating Web Sites with RSS Feeds
  For Dummies
  0-7645-8848-6
- Yahoo! SiteBuilder For Dummies
  0-7645-9800-7

NETWORKING, SECURITY, PROGRAMMING & DATABASES

0-7645-7728-X

0-471-74940-0

Also available:
- Access 2007 For Dummies
  0-470-04612-0
- ASP.NET 2 For Dummies
  0-7645-7907-X
- C# 2005 For Dummies
  0-7645-9704-3
- Hacking For Dummies
  0-470-05235-X
- Hacking Wireless Networks
  For Dummies
  0-7645-9730-2
- Java For Dummies
  0-470-08716-1

- Microsoft SQL Server 2005 For Dummies
  0-7645-7755-7
- Networking All-in-One Desk Reference
  For Dummies
  0-7645-9939-9
- Preventing Identity Theft For Dummies
  0-7645-7336-5
- Telecom For Dummies
  0-471-77085-X
- Visual Studio 2005 All-in-One Desk
  Reference For Dummies
  0-7645-9775-2
- XML For Dummies
  0-7645-8845-1